Projecting the End of
American Dream

Projecting the End of the American Dream
Hollywood's Visions of U.S. Decline

GORDON B. ARNOLD

PRAEGER

AN IMPRINT OF ABC-CLIO, LLC
Santa Barbara, California • Denver, Colorado • Oxford, England

Library of Congress Cataloging-in-Publication Data

Arnold, Gordon B., 1954–
  Projecting the end of the American dream : Hollywood's visions of U.S. decline / Gordon B. Arnold.
    pages cm
  Includes bibliographical references and index.
    ISBN 978-0-313-38563-6 (cloth : alk. paper) — ISBN 978-0-313-38564-3 (ebook)
1. American Dream in motion pictures. 2. Motion pictures—Social aspects—United States—History—20th century. I. Title.
  PN1995.9.A4835A86   2013
  791.43′6587392—dc23   2012037945

ISBN: 978-0-313-38563-6
EISBN: 978-0-313-38564-3

17 16 15 14 13   1 2 3 4 5

This book is also available on the World Wide Web as an eBook.
Visit www.abc-clio.com for details.

Praeger
An Imprint of ABC-CLIO, LLC

ABC-CLIO, LLC
130 Cremona Drive, P.O. Box 1911
Santa Barbara, California 93116-1911

This book is printed on acid-free paper ∞

Manufactured in the United States of America

Contents

Preface

This book examines various ways that American film has envisioned the demise of the United States in the years since the 1940s. Its purpose is to explore how unfolding events and circumstances have shaped literal and metaphorical film portrayals of the United States' ruin and the end of the American Dream. It also considers how the long succession of such works from Hollywood has influenced the continuing construction of the American narrative.

Hollywood and the idea of the American Dream are deeply intertwined with each other. The American Dream, an amorphous collection of hopes, ideals, and aspirations, is woven into the fabric of many stories that mainstream American films tell. It may not always be the most obvious part of such stories, but it is often a taken-for-granted part element in movies across a wide range of genres. The notion that the United States is a good and just nation and that its way of life will persist into the future, overcoming any challenges, is an underlying perspective that has been repeated in countless American films.

But as much as Hollywood has reflected, and perhaps reinforced, this important part of the unfolding American narrative, the U.S. film industry has also reflected a much more anxious picture of the United States' condition. In this alternate view, which in some ways is the flip side of the American Dream, the United States is not secure and its way of life is under challenge. In this vision, which is also embedded in many Hollywood productions, the United States is in a perilous moral state and seems to be hurtling toward an apocalypse, either literally or figuratively.

These opposing perspectives about the recent and future condition of the United States have coexisted in political and popular culture since at least the middle of the last century. On the one hand is the swaggering, triumphal view. This is the dominant framework for understanding the United States for many Americans, and it is regularly declared in speeches and public statements made by U.S. leaders. Hollywood also has a long history of repeating this worldview, in movies that celebrate American virtue and ideals and that marvel at U.S. power. In politics and on screen, then, this view shows the United States as the home of the good life and of ideals that are the envy of the world. It is a view that is embodied in what is often called the American Dream—a collection of ideals that extols everything that is good about the nation for past, present, and future generations.

Beyond this positive outlook, American culture also possesses a darker undercurrent, which sometimes comes to the surface but is often camouflaged. This subtext to the more optimistic American narrative is filled with anxiety and dread. It is an expression of fear that much, or even everything, that Americans have loved and cherished about their nation could fall into ruin. In this metaphorically apocalyptic narrative, the military and economic might of the United States is precarious and the American Dream is under challenge. But more than this, the United States' moral stature—a linchpin in the self-construction of American identity—is threatened by a host of potentially ruinous forces—crime, communism, drug addiction, rebellion, immoral behavior, and more. Both Hollywood and American politicians and commentators have frequently focused on this narrative frame as well, in ways that sound an alarm about the direction that American society is heading.

APPROACH

The following chapters trace the evolving ways in which Hollywood has reflected the theme of American ruin within the broader context of changing political culture. To do this, the discussion is situated in the shifting contexts of national and domestic events that have shaped the world since the middle of the twentieth century. The chapters set out to restore for the reader some of the milieu in which various motion pictures were produced and viewed by their original audiences. Adopting a bird's-eye view, the text considers many American films from a number of times and genres, all with a view of illuminating the forces that shaped public awareness and perceptions in their day. What is reflected in both cinema and the political realm is a subtext to the American narrative dominated by fear and anxiety of the nation's demise.

The book is a hybrid analysis of a cultural theme that focuses on fears about national ruin and the demise of the American Dream. Films, as well as broader historical developments, are the means of exploring the theme. While there are other ways one might approach the topic, a basic argument of this book is that when historical context is taken into account, American films reveal much about the sense of anxiety and dread that has been a persistent undercurrent in American consciousness since the dawn of the atomic era many years ago. The book interprets the portrayals of national ruin as broad cultural metaphors that are connected to long-standing uneasiness among some Americans with regard to the moral fate of their nation.

The following chapters are organized primarily in chronological sequence. This allows the historical contexts of American society and politics to be seen alongside the developments in American film that coincided with the given eras. The political and cultural history in the chapters is necessarily incomplete and not intended as a substitute for readings that cover these topics in more breadth and depth. Instead, the material included here serves to provide readers with signposts to broader historical and cultural forces that the reader may wish to explore in more detail elsewhere.

This book also discusses many films as a means to examine the theme of American doom. These examples are intended to be illustrative of the book's overarching topic. The specific films included here are not the only relevant examples in such a discussion, of course. Rather, they are only some examples from a larger universe of possible examples. And of course, the films discussed here can usefully be interpreted in more than one way. The discussion here remains focused on those aspects that reflect the book's thematic emphasis.

AUDIENCE

This book is aimed at several audiences. These include general readers, high school students, college and university students, as well as scholars in areas related to the general topic.

Readers from these groups with interest in the history of film, the American Dream, or the apocalyptic subtext in modern American history will find those subjects discussed in these chapters, along with notes that direct them to other sources for readings on more specific aspects of these topics.

Acknowledgments

As with all such projects, the preparation and writing of this book benefited from the direct and indirect assistance of many people. I am grateful to Praeger and ABC-CLIO for their interest and support of this project since its inception several years ago, and particularly to Jane Messah, with whom I worked as the manuscript was being completed.

My colleagues at Montserrat College of Art were very helpful and supportive throughout the months of research and writing. I especially thank Kimberlee Cloutier-Blazzard and Erin Dionne, as well as Marjorie Augenbraum, Charles Boyer, Martha Buskirk, Ethan Berry, Rob Roy from the faculty of the college, as well as Dean of Academic Affairs Laura Tonelli and President Stephen Immerman.

My students at Montserrat College of Art have inspired me for many years. I thank them all for their keen observations and curiosity. Conversations with several former students were particularly helpful during the period in which I was working on the book and deserve special note. I offer special thanks to Katherine Irving, as well as to Katie Weismann, Meghan Hawkes, Katherine Romansky, and many others for their insights and engaging conversation.

This book is built upon the insights and observations of many other writers and scholars. I am grateful to several libraries, which have been instrumental in providing access to a wide range of materials available over the past few years. I especially thank Librarian Cheri Coe of the Paul M. Scott Library at Montserrat College of Art. In addition, the staffs of the Westborough Public Library, Shrewsbury Public Library, Northborough

Public Library, and Beverly Public Library have also offered helpful assistance and services.

And finally, I offer a word of thanks to my family for their interest and
support over the many months that this project was in process.

CHAPTER 1

American Ruin, the American Dream, and Hollywood

For more than six decades, Hollywood has repeatedly turned to the theme of the United States' ruin as a central idea. It is a common thread in films that span many genres, in hundreds of cinematic incarnations. It is a popular theme in its own right, but it is also an underlying narrative element in movies that, on the surface, seem to be about something else. Embodying anxieties that have developed throughout American culture in the period after World War II, the theme appears as a powerful metaphor in films of many types, across multiple genres.

The doom and gloom in these films is part of a broader cultural theme: a creeping fear of American decline. It is a general anxiety caused by the idea of pervasive American failure—or, more specifically, by a fear of the nation's moral collapse and fall from the position of power and influence that it attained at the height of the so-called American century and especially in the era that immediately followed World War II. More than this, it is also the feeling of distress that is related to dread that an entire way of life—the American way of life—may disappear in a highly volatile world.

This fearful vision of the United States sliding toward ruin, which in its most extreme manifestations takes on an apocalyptic tone, did not emerge in isolation. Rather, it is a dark alternative to the much more positive theme of the American Dream. Indeed, the various cultural incarnations and cinematic representations of American failure—of literal or metaphorical demise—derive much of their cultural power because they represent the negation of the more positive and triumphal American Dream idea, which is a dominant interpretive framework in U.S. society. This ruination is a picture conjured up by perceptions of things gone horribly wrong, as symbolized by crime waves, decaying families and communities, loss of common values, epidemics of addiction, feelings of international failure, and so forth. The envisioning of American ruin conjures not only a picture of a moral wasteland, then, but also one of a deeply felt loss of a cherished way of life.

The thought of American doom is a dramatic idea. It provides raw material that Hollywood has frequently adapted for cinematic use in a wide range of narrative frameworks. It is not difficult to understand why American filmmakers and their audiences would view the potential collapse of their society, or major aspects of it, with a sense of foreboding. People who are comfortable with their way of life obviously do not wish to see that way of life change in ways that would be perceived as negative. And while not everyone or every group in U.S. society has felt the same sense of devotion to the American way of life, after World War II many Americans came to understand their society in largely the same resplendent manner. To many of those in the majority, victory in World War II cemented the notion—which was hardly new even then—that the United States had fully arrived on the global stage as a superpower. It was also interpreted as a kind of proof that the United States had become a moral beacon, a country providing a shining example to the rest of the world.

These postwar perceptions about the positive attributes and potential of the United States, which were bound up in the idea of the American Dream, represented a noble, idealized way of thinking about the U.S. culture and political system. To speak of the American Dream was therefore to speak of a way of life that was perceived as leading to "the good life," a life symbolized by material bounty, security, and moral superiority. It was a national self-perception in which the stakes were very high.

The material comfort and sense of security that are the cornerstones in the idea of the American Dream are important and often observed, but it is the idea's moral dimension that gives it deeply emotional meaning. As a declaration of moral superiority, the concept of the American Dream refers to a way of life in which positive outcomes are linked to inherent virtue. In this respect, the American Dream idea dovetails with an "exceptionalist" view of the United States.

The exceptionalist idea asserts that the United States is a success at least in part because it is a nation that is unique in human history. The basic assumptions of this way of thinking about American life can be traced to the colonial period of American history. It is a perspective that owes much to a speech delivered in 1630 by John Winthrop, governor of the Massachusetts Bay Colony, in which he said:

We shall find that the God of Israel is among us when ten of us shall be able to resist a thousand of our enemies, when He shall make us a praise and glory, that men shall say of succeeding plantations: "The Lord make it like that of New England." For we must consider that we shall be as a city upon a hill, the eyes of all people are upon us.[1]

The "city upon a hill" language, which is taken from the Christian Bible, has found repeated resonance in American discourse. It is an idea that is thoroughly woven into the American Dream concept.

This exceptionalist aspect of the American Dream, which focuses attention on perceptions of the nation's deeply moral character, is widespread and deep-seated. The major political parties have regularly reiterated this way of looking at the American experience in the world. More than that, in many facets of American culture the idea is taken for granted, accepted as a truism that is beyond serious questioning. As a consequence, many Americans believe not only that the United States possesses a unique goodness but also that it has a special obligation to protect and spread that virtue throughout the world. Many Americans thoroughly agree with the sentiment expressed by George W. Bush, who once said that American-styled democracy is God's gift to the world. Indeed, the presumption that the American way of life should be spread across the entire world is seldom questioned in the public sphere of the United States.

Perhaps because the American Dream is so important when Americans think about their way of life, the thought of losing what it entails is seen as very troubling. Situations and events that placed the American Dream under stress—examples include military or political challenges from abroad, domestic civil disruption, and perceptions of breakdown of traditional American institutions—are seen as more than challenges to life's material aspects and personal well-being, though they are that also. More than that, such challenges chip away at American confidence at a deeper level, presenting disturbing scenarios in which the moral foundations of the American Dream are put in doubt. This usually has been perceived as very threatening by the American people.

OUTWARD CONFIDENCE, INNER DOUBT

Since World War II, Americans have been accustomed to thinking of the United States as the most powerful and righteous nation on earth. Yet the world is complex, and maintaining the nation's place at this pinnacle has proven to be difficult. And at times, Americans not only have had difficulty persuading the people of other nations to share their towering view of the United States, but also have had trouble convincing themselves that this exalted, idealized way of thinking about their nation remained true. The latter phenomenon appeared, for instance, in such differing circumstances as the social and political unrest of the 1960s and, in a very different manifestation, two decades later in the so-called culture wars that were prominent in the 1980s.

The reasons for this have been many. But generally, the perceived challenges to American confidence have come from two types of sources. In some ways the most obvious of these has been the challenge that the nation has faced from the outside, whether of a military or an economic nature. In this sphere, it is obvious that other nations routinely have contested American power, and to the extent that these have been perceived as genuine threats, the dampening effect on American confidence has been evident. Still other threats come from within. These have been perceived as deeply troubling and have often evoked highly charged, moralistic rhetoric in response. Shifts within American culture and politics that have veered from traditional American values or behaviors have added much stress to the American psyche, at times leading to pronounced reaction. As such challenges have seemed to mount, cultural anxiety has been a common response. The main worry has been that a lessening of American power and influence abroad and deviation from traditional norms at home are the harbingers of future disaster.

It is not belief in American exceptionalism itself that has been the subject of extensive public debate in the United States, but rather the question of whether the United States is able, or will be able, to maintain this distinct identity. This aspect of American exceptionalism has remained a contentious subject in the polarized world of American politics. The *Los Angeles Times* published an essay in 2011 that probably captured a feeling that many Americans have secretly feared may be true: "Decline is upon us, and every assurance that it isn't only serves, however subliminally, to reinforce that reality."[2] The topic is more than mere politics, however. It is a deeply emotional idea that is at the heart of the American sense of identity. And anxiety prompted by the fear that what is exceptional is, or already has, somehow slipped away has found many outlets for expression, of which film and television are prominent examples.

This has been true since the middle of the twentieth century. At that time, just as the United States rose to the forefront of the world stage, symptoms of unease and anxiety began to appear with some regularity in American life. These symptoms grew more obvious and more frequent for the rest of that century and into the next. They appeared in many guises and contexts, sometimes reflecting what on the surface seemed to be different underlying conditions. For a long time, most Americans treated them as isolated and unrelated. Few observers saw meaningful connections between these symptoms. Slowly, however, a clearer pictured emerged in which many layers and manifestations became apparent. The picture that came into focus was a landscape in which fear and apprehension often held a prominent place. Often, such metaphorical depictions portrayed the United States' fall from grace. The nation's military power and moral authority, which Americans perceived as having been won in the victory of World War II, at times seemed poised to evaporate.

Yet on the surface the United States usually seemed confident, and the darker, more anxious national vision was often, though not always, hidden. Looking back decades later, it is difficult to imagine just how commanding and supremely confident the face that the United States presented to the world has been at times. When anxiety and fear have been held at bay, the picture projected has been that of a nation and a people at the pinnacle of success. This is the picture of a triumphant nation that prevailed in global conflict, crushing enemies across two oceans in World War II. And in 1945, as Americans looked out on the newly remade world, only the United States held what seemed to be the ultimate trump card: nuclear weaponry. When, a few years later, the Soviet Union acquired nuclear weapons, the shock was palpable. And arguably, a similar sense of shock—the shock that any other nation would seek to rival American might and goodwill by acquiring atomic weapons—has been one that still holds great power in the American mind-set many decades later.

But in 1945, such future challenges had not yet materialized. This image of confidence and success, of almost inevitable supremacy, that the United States presented to the world was very similar to what Americans saw when they looked at the presumed promise of their own society. Just as the people of the United States had little doubt about what they saw as their nation's rightful place on the world stage, leading the world to a better future, most Americans had little doubt that they were standing at the gates of a promised land at home. The might of American industry, ingenuity, and tenacity had blossomed amid the nationwide mobilization of the war years. Now these forces, which had propelled the American military to supremacy on the battlefield, could be harnessed for domestic production.

Soon after the end of fighting in 1945, the spoils of war spurred the rise of a consumer culture unlike anything that came before. Across the United States, a new world of suburbs and highways sprang up. This rise of the middle class brought a world of modern conveniences, such as washing machines, refrigerators, and televisions, and the neat rows of houses, with manicured lawns and picket fences, in which to put them. It seemed to be the American Dream come true.

On the surface, then, there was little evidence that Americans had second thoughts about the direction in which they were going. It seemed obvious that the "American way" was the way, the singular way, for the future if humankind was to survive and flourish. There was a price to pay, and Americans realized that the success of the American Dream idea at home and abroad had come at a cost. From their perspective, however, they had already shown they were willing to pay that price by the many sacrifices that had been made during World War II. As a result, they reasoned, their nation was now poised to lead the whole world to a brighter tomorrow. So yes, Americans knew there was a price. What many people failed to recognize, however, was that the cost would not be paid in full upon delivery. There were recurring and hidden costs to this vision of a worldwide American Dream. Although they may not have realized it in the beginning, they would be asked to continue paying more, and in ways old and new, well into the future. The full extent of costs—financial, cultural, and social costs—and the burdens that those costs were to create, would take decades to become clear.

In fact, there was a flip side to the very things that fueled American confidence and made possible the increasing material comfort of everyday life. For the most part, however, it seemed that few voices were willing to openly call attention to the potentially negative long-term and far-reaching consequences that were inherent in the success of the American way. Surely, no successful political leaders dared—or were inclined—to question the unbridled growth of the American Dream and all it entailed. To have done so, in fact, would have seemed a betrayal of American ideals and an act of disrespect toward all those who had sacrificed in war, both in the real war and in the long and ongoing metaphorical war for the United States' soul. And at mid-century the dominant institutions of American life—government, business and industry, schools, and religious institutions—strongly reinforced American ideals. Such was the power of the American vision, which by this time had developed and taken hold over a very long period of time, extending back decades.

Thus the United States asserted its moral and political leadership as a sort of manifest destiny in the post–World War II era. But this was accompanied by an undercurrent of apprehension, which focused on the thought that the United States' mighty position might not persist. This emerged as a very real, if somewhat suppressed, fear of American ruin and demise. And during the era in which the United States rose to a position of power and influence that was perhaps unparalleled in any previous time, the nation's popular culture sometimes became a fertile ground for the growth of deep-seated anxiety and uncertainty.

And although the powerful, sometimes boastful vision of American triumph and grandeur has never completely faded away, that way of imagining the world was accompanied by a far bleaker and more negative vision, in which the American Dream becomes a nightmare. This alternate, sometimes apocalyptic strand of the American narrative envisions the fall of the United States from the heights that it reached in the post–World War II era. It has been a disturbing, nagging image of American doom looming on the horizon.

PROJECTING APOCALYPSE AND AMERICA'S FALL

The positive and uplifting content that often appeared in American films after 1945 has long been noted. The parallel appearance of a bleaker vision of the United States, in which its fate is decidedly negative, has received somewhat less attention. This latter undercurrent in American film was especially noticed as an artifact of the strain placed upon public confidence in American institutions and aspirations that became pronounced during and after the 1960s.[3] But this tendency has roots prior to that era. In fact, the fear of national decline was already well established by that period. Anxieties about American ruin had emerged even before 1945. A dark narrative strand was an undercurrent in the American cinema, for example, and was sometimes present even during the years before the turbulent 1960s, in an era when Americans were supposedly brimming with unquestioned self-confidence.

In fact, visions of failure and impending apocalypse, real or metaphorical, have coexisted with more positive American Dream narratives in various forms throughout American culture. They are, for example, regular fixtures in political rhetoric and can be found on the campaign trail, in official speeches, and in discussion of political issues across the nation. These narratives are also prominent in popular culture, where they sometimes find expression in widely novel and imaginative ways. Although these narrative ideas have been expressed in a wide range of popular-culture forms, since the middle of the last century they are perhaps nowhere more strongly and frequently repeated than in film.

The American film industry, which is often simply called Hollywood, almost always presumes that audiences share an understanding and appreciation of the American Dream. These central ideas have been replicated in various manifestations in American cinema and have been portrayed in both literal and metaphorical ways. As for the narrative of ruin and decline, it is often implied in stories in which some part of the American Dream has gone awry. In other words, it is seldom literal catastrophic ruin that is suggested. Rather, the idea usually appears in more oblique and metaphorical portrayals, with the suggestion that bad things have happened, or are about to happen, as the result of moral failure. The stories have the common thread of imagining a United States with a very questionable future.

There is, of course, something ironic about Hollywood as a purveyor of mythic American narratives with any sort of moral dimension. Since its earliest days as the center of American cinema at the beginning of the twentieth century, the U.S. film business has often been regarded as decadent, even immoral. Few people appear to have looked to it for moral guidance.

Hollywood's appeal to ordinary people and its willingness to entertain them in ways that sometimes offended those of high social stature have frequently resulted in condemnation. Indeed, cultural and political leaders have often regarded Hollywood with disapproval and skepticism. The harshly critical attitude about the film business during the McCarthy era of the 1950s, for example, is only one of many examples of external pressures that Hollywood has faced. And more than that, a long series of scandals, which have been widely reported in the press and eagerly consumed by the American public for generations, has helped generate a view of Hollywood as an almost outsider, renegade element in American culture.

Yet this surface appearance is deceiving. It is true that Hollywood does have a long tradition of publicizing the often extravagantly atypical behavior of actors, actresses, and other celebrities in its orbit. And it has a history of producing works that at times push socially accepted boundaries in the depiction of topics such as sex, violence, drugs, and other behaviors that are widely perceived as possessing a moral dimension. But despite this apparent sensationalism, the movie business usually embraced a very American view of the world. In fact, its success has in no small measure depended on its ability to draw upon a commonly understood worldview on the part of its wide audience. For the most part, Hollywood has produced stories that are consistent with the standard ways in which Americans view their nation, often tracking changes in social and political attitudes that have evolved over time.

Despite the other ways in which people have thought about it, Hollywood is a business. Its audience is therefore not simply an audience; it is a market. The studio executives who are responsible for overseeing the business aspects of the industry seldom forget this fact. Therefore, as much as filmmakers may desire critical acclaim, their productions usually have remained squarely business ventures that must be able to attract mass audiences to be financially viable. There is a strongly felt need to generate a return on financial investment. As a practical matter, this tends to channel Hollywood productions along paths that do not stray very far from the sensibilities and attitudes of the intended audiences. This is because making films with stories and themes that veer too far from what audiences are willing to accept is not only a risky artistic venture but also a risky business idea. Hollywood may explore the boundaries of acceptability in efforts to find some exciting or enticing story to tell, but it generally has not ventured too far ahead of its audiences in the choice of what stories to tell and how to tell them.

Underlying this reality is the matter of ideology, a topic that is often glossed over in discussions about Hollywood and the entertainment business more generally. For despite the somewhat regular complaints from Washington, newspaper editorialists, and radio talk show hosts to the contrary, Hollywood productions have not typically challenged the foundational ideals that are inherent in the traditional American cultural narrative. Most often, in fact, movies have tended to presume an audience that is very familiar with, and accepting of, the general shape of the nation's story as understood by mainstream Americans. And among the most powerful strands of such storytelling are the American Dream and apocalyptic narratives.

Despite having generated movies about some of the darker aspects of American life, then, the U.S. cinema generally has supported and reaffirmed the wisdom and morality of American ideals. Even genres devoted to deviant behavior—genres such as film noir and gangster movies—typically present stories that require recognition of accepted social boundaries, even if characters in the stories violate them. And one would be hard-pressed to find very many films that approvingly depict social, economic, or governmental systems that stray far from the American ideal. In fact, narratives of good and evil—of protagonists and antagonists—usually presume as a backdrop a society that is like an everyday United States, sharing its norms, ideals, and moral condition.

But although Hollywood has usually repeated flattering perceptions of the American way in terms of an ideal—presenting this as the norm, in other words—its productions have reflected other cultural trends as well. Even as it extolled American virtues and superiority in the period immediately following World War II, for example, some of its output began to reveal the anxieties and insecurities that were becoming visible in the wider society. And as time wore on, films increasingly employed stories in which the American Dream was beginning to unravel, particularly around the edges of American life. It marked the beginning of a long but continuous emphasis on a darker cinematic worldview.

Perhaps a shift to the underside of the American Dream, as a thematic strand deeply embedded in screen narratives, was inevitable. After all, dreams are not always happy. And just as the American Dream, as a metaphor, might suggest, there was always the possibility of a darker, and perhaps more night-marish, counterpart to the happy and heroic vision of life that it evoked. The flip side of the American Dream was a bleaker picture, drawing on the apoca-lyptic narrative as a counterpoint to its normally brighter surface.

This darker theme has been dispersed across Hollywood productions since the 1940s, appearing with regularity within a few decades after World War II, as the apparent confidence in the power and influence of the United States, and in the way of life it embodied, gradually revealed cracks and strains. Hollywood reflected these changes as it became increasingly apparent that many of the same things that led to the success of American Dream ideals in the post-war period were two-edged. And although at first these things helped build and maintain American life and influence, eventually it appeared that they contrib-uted to weakening the very things they had helped make possible. Indeed, exces-sive consumerism, sprawling suburbia, and other mainstay features of postwar domestic American life had implications that would eventually become apparent. And over time, the nation's projections of power abroad also revealed unin-tended consequences, and in some parts of the world the United States came to be regarded with increasing skepticism. And within American society, broad cultural changes and shifting social behaviors seemed to indicate that the cher-ished ideal of personal freedom could have unanticipated effects. In such cases, things that once were viewed as positive later became seen as negative, or at least as problematic. There is, of course, more to the story, but by the beginning of the twenty-first century, it was very clear that some challenges and anxieties to the American Dream, writ large, emanated from within the system that built it.

As such strains emerged, Hollywood productions began to reflect the darker underside, real and imagined, of the American vision of life it other-wise took for granted. As films increasingly told stories with such themes, nar-ratives that implied American demise and ruin became more common, albeit with many variations. Frequently, such narratives were cloaked in other forms. In fact, it is not at all apparent that many of the films that in retrospect seem to be commenting on the American Dream were originally intended to have that purpose per se. For example, the 1956 movie *Invasion of the Body Snatchers* appears to be a straightforward science fiction story. Yet considered within the context of its era, it has often been interpreted as an allegorical tale that comments on the fierce anti-Communist xenophobia of that era. In retrospect, it is difficult to escape that reading of it, especially considering the anxiety-ridden political culture in the mid-1950s.

Two decades later a very different kind of film, Martin Scorsese's *Taxi Driver* (1976), can be viewed on one level as a portrait of Travis Bickle (played by Robert De Niro), a troubled Vietnam War veteran who was emotionally scarred by his experiences in that conflict. But a broader consideration of the film as a whole reveals a disturbing picture of urban society in the 1970s. Overall, the film portrays a society in decline. Scorsese shows audiences a world that has become corrupt and dark, a world that so repels the main character that he lashes out against it.

Beyond these, there are many examples of films that, intentionally or not, present viewers with a vision of the American Dream disrupted or worse. The cumulative effect of so many productions revealing aspects of this theme is startling, but not surprising. As products of specific cultural conditions, after all, films sometimes reflect those conditions whether or not the makers of these productions had that explicitly in mind.

There are other ways to interpret Hollywood's output over the past 60 years, of course. The potentially apocalyptic underside to the American Dream is a major thematic strand in its output, but only some of Hollywood's productions possess it as a central feature. The film and television industry is voracious and constantly probing for themes and approaches that will capture the public's imagination, especially in an era when other forms—video games and the Internet, for example—are competing for attention. Still, the bleak vision of American life on the brink of ruin has been a persistent theme, regularly appearing in American cinematic productions.

AMERICAN DREAM, AMERICAN APOCALYPSE

A closer look at the idea of the American Dream and its inverted image, that of demise and ruin, can reveal how deeply embedded and powerful these linked concepts are in U.S. cultural life.

The American Dream is an old idea. As the concept has evolved over time, one constant has been that it envisions the good life according to traditional cultural ideals of the United States. The writer-historian James T. Adams popularized a then-contemporary articulation of the idea, and the label, in a 1931 volume entitled *The Epic of America*. In this book, Adams described the concept as "that dream of a land in which life should be better and richer and fuller for every man, with opportunity for each according to his ability or achievement."[4] This view of things emphasizes the idea of increasing comfort, security, and happiness. The gist of the idea is that these positive results are the direct outgrowth of the American way of doing things. It is a declaration that the American way of life—its manner of government, social and economic organization, spirit of individuality, and so forth—have produced a way of life that is, and should be, the envy of the world.

In the narrowest sense, the American Dream refers to simple goals and especially to home ownership. Indeed, acquiring ownership of a home is often regarded as proof that the American Dream has been achieved. It is not simply that one can enjoy the presumed benefits of owning property. More than that, it symbolizes and reinforces in a broader sense the view that bounty and good fortune are the result of the American system of free enterprise and private property.

Home ownership is such an important cornerstone ideal of the American Dream that the implications of it are sometimes overlooked. But consider the practical realities of purchasing a home in the United States. Typically, "home owners" do not fully own their property. Usually a home is purchased with borrowed money and not fully "owned" by the borrower for many years. Yet Americans in such circumstances tend to consider themselves home owners, even if their equity in their property is actually very small at the outset. (Of course, such "home owners" fully realize this state of affairs and in any case are reminded of it every time they make a mortgage payment.) Still, the idea of home ownership—the very language of it—is a powerful symbolic statement, a way of judging that a person has achieved one of society's goals. Therefore discussions of the American Dream often focus on this aspect of it.

But the American Dream idea is much bigger than this. In a way, home ownership is not only a way that people achieve a sense of comfort and security, or even only a way by which they judge themselves and each other in terms of achieving the Dream. Perhaps just as importantly, home ownership and the widely shared and articulated beliefs and feelings about it serve as ways to reinforce, through frequently repeated individual examples, the broader ideals of American government and society as a whole. Each successful instance of home ownership, then, functions as further evidence of the rightness and appropriateness of the U.S. system. It is not the home itself that is important from this perspective, then, but rather the system that makes acquisition of the home possible.

This enlarged sense of the American Dream is a very powerful idea. The thought that the United States has developed a superior system that generates a good life—a life of plenty, of justice, of fairness—is a commanding moral framework that is widely accepted as an interpretative lens for modern life among Americans. Even for those who find fault with, or are even harshly critical of, certain outcomes in American society, undesirable results are commonly viewed through the American Dream lens. Indeed, poor results are often interpreted not in a way that dismisses the idea of the American

Dream but rather in a way that something has gone wrong, preventing the Dream from being more fully realized. So, even critics of the system largely accept that American Dream ideals are the basis on which to make judgments. Although advocates of some political ideologies—socialism, for example—have expressed skepticism about, and even hostility to, the U.S. system and the ideas on which it is based, such critiques have never found widespread resonance with the American people as a whole. Instead, most people seen as critics of the United States accept the ideals, such as private property and democratic governance, even if they criticize the ways in which the ideals have been implemented. This aspect of American political life is perhaps not always recognized. This seems especially the case with some highly partisan political activists, who often fail to acknowledge how much they have in common with the views they criticize.

The result has been that despite differences of opinion about some aspects of the American Dream—differences that are sometimes loud and bellicose—the idea has remarkable potency. As scholar Jim Cullen writes, "The American Dream has functioned as shared common ground for a very long time, binding together people who may have otherwise little in common and may even be hostile to one another."[5] From a slightly different vantage point, the idea suggests a powerful story. In articulating ideals and suggesting how to think about them, it provides a way of making sense of the entire sweep of American history. Indeed, the idea of the American Dream offers a lens through which to interpret the whole of U.S. history, a way to make sense of sometimes surprising twists and turns in a way that is forwardly oriented and that is positive and aspirational. It is no wonder, then, that politicians frequently use this commonly understood way of thinking about the country in public declarations, whether the idea is identified by name or not.

American Nightmare

The narrative of the United States' ruin, which has many variations and appears with different degrees of intensity, can be conceived as a dark flip side of the American Dream. And like the more positive idea to which is it conceptually bound, it is a major interpretative strand in American culture, providing a means to express cultural anxiety and find meaning in troubling events. In a chaotic and confusing world that seems always in flux, the negative narrative frame is a way to sort out and process experiences, especially experiences that evoke anxiety and dread.

Like the American Dream idea, it therefore serves a purpose similar to that of ancient myths, which, as once explained by Joseph Campbell, "are stories of our search through the ages for truth, for meaning, for significance."[6] Thus, as disturbing as the idea of catastrophic ruin may be, even in a secular sense, this narrative provides a mechanism for establishing order when events seem most troubling and incomprehensible.[7] It is not surprising, then, that the apocalyptic framework is widely employed in American culture, especially in times of social or political turbulence. And whereas the American Dream is a powerful theme that has provided generations with a lens through which to look at the world and make judgments, the dark narrative is frequently found in cases where there is some real or perceived negative development that is experienced as a rupture with ordinary life and its expectations.

Negative events, especially those that are dissonant with the dominant ideas that people have about the world in which they live and that cannot be explained away as isolated occurrences, demand attention. As the cultural anthropologist Clifford Geertz has written, "The drive to make sense out of experience, to give it form and order, is evidently as real as the more familiar biological needs."[8] Like ancient myths, cultural narratives provide a mechanism for speculating about such dissonances—for example, about crime, war, or human suffering—and asserting various potential ways of interpreting them. While this can be done directly, fictional narratives also provide a context in which this process can unfold. In a film or a novel or a comic book, therefore, reasons and judgments about similar events are proposed. These often place the dissonant event within the context of more easily understood terms, consistent with the stories that the culture tells about itself. Such explanations are sometimes the subject of argument or skepticism, but importantly, these interpretations are asserted nonetheless. This is true perhaps even more than in the case of negative events, which are otherwise dissonant with prevailing ways of cultural self-perception, than in the case with more positive experiences.

Apocalypse, Religious and Secular

In mainstream U.S. culture, it is not a coincidence that a sense of impending doom is sometimes seen as an "apocalypse," a term with obviously biblical overtones. Even a cursory look reveals that much of American politics and culture is informed by religious—more specifically, Christian—traditions. Indeed, despite the constitutional edict, expressed in the First Amendment, that "Congress shall make no law respecting an establishment of religion," Christian thinking is deeply and obviously embedded in the mainstream experience of the United States.

This very strong and long-standing Christian orientation is intertwined in the narrative that many Americans use to interpret their country's story. It is found, for example, in the "five foundational myths" that religious history scholar Richard T. Hughes has identified within the standard American narrative.[9] Hughes identifies five widely held ideas in which this view of the United States is revealed. The ideas are that the United States is a nation chosen by God, that it is a Christian nation, that it is nature's nation, that it is a millennial nation, and that it is an innocent nation.[10] In Hughes's analysis, these strands of American self-perception, while composed of somewhat independent lines of thinking, mutually reinforce the exceptionalist view of the United States as a nation unlike others past or present and unique in history.[11]

In the United States, it is a widespread article of political, as well as religious, faith among leaders and citizens alike that the nation has a special place in creation, a place that might more or less be described as a divine purpose in human history. The speeches of political leaders frequently assert the view that the United States has a unique and morally superior place in world affairs and that the American way of life is at the apex of human achievement. Belief in the divine purpose, in the Christian sense, of the American nation suggests other moral dimensions to this American story. For some Americans, especially for some Christians, this means that the United States plays a key part in unfolding Christian prophecy not just metaphorically but literally.

This background informs the more ordinary way in which the idea of apocalypse is used in everyday American culture. In the everyday sense, the religious dimension may or may not be part of the way the term is interpreted. Yet even in secular contexts, the term "apocalypse" implies something more than a simple defeat or a diminishment of power and influence. Rather, "apocalypse" is a word that implies harsh, certain, irrevocable moral judgment. For a society to suffer an apocalyptic fate is not just to suffer from a random disaster or from the effects of bad policy or poor foresight in such a context. It is a damning moral judgment and rebuke.

Even a cursory look at use of the term reveals how widespread its application has been. Soon after the use of atomic weapons at Hiroshima and Nagasaki, nuclear began to be talked about in apocalyptic terms. Even when the tone was otherwise moderate, the ideas of the atom and apocalypse were at times closely linked. In 1946, for example, newspaper columnist Dorothy Thompson wrote, "The great, creative co-operation which produced an apocalyptic weapon of destruction is not on hand to develop, with anything like equal unity and energy, the peaceable potentialities of atomic science."[12] This rhetorical linkage remained evident for many years. It also crossed national borders. In 1957, for instance, West German chancellor Konrad Adenauer said humans faced "an apocalyptic fate" if nuclear war were to occur.[13]

The concepts of nuclear war and apocalypse remained closely connected in subsequent decades. Consider, for example, this quotation from a 1963 newspaper report: "On the Kennedy measuring rod the world stands considerably short of the millennium and still just a step away from the apocalypse of nuclear war."[14] And some years later, in the 1980s, when the Cold War was reignited during the Reagan administration, the old, familiar language was often employed in media reports. In one instance, an editorial piece in an Albany, Georgia, newspaper, stated: "The question of apocalypse has reawakened fears of nuclear arsenals."[15] And some foreign policy situations raising the prospects of military conflict continued to evoke use of apocalyptic language even after the Cold War ended. In 2000, the headline of an opinion piece by syndicated columnist Cal Thomas read: "Clinton policies bring Israel's apocalypse near."[16]

In the years since the attacks of September 11, 2001, references to apocalypse have been frequent. A newspaper article written several years after the 9/11 terrorist attacks, for example, noted, "There is also something about the scale of that day's horror that makes it hard to continue viewing it as the handiwork of a few determined terrorists rather than as some larger, preordained apocalypse."[17]

Yet it has not only been war and the prospects of armed struggle that have been described in apocalyptic language. Indeed, many disparate types of events and situations have prompted use of this linguistic frame. The idea of apocalypse, even in the secular sense in which Americans often use the term, carries the undertones not only of widespread disaster but also of moral judgment. Such disasters include not only natural events—such as hurricanes or tornadoes, or even plagues—but also cultural developments that are perceived as highly negative. These wide-ranging disasters are often described in terms of apocalypse, even if sometimes in a subtle way, with the implication that these events are linked to moral failure.

Of the many possible examples, a few from the years since 2000 make this point. In one instance, a *New York Times* article from 2001 reported, "One reason for the worldwide movement on AIDS is that the dimensions of the apocalypse are beginning to sink in."[18] An update about a major tsunami, published in the *New York Post* in 2004, was entitled, "Apocalypse gets worse as epidemic may double death count."[19] Prior to the economic meltdown of 2008, an article for the *Sarasota Herald-Tribune* stated, "Bush administration officials continue to warn of a looming economic disaster, an apocalypse akin to the Great Depression of the 1930s."[20] And in a discussion of the 2011 European monetary crisis, an article in *The Economist* said, "European leaders can still avoid the apocalypse, but only if they act boldly."[21] The moral dimension embedded within the notion of apocalypse is an important aspect of the idea with widespread application and implications.

When moral failure is linked to negative events—especially those of massive scale—Americans have tended to look for judgment and to ascribe blame. An important implication in the idea of perceiving negative events in an apocalyptic framework is that such a way of making sense of these events quickly leads to seeing events in dichotomous ways, in terms of innocence and guilt. Once events are viewed in this way, the manner in which the events are told can soon become a narrative of good and evil. In telling and retelling the story of a disaster, for example, victims may be seen as suffering their fate because of their own moral shortcomings or at least because of the immoral actions of someone else.

FILM AND PUBLIC PERCEPTIONS

The vagaries of American politics and culture have generated an evolving cultural environment in which the theme of American failure—of American apocalypse—finds much resonance in many ways, at many levels. In popular culture, film has been an important vehicle by which this theme has been spread throughout the social sphere.

For the past century, the cinema has been a hugely successful mass medium, fulfilling entertainment, informational, and persuasive purposes. But motion pictures—whether theatrical films, television, or video—are more than simply entertainment, or aesthetic works, or items of commerce. They are cultural artifacts that reveal much about the people who produce and consume them. Mainstream productions—the sorts of productions that are thought of as the output of "Hollywood," whether or not they were actually created there—not only reflect, in some way, the cultural attitudes and interests of their intended audiences, they are products of that same culture. As cultural artifacts, therefore, screen media embody the sorts of ideas, assumptions, hopes, fears, and dreams of the broader culture. And in recent decades, Hollywood films have often reflected the dark, ruinous vision of the United States.

The stories that Hollywood tells, to be successful on the industry's own terms, must somehow reach and resonate with an audience. There must be something about the story that is understandable to the audience and that draws the audience in and holds its interest. Hollywood is, after all, built on the idea of broad appeal and populist impulses.

This is not to say that Hollywood is simply a mirror. Filmmakers seldom wish to simply replicate on screen the ordinary life that constitutes everyday existence. But film is still a mirror of sorts, or more accurately a collection of mirrors, each of which may distort or exaggerate, reflecting some things clearly and other things hardly at all. Thus movies reflect multiple aspects of the culture in which they are embedded. This is true across the many types of stories Hollywood tells and across the many goals that filmmakers might have for the works they produce. Sometimes a director comes to a project wishing to convey a specific message in a film. At other times, the goal is simpler, aimed at providing a couple of hours of escape from life. Yet there is much common ground here. The makers of mainstream movies are aiming to hold the interest of at least some segment of the public. The economic realities of filmmaking demand it.

The important role that movies play in shaping the public's understanding of the world has been widely noted. Cinematic productions, like literary works, may seek to portray a sense of emotional authenticity as a means to say something useful about a historical topic. As George Orwell once said, "For a creative writer possession of the 'truth' is less important than emotional sincerity."[22]

Yet films evoke more than words of emotional sincerity. As Tara J. Yosso and David G. García have observed, "Hollywood studios recognize and capitalize on the power of films to influence public perceptions and social policy."[23] Cinematic productions have a visual and aural specificity that limits how much is left for audiences to imagine about the past. Importantly, viewers are presented with tableaus that depict specific ways of envisioning stories, fact or fiction. Consequently, film experiences can make indelible impressions, lasting for a very long time.

The role of film in shaping and reinforcing perceptions about war has been studied at length. In the book *Projections of War: Hollywood, American Culture, and World War II*, for example, Thomas Doherty concludes that Hollywood was "the foremost purveyor and chief custodian of the images and mythos of 1941–45" that "maintained a unique bond with its adored and idealized 'public.'"[24] Similarly, in their book *World War II, Film, and History*,[25] John Whiteclay Chambers and David Culbert examine how films that were produced about that conflict as it unfolded were influenced by perceptions about events at the time, but also later played a role in shaping collective memory of the war. As they demonstrate, cultural memory of events draws upon many sources. The potent visual and aural capabilities of screen media, combined with film's ability to powerfully deliver narrative messages, play a role in how an event is recalled, both in terms of historical "facts"—that is, in perceptions about what actually happened—and also in terms of how events are interpreted.

In another example, John Emmett Winn argues that the American Dream has been consistently reinforced by a long series of Hollywood productions that repeat core ideas about the United States.[26] His study cogently argues that film has shaped perceptions of the nation's class structure and of society more generally.

Indeed, scholars note that screen portrayals can have a profound impact on public perceptions across a host of issues. One study, for example, showed "how dystopian sci-fi stories, films, and images influence public attitudes towards cloning."[27] Other studies have shown how films have fueled public cynicism, reinforcing suspicions that malevolent forces conspire against ordinary citizens in numerous ways.[28]

Such messages are disseminated via the cinema in multiple ways. The most obvious mechanism is through individual narratives in which the story of a film conveys the idea. Most Hollywood movies are individual projects that are created, viewed, and interpreted as separate entities. (The primary exception to this is the practice of producing sequels.) Movies are generally freestanding works, therefore. Much of what a viewer needs to know to understand a film or television show is provided in the production. Filmmakers are usually careful to make it possible for viewers to easily understand the story being told without much additional knowledge. On the surface, then, such productions seem to be unique experiences, something like the media equivalent of disposable consumer goods that fill an immediate purpose.

But taking a step back, the picture can be quite different. When viewed more panoramically, it becomes evident that cinema transmits and reinforces cultural themes in a more general way, amplifying the effect of individual films. From a distance, what initially appears to a jumble of unconnected film projects, which express unrelated themes, can begin to take on a different look. Cultural themes that may previously have been unrecognized, or at least underappreciated, in individual films start to become clearer when the broader sweep of Hollywood productions is considered. Analyzing thematic connections among apparently separate productions, perhaps even among widely differing genres, may not supplant the usual way of discussing film and television as distinct entities or narrow genres. But this more expansive view, by exposing overarching thematic trends, has the potential to reveal something not only about the screen media themselves but also about the culture that produced and consumed them. From this starting point, the following chapters explore the appearance and meaning of visions of the United States' fall in Hollywood productions since the first half of the twentieth century. Considered against the overarching backdrop of the American Dream, this examination explores the projection of American anxieties and fears on screen and across the cultural landscape.

CHAPTER 2

Backstory

In the years since 1945, an anxiety-prone reflection of life in the United States, and visions of American doom, developed as a response to world events and changes in American political culture. But this dark, sometimes apocalyptic vision of the United States' fate did not emerge from the ether. In fact, the story of its development as a persistent cultural theme began well before World War II. During the years prior to the war, the relationship between Hollywood and its audience evolved in ways that would later be conducive to expression of this theme of the United States' demise.

Throughout the 1930s, the glamorous movie business made a significant impact on American culture. Hollywood continued to produce a wide variety of films that appealed to many public tastes and interests. Indeed, movie-going was a staple of American life throughout the decade, despite the hardships of the Great Depression, when money was tight and the mood was at times downbeat. In that era, movies often provided a diversion from real-life woes. Some writers have suggested that Hollywood did more than this, playing an important part in bolstering public unity and in promoting the New Deal social policies that the administration of Franklin Delano Roosevelt championed in response to the crisis.[1]

Movie audiences found refuge in genre movies of many types. With their escapist stories and good spirits, comedies and musicals were popular. Films such as *The Golddiggers of 1933*, *A Night at the Opera* (1935), *Top Hat* (1935), *Bringing Up Baby* (1938), and *The Wizard of Oz* (1939) offered entertaining respites from the concerns of everyday life. Other popular box-office successes of the 1930s included wide-ranging features, such as

Frankenstein (1931), *King Kong* (1933), the animated *Snow White and the Seven Dwarfs* (1937), *Mr. Smith Goes to Washington*, and *Gone with the Wind* (1939). Still other films, such as *Stella Dallas* (1937), focused on the trials and tribulations of ordinary women and men. What most of the movies had in common was that they whisked viewers away to other realities, offering respite from day-to-day life.

One very popular genre in this period was the Western, which reenvisioned frontier days in the nineteenth-century American Old West, usually in over-simplified and stereotypical ways. Actors in the genre, including such well-known stars as Gene Autry, Roy Rogers, and Tex Ritter, became household names on the basis of their screen portrayals of cowboy heroes. More famous still was actor John Wayne, whose appearance in director John Ford's *Stagecoach* (1939) established him as the prototypical Western star for deca-des to come. Such films provided opportunities to present the Old West as mainstream morality plays, with heroes and villains clearly delineated. And if any moral ambiguity was present beneath the surface of such tales, it was not much noticed at the time.

Yet some popular movies from the 1930s focused on less-positive aspects of then contemporary American experience. Films with crime themes, for example, showed a darker, almost parallel version of the United States. They depicted people seeking riches and the good life, which was an aspira-tion that most Americans would have recognized as a common goal. But in these movies, the characters attained the good life not by honesty and hard work, or even by good luck. Instead, they achieved success by violating society's most cherished values. In other words, although these characters achieved a version of success that was mostly consistent with American cul-tural ideals, the means they chose to achieve this ran counter to prevailing norms and values. In a way, fascination with this sort of narrative helped pave the way for future cinematic visions that focused on the American way break-ing down, either becoming wholly subverted or being diverted in unex-pected, often negative ways.

In the 1920s and 1930s, Americans were fascinated with organized crime and the colorful and violent figures at the center of this "underworld." Real-life crime figures, who were known through news accounts and rumor, provided models for pulp fiction writers and Hollywood scriptwriters. Prominent examples of Hollywood's interest in this theme can be found, for example, in the early days of the sound motion picture era, which did not begin until the late 1920s. In director Mervyn LeRoy's *Little Caesar* (1931), for example, viewers see the rise and fall of fictional mobster Enrico "Rico" Bandello (played by Edward G. Robinson), an ambitious man whose material success and vanity are fueled by ruthless criminal activity. This movie set up many elements that run through films about organized crime in the years since its release. (The basic outline of the plot can be seen in many films from this genre, including, for example, Francis Ford Coppola's 1972 classic, *The Godfather*, and its sequels.) Other crime world films of the era included *Scarface* (1932), a movie starring Paul Muni and directed by Howard Hawks. It told the sordid story about criminal gang warfare in the urban United States.

One important aspect of gangster films, in terms of their relationship to the dominant American narrative of the era, was that crime was portrayed as a means to achieve a dysfunctional yet still recognizable version of American success. Unchecked passions and the quest for exciting lives are shown as a socially unacceptable but still fascinating pathway to material comforts and to a warped measure of prestige. That these are achieved by violating the law and norms of civility does not take away from the fact that criminal activity was portrayed as a means to traditional success in American terms.

Both of these films were released shortly before the end of Prohibition, the era in which the manufacture, sale, and possession of alcohol was illegal in the United States. Prohibition had been adopted in the United States with the ratification of the Eighteenth Amendment in 1919. It set into law some of the conservative social attitudes of the temperance movement. Chief among these was the view that alcohol consumption was the cause of much immorality and constituted a corrupting influence on American society.

During the height of Prohibition, official attitudes about those who disagreed with the law were harsh and dismissive. Opponents of temperance, which had been cast as a moral issue, were criticized almost as deviants of society. As Joseph R. Gusfield writes,

> Temperance materials of this period stressed the "unAmerican" [*sic*] connotations of Wet opinion and depicted the violator of the Dry law as unpatriotic, a nihilist without respect for law, and an opponent of constitutional government. Speaking before the annual convention of the National Woman's Christian Temperance Union in 1927, Senator Capper said that refusal to obey a law is equivalent to treason.[2]

But although alcohol was criminalized, Prohibition policies were widely ignored. Continuing demand for alcohol fueled the rise of vast real-world criminal organizations, which used the public's appetite for alcohol as a cornerstone in their wide-ranging criminal activities to amass money, power, and influence. As the eminent historian Samuel Eliot Morison noted many years ago, Prohibition led to "the encouragement of lawbreaking and the build-ing up of a criminal class that turned to gambling and drugs when Amendment XVIII was repealed in 1933."[3] These side effects also propelled some criminals, such as the Chicago gangster Al Capone, into nationally known figures, in a way that is similar culturally to the notoriety achieved by some legendary gunfighters of the American Old West in the nineteenth century.

Films such as *Little Caesar* and *Scarface*, which were released near the end of the Prohibition era, were some of the last produced before the full weight of the American movie industry's self-censorship set in. Even before the early 1930s, Hollywood was already examining ways to ensure that it depicted themes more consonant with traditional and approved American values. Yet the public's continued interest in movies with crime themes revealed a fasci-nation with darker possibilities inherent in American life.

HOLLYWOOD'S DOUBLE-EDGED REPUTATION

For years, Washington had been skeptical of Hollywood's appeal to work-ing- and middle-class audiences. To many American politicians and moral lead-ers, the film industry often appeared to produce films that had lurid, immoral, and even unpatriotic elements. But such concerns went beyond the films them-selves. The glamorous Hollywood lifestyle was often regarded with suspicion. Sensationalized news accounts of Hollywood excesses fueled such skepticism. In the early 1920s, for example, a major scandal involving Roscoe "Fatty" Arbuckle increased suspicions about Hollywood's moral state. Arbuckle, who had been a popular actor in the silent film era, was tried on charges stemming from the rape and murder of a young actress. He was subsequently acquitted of the charges, but by then public uproar over the matter had already cast an unflattering light on the Hollywood establishment.

Such episodes helped cause industry leaders to conclude it would be advantageous for the film business to clean up its image and to repair public perceptions of Hollywood. By the 1930s, even as the failed experiment of the Eighteenth Amendment came to an end, there was a backlash against the perceived immorality of previous years, which was arguably part of the same broad social milieu that had led to Prohibition. Indeed, in some ways the Great Depression was a heyday for critics of American life, who perceived immorality in many parts of that life. Hollywood had already been a target of suspicion, and the cultural climate of the era had little to suggest that the industry's reputation would improve anytime soon on its own.

The movie business was, of course, concerned about potential intrusions into its world, and especially about changes that might be imposed by new laws or legal restrictions on the films it produced or on the industry's business practices. Already, the motion picture business was subject to closer regulation than some other media businesses of the day. In 1915, for example, the Supreme Court had ruled that movies were not covered in the free-speech protections of the First Amendment. The legal environment was therefore conducive to the potential regulation of film content, particularly with regard to obscenity and moral issues. (The case that set this precedent, *Mutual Film Corporation v. Industrial Commission of Ohio*, was not overturned until 1952.) In this context, Hollywood executives were especially eager to forestall the possibility that the federal government would take a role in censoring its films.

Leaders of the movie business therefore undertook a major plan under which Hollywood would censor itself. This would have significant impact on the types of stories that movies could tell and how they could be told, but it would keep the federal government more or less at bay, thereby giving the industry more control over its own destiny. Or such was the plan.

A new industry organization, the Motion Picture Producers and Distributors of America (MPPDA)—the forerunner of the Motion Picture Association of America (MPAA)—took the lead in Hollywood's self-censorship efforts. It espoused a very traditional version of American morality. In 1927, for example, it published a list of practices under the title "Don'ts and Be Careful's," which was designed to guide productions along approved paths.[4] Among the items that were forbidden outright in this document were "pointed profanity," "illegal traffic in drugs," "any licentious or suggestive nudity," "any inference of sex perversion," "ridicule of clergy," and "willful offense to any nation, race, or creed."

Beyond such explicit bans, the document cautioned filmmakers to use "special care ... to the end that vulgarity and suggestiveness may be eliminated and that good taste may be emphasized." Among other topics on the "Be Careful" part of the list were "use of the [American] flag," use of firearms," "brutality," "sympathy for criminal," "attitude toward public characters and institutions," "sedition," rape or attempted rape," "men and women in bed together," "the institution of marriage," "the use of drugs," and "excessive or lustful kissing." On the whole, then, the introduction of MPPDA standards established the idea that there were limits on what could be produced. In so doing, Hollywood clearly set out to bring its movie output into conformity with the prevailing morals and sensibilities of presumably average Americans.

Once initiated, the industry's self-censorship efforts continued to evolve. A few years later, the MPPDA adopted a more comprehensive set of rules to oversee the content of American films in 1930 called the Motion Picture Production Code. It was wide-ranging and more forcefully covered what could and could not be depicted or said in a motion picture.

These new self-censorship policies were a major change in the way Hollywood conducted business, and the full effects did not materialize immediately. For the first few years, the Production Code was not consistently or effectively applied. By 1934, however, regular procedures were in place. As a result, mainstream American films produced between that time and the 1960s, when the Production Code faded from the scene, were required to meet the Code's standards in order to secure approval for traditional distribution to American theaters.

Most Hollywood movies easily, and without controversy, fit within the Code's guidelines. Eager to secure popular appeal and reluctant to upset the success that the industry had built, Hollywood studios usually had little difficulty producing stories that stayed far away from what the Production Code forbade. And in cases where changes were mandated, filmmakers usually found alternate ways to convey film narratives that were permissible. The Code quickly became established, and dealing with it was understood as a mundane fact of life when making movies.

For the most part, audiences seemed satisfied with the situation, to the extent they even thought about it. Movies continued to be popular, as the motion picture business that the audiences supported largely replicated the moral universe in which they comfortably lived. In retrospect, there is nothing surprising about this. After all, the movie industry depended on the goodwill of the public, which expected to encounter entertainments meeting its approval in theaters.

The Production Code articulated norms that were embedded within leading elements of American society at the time. They amply showed the apprehension with which certain negative aspects of life were regarded and the degree to which Hollywood conformed to practices that were viewed as shoring up traditional American values. The Production Code was, then, an implicit acknowledgment that movies had the potential to affect the direction of society in very negative ways. The self-censorship practices reveal nascent fears about the power of movies to subvert American values and even aid in the destruction of the nation's promise and achievement.

The populist nature of movies, which had appealed very directly to ordinary Americans since the earliest days of the medium, had always caused some wariness on the part of the elites of society. The Production Code, and the attitude it represented, thus provided a way to keep the cinema's capacity for negative effect in check. It was already realized that film's visceral qualities—the immediacy of its moving images and the newer capability of synchronized sound—held the power to influence what people thought and what they thought about. And it had been known for years that movies could inflame passion and social unrest. (D. W. Griffith's scandalous silent film *The Birth of a Nation* from 1915, for example, had spurred protests and demonstrations upon its release, which had amply demonstrated this point.) The Production Code therefore can be seen as an attempt to control and channel film's power along socially acceptable paths. It sought to rein in the capacity of movies to depict people, situations, and themes that might be alluring to many people, but that might chip away at the presumed moral consensus that kept society more or less in balance, despite many tensions.

THE DARK SIDE OF AN AMERICAN SUCCESS STORY

A serious film that was perhaps less obvious in its critical, apprehensive view of American society was issued in 1941, just before the United States entered World War II. This movie, *Citizen Kane*, was the product of upstart media sensation Orson Welles, who was only in his mid-20s at the time. The youthful director-actor had risen to fame on the basis of a successful radio show, *The Mercury Theatre of the Air*, which he had founded with fellow actor John Houseman. *Mercury Theatre*'s 1938 radio play adaptation of H. G. Wells's science fiction novel, *War of the Worlds*, was nationally broadcast in October 1938 and reportedly caused a widespread panic among listeners, who apparently believed that the fictional play was an actual news account of an invasion from Mars. This scare was subsequently sensationalized, and no doubt exaggerated, but the publicity nonetheless propelled Welles to fame. He soon obtained a movie deal and set out to make a motion picture that would be equally attention getting, even if in a different way.

The subject of *Citizen Kane*, Welles's first and most well-known film, borrowed heavily from the life story of the media mogul William Randolph Hearst, whose legendary successes and excesses had made him perhaps as famous as the newspapers and radio stations that he controlled. The idea of fictionalizing Hearst's life as a movie project had originally been developed by scriptwriter Herman J. Mankiewicz. Welles latched upon this as the subject for his movie and then also worked on the script with Mankiewicz. The resulting film, which is now widely regarded as among the best ever produced, initially met with mixed reaction.

Hearst was a powerful and well-connected man, and he was angered by the thinly veiled portrayal of his life, even if it was cloaked in a work of fiction. His opposition meant that the film would not be advertised or publicized in the many newspapers that he controlled across the country. The studio was taken aback by Hearst's response, and its executives were anxious about the potential for the mogul's anger to translate into damaging future effects on its other films. And Hearst was very angry. He made concerted attempts to squash *Citizen Kane*.

Citizen Kane was moderately successful in financial terms. And while the film did earn critical praise, it remained controversial. Hollywood gossip columnist Hedda Hopper, for example, characterized the movie as "a vicious and irresponsible attack on a great man."[5] The film did not garner the audience that might have been expected, given Welles's notoriety and self-promotional skills. In fact, despite the formidable reputation that *Citizen Kane* was to enjoy in future years, this was a much after-the-fact development. It did not initially receive the widespread acclaim that later became common.

Beyond the problems with Hearst, the narrative of the film was also jarring in the context of the early 1940s. The fictional Charles Foster Kane was, at first blush, the epitome of an American success story, rising from obscurity because of an inherited fortune. As a young man, Kane seems to find a purpose in his life when he takes a controlling interest in a small New York newspaper, which he has acquired as part of another business transaction. He famously decides, "It might be fun to run a newspaper," and takes over the editor's role himself. Using his power and influence, Kane then becomes determined to champion the common person and fight corruption in business and politics. He goes so far as to publish a "Declaration of Principles" that he envisions as a guiding light for his crusading journalism.

Yet the story shows how Kane gradually becomes bitter and corrupted by his vast wealth. His vanity overtakes him, his judgment becomes suspect, and whatever altruism had been expressed in his early days at the newspaper is gone. Eventually, even his closest friend, an associate he had known since childhood, abandons him. By the close of the story, Kane is a lonely, broken old man. He still possesses some of his fortune, but he has also been destroyed by it.

The story portrayed in *Citizen Kane* is hardly the kind of success that is consistent with a vision of the American Dream. Kane possesses great wealth and material comfort, to be sure. But these do not bring Kane happiness, and in fact seem to haunt him. Indeed, much of the story of *Citizen Kane* seems to show the underside of what might otherwise be regarded as a very successful life. As one writer has concluded, the film suggests that "mere association with affluence may ultimately erode one's spirituality and lead to moral corruption."[6]

Over the course of the film, viewers witness Kane's increasingly ugly behavior. Women are treated badly; electoral politics are shown as manipulation; high society is depicted largely as a sham. All in all, the movie implies a dark picture of the rich and powerful. *Citizen Kane* was not the first movie to make reference to such ideas, but it was among the most direct in its presentation of the subject. From one perspective, many of the ideas in the film seem dissonant with the idealized ways that Americans often talked about their way of life. The only American virtue that it seems to reinforce, by way of negative example, is moderation, a quality Kane clearly does not possess.

THE YEARS OF WORLD WAR II

Ironically, one scene in *Citizen Kane* shows the character confidently stating that there will be no new world war, which was a bold pronouncement given that Europe was already engaged in hostilities when the film was released in May of 1941. In real life, the attack on Pearl Harbor on December 7, 1941, finally pushed the United States into ongoing conflicts in the Pacific region and in Europe. As the United States went to war, so did Hollywood.

When the United States declared war on Japan and also on Germany, the global conflict, which had already begun, grew significantly larger. Over the next four years, the ranks of the American military grew to more than 16 million. Of these, the war eventually took an immense toll. In the next four years, over 290,000 American military personnel died in battle, and another 113,000 perished in "nontheater" service. Still another 670,000 suffered injury. The pain and suffering was shared across the country; few communities were spared.

In the United States, the war effort generated unprecedented demand for military supplies and equipment, sweeping away whatever remnants of industrial lethargy had lingered from the Great Depression years. Factories around the nation rushed to fill orders, creating many new opportunities for employment. The war was, then, something in which the whole of American society was deeply involved. But this was not surprising since the conflict was viewed not just as any war but as a titanic struggle for the very survival of the United States and its Western allies. The stakes were thus very high, giving the war a potentially apocalyptic character.

The American movie industry was intimately involved in the war effort, as well. This was a relatively new development for Hollywood. The American film business had been in its infancy when the Great War—later called World War I—engulfed Europe and other parts of the world from 1914 to 1918. Despite the breadth and intensity of that conflict and its profound impact internationally, the United States did not formally enter the war until spring 1917. The American film business was still young, and filmmaking technology and technique still in early stages of development, but the potential of film to inform and persuade was noted even then. The publication *Motion Picture News*, for example, called on the industry to "spread that propaganda so necessary to the immediate mobilization of the country's great resources."[7] Indeed, some films promoting American entry into the war were produced, and others presented a heavily anti-German message.[8] Still, American involvement in the war came late, and the opportunity for the U.S. film industry to become fully enmeshed in the war effort was somewhat limited.

Hollywood's explicit and implicit involvement in the American war effort during World War II, however, was more pronounced. In this second worldwide conflict, the American film business was deeply involved in promoting war-related messages. Indeed, Hollywood productions throughout the war helped shape the already negative public perceptions of the German and Japanese enemies, while simultaneously portraying the American war effort as a moral and noble purpose. Of course, previous American war efforts had also been bolstered by propaganda-like media messages. (Consider, for example, World War I–era government posters, which portrayed German soldiers as inhuman, sadistic "Huns.") But by the time of World War II, film techniques were highly evolved, and movies were very well situated to deliver effective progovernment policies messages.

The particular savagery of World War II is beyond question, and it was no doubt not difficult for Hollywood to marshal its resources to produce works that highlighted the negative aspects of the United States' enemies, even in the years before the specifics of such atrocities as the Holocaust were widely known. Hollywood had already gained significant experience producing Westerns, in which the "bad guys" are truly and unambiguously evil. Stories in which war enemies were equally or more evil were not conceptually far from this narrative model. In both cases, American heroes were thwarting evil and restoring morality.

Movies of this type depend on evildoers and villains for their narrative power. These stories therefore involve struggles against a destructive "other," and they often become stories in which the outcome has powerful implications. The defeat of heroes in such stories is more than just a setback, therefore. Defeat has enormous moral consequences. Enemies loom large and are the potential embodiments of evil.

Indeed, during World War II Hollywood produced many films that directly and indirectly supported the war effort and replicated official attitudes. For example, famed director Frank Capra was commissioned by Washington to oversee production of movies that supported the war effort. Capra was already well known for such hits as *Mr. Deeds Goes to Town* (1936), the idealistically patriotic *Mr. Smith Goes to Washington* (1939), and other films. In his new capacity, which extended from 1942 until 1945, he oversaw production of a series of films that was issued under the collective title of *Why We Fight*. These movies, which were ostensibly informational in nature, explained and justified why the United States should fully support the burdensome sacrifices of massive war on two fronts. With portions narrated by the well-known actor John Huston and also containing animated sequences supplied by the Disney studios, the *Why We Fight* movies were part of a successful domestic propaganda campaign made with the participation of the War Department.

Capra directed the first of these films, *Prelude to War*, which was released in 1942, not long after the United States entered the war. The War Department hoped to bolster support and enthusiasm for the struggle by presenting military personnel and the general public with an easy to understand picture of the fascist enemy. Of course, chipping away at the American public's long tendency to isolationism in foreign entanglements was also a factor that had motivated production of these films.

Several more *Why We Fight* movies were issued throughout the war: *The Nazis Strike* (1943), *Divide and Conquer* (1943), *The Battle of Britain* (1943), *The Battle of Russia* (1943), *The Battle of China* (1944), and *War Comes to America* (1945). Taken together, these films formed an important part of the domestic war effort and were recognized as important at the time. The first of the series, *Prelude to War*, was awarded the prize for Best Documentary by the Academy of Motion Picture Arts and Sciences in 1943.

During the war years, more traditional Hollywood productions also portrayed the conflict, directly or indirectly, in ways that were overtly supportive of the war effort and government policy. Of course, the war was also a compelling, ready-made subject with built-in dramatic potential, and the sort of story line that Hollywood could easily utilize.

Some of the best and most enduring of these films, such as *Casablanca* (1942), treated the war as a backdrop. The struggle provided a moral context against which people in the story would find and reveal their own true character. In the film's narrative, the love affair between Rick Blaine (played by Humphrey Bogart) and his former lover, the now-married Ilsa Lund (played by Ingrid Bergman), is played out in the remote location of Morocco. But overtones of the war are everywhere, as are German military personnel in a city nominally under French control. In the climatic final moments of the film, the main characters sacrifice their love so that Lund can support the work of her husband, who is active in the anti-Nazi resistance movement.

The unambiguous message of the film is that personal sacrifice is a small thing to make in the midst of a struggle against global evil. Especially given the context in which it was initially released in 1942, *Casablanca* is therefore squarely a film that bolstered sympathy for the United States' entry into the war. That it does so without resorting to the portrayal of American combat troops or without really seeming to be primarily a "war movie" is noteworthy. But more than that, *Casablanca* shows an idealized, patriotic vision of the United States and illustrates, as noted by writer Aljean Harmetz, "America's mythological vision of itself—tough on the outside and moral within."[9]

More traditional war movies were part of Hollywood's agenda in these years, as well. The titles of such movies provide a strong indication of the pro-war, pro-American stories that viewers would see. Among the more well known of these features were *Dive Bomber* (1941), *A Yankee in the R.A.F.* (1941), *Wake Island* (1942), *Guadalcanal Diary* (1943), *Bataan* (1943), and *Thirty Seconds over Tokyo* (1944).

The list of movies of this type also included *They Were Expendable*, a 1945 feature directed by John Ford and starring Robert Montgomery, John Wayne, and Donna Reed. In the film, the characters played by Montgomery and Wayne actively seek out naval combat assignments for their small, swift-moving PT boats. As was typical for films of this type, ample assistance was given to the production company by the American military.

Films in other genres also bolstered support for the war. *To Be or Not to Be* (1942) was a comedy starring the popular comedian Jack Benny. Its story was about a stage troupe that outwits Nazis occupying Poland. In another genre, Universal updated a popular series of movies based on Arthur Conan Doyle's famous Sherlock Holmes character. Originally set in Victorian England, the stories now showed Holmes (played by Basil Rathbone) and his assistant, Dr. Watson (Nigel Bruce), battling Nazi spies in wartime Britain, as was the case in such films as Universal Studio's *Sherlock Holmes and the Voice of Terror* (1942) and *Sherlock Holmes and the Secret Weapon* (1943). In *Sherlock Holmes in Washington* (1943), the detective crosses the Atlantic Ocean to fight the enemy on American soil.

These are only some of the many films that were related to the American participation in World War II. But they demonstrate the depth and scope of the industry's involvement in the war effort, and they give some indication of how often American moviegoers saw productions that were designed, at least in part, to maintain public enthusiasm for the war. As the war transpired, then, there was little question about Hollywood's support for the war, though this would sometimes be questioned in years after the fact. But in the early 1940s, it seemed clear that the American movie business was an important part of the war effort, producing movies during the war years that were generally supportive—usually enthusiastically so—of the United States and its allies.[10]

AMERICA AT THE END OF WORLD WAR II

Americans celebrated when the end of World War II finally came in 1945. After President Truman announced the surrender of Japan on August 14 of that year, euphoria quickly spread. In New York City, 2 million people jammed into Times Square, filling the air with a roar of jubilation.[11] That moment was a deeply emotional moment in American history. The nation had won an all-out war, which it had viewed as a fight for the survival of its way of life. The price was very high, but the United States had persevered. The triumph seemed to be a righteous outcome that validated the ideals that Americans had come to use when talking about themselves.

In the eyes of many people, the United States had achieved its commanding position in the world thanks to the sacrifices of an extraordinary group of people. These were the young Americans who fought the war, both at the front and in support positions at home. They were, in the later words of television journalist Tom Brokaw, "the Greatest Generation." And as Brokaw wrote some decades later, no sooner had the war ended than these young, idealistic Americans set about to the "task of rebuilding their lives and the world they wanted. They were mature beyond their years, tempered by what they had been through, disciplined by their military training and sacrifices. . . . They stayed true to their values of personal responsibility, duty, honor, and faith."[12]

With its triumph, the United States had achieved a lofty position of power and recognition. The people of the United States savored peace and victory. They were eager to put the trials and tribulations of war behind them. Looking forward, they were ready for a bright, new future and a return to normalcy as they imagined it.

In reality, however, it had been a very long time since things had been "normal." By the time the United States had entered the war, life had already been altered by the years of economic hardship. The war was a crisis of monumental proportions, but in the decade prior to the war, the years of the Great Depression had devastated the nation. The economic catastrophe stretched the fabric of American society thin and ruptured national confidence in the 1930s.

Yet in 1945, Americans could look at the devastation in Europe and Asia, where the bulk of the fighting had taken place, and notice how that stood in stark contrast to conditions in the United States, which had been mostly spared the firsthand effects of war on its home soil. So when Americans took stock immediately after the war, they realized that despite the many sacrifices, they had come through the war more intact than many other countries. Given the collective sense of relief felt throughout the nation, it is perhaps not surprising that for many Americans it seemed as though it was the dawn of a golden era. In many respects, then, Americans were brimming with enthusiasm. They were proud of their achievement and largely thought of their nation as a moral beacon for the rest of the world. And they believed that winning the war made it possible to create a bold new world, fulfilling, in a way, a vision of the United States that seemed to be its destiny.

Perhaps no previous victory was as sweet as that won by the United States and its allies in 1945. Indeed, the war provided an opportunity for the United States to take the center of the world stage at a historic moment, cementing the country's status as a superpower among nations. The war had been experienced as a titanic struggle that tested American will and moral character when the nation was at one of its lowest points. Like an ancient hero tested when the outlook seemed bleakest, the national ordeal of World War II was experienced not just as a massive conflict, but also as a do-or-die situation. It was an unexpected (and surely unwanted, given the toll it took) opportunity for the United States to prove to itself and to the world of the rightness of its story. Victory was much more than victory, from this point of view. It was the validation of the American Dream narrative that had origins in a much earlier era.

Although the idea of the American Dream had already been established in U.S. culture, the circumstances at the end of the war provided a context when the idea could more firmly and thoroughly take root. If the Great Depression and World War II were the tests, then the rise of the American Dream was, in this way of looking at things, the deserved result.

With victory came a distinctly national point of view about the rightful place of the United States in world affairs. Success in the war further reinforced American exceptionalist self-perceptions, of the nation's role as a special outlier in world history with a rightful place at the head of nations. For many Americans, the leading role of the United States was (and is) a moral right, based on the idea that the American brand of democracy has innate virtues that are self-evident and self-justifying. Some people took this reasoning further, suggesting that the United States' place as world leader is a divine right, sanctified by God.

Indeed, winning World War II significantly added to and enhanced the American narrative, providing a heroic dimension to the existing American myth. In some ways, the story that Americans told themselves about their nation was a story of the United States the good, the United States the just. There was a commonly perceived sense of moral clarity about the American role in World War II. Domestic opposition to U.S. participation in the war had been negligible. Instead, the prevailing attitude was that the United States was upholding its duty to do good by fighting truly evil enemies.

ENEMIES AND THEIR USES

In wars, it is obviously typical to regard the enemy in very negative ways. But the United States' foes in World War II were regarded with special enmity and as threats to the very survival of the United States and its way of life. Though it is sometimes forgotten, not all wars are perceived as possessing such existential consequences. Sometimes wars are more about territorial expansion or other matters that, while perceived as important to the warring nations, do not threaten the survival of the nations involved. (One would be hard-pressed to find people who seriously thought the Falkland War between Argentina and Great Britain in 1982 was a fight for the survival of either nation, for example.)

World War II was a conflict in which the stakes rose to the highest level, however. Germany and Japan were seen as enemies that presented clearly existential threats to the survival and well-being of United States. This conceptual framework, with its stark moral divide between the United States as a force of good and its enemies as the embodiment of evil, reinforced a conceptual dynamic that persisted long after World War II. Much political rhetoric in the years since has tended to define the United States' moral character by comparing the United States to what it is not. In this way, powerful enemies have been important instruments in the creation and maintenance of American self-perceptions.

Thus consensus perceptions of the United States' World War II enemies as embodiments of danger and evil helped further a widespread feeling of unity among Americans. The threat of these external foes provided a compelling reason for Americans to largely set aside—or at least minimize attention to— many of their differences and instead join together in a spirit of camaraderie. Indeed, enemies can serve important political purposes. They can have the effect of uniting nations and driving national consensus. As political scientist Murray Edelman has written, "In constructing such enemies and the narrative plots that define their place in history, people are manifestly defining themselves and their place in history as well; the self-definition lends passion to the whole transaction."[13]

A wartime foe that represents a different way of life or a different set of interests can instantly allow a people to see themselves as a people and to view conflict through a lens of good and evil. Political leaders have long recognized the power of conceiving things in this way. They have often relied upon the popularity of the war metaphor in American politics (e.g., "war on drugs," "war against poverty") in order to add clarity (perhaps not always successfully) and a moral dimension to otherwise complex problems.

The call to war, whether in a real or metaphorical sense, also heightens the stakes at an emotional level. It is not a call to examine some problem; it is a call for decisive action. The language of war is therefore useful for mobilizing citizens who might otherwise be content to let some situation stand as it is. But the heightened emotional stakes in war rhetoric can be used for less than noble purposes, as well. In the frenzy before and during war, rationality can take a backseat, and the potential for manipulation can be very real.

Enemies also serve potent ideological and national purposes. Just as villains heighten drama and create situations in which the heroes of literature can become heroes, the threat of villainous nations or international entities creates a context in which the virtues of a nation can be played out. Enemies provide a counterpoint that helps confirm national identity. They are negative examples that demonstrate to a people, as well as to other members of the world community, who they are by showing who they are not. From one perspective, then, enemies are a vital part of modern political culture. So, while a people may yearn for peace and tranquility both within and outside national borders, there is nonetheless a cultural usefulness for opponents, the existence of which can draw people together and help a people define who they are.

Uneasy Alliance with the Soviet Union

But with the end of the war in 1945, Germany and Japan, which had been viewed as the embodiments of evil, were defeated. What would happen to the sense of unity that the monumental struggle against them now that they were vanquished? The answer to this question was already apparent.

The Soviet Union had been an ally of sorts during the last part of the war. But even before the war was fully concluded, American political leaders were wary of the USSR's motives and disdainful of its ideological inclinations. The alliance between the United States and the Soviet Union during World War II was uneasy, at best, and never much more than a convenient relationship during a time when there was a common enemy. The tensions between the two nations were never far from the surface.

Despite the mutually shared goal of defeating Germany, the Soviet and American governments had remained deeply suspicious of each other. Even before the war ended, the two nations were often already working at cross-purposes. In 1945, as the allied army of the United States approached Berlin from the west and the Soviet army approached from the east, each power sought to manipulate the circumstances of the war's impending conclusion to gain a potential advantage in Europe when the fighting was over.

When Berlin fell in 1945, the common enemy was vanquished, and the weak alliance between the United States and the Soviet Union quickly evaporated. What soon emerged was the Cold War, which would extend for nearly a half century. These conditions, and others that would emerge over time, fueled an anxious and fearful way of thinking about American life that was often perceptible, even in times when the more promising vision of the American Dream was widespread.

Thus, in the period immediately following World War II, the external threat that Germany and Japan represented during the war was soon replaced by the USSR, a powerful enemy that, if not exactly new, was at least envisioned in a newly dangerous way. It would not be long until this enemy would be regarded as even more dangerous than the enemies that had come before. Over time, the identification and positioning against enemies helped Americans reinforce their ideas about themselves and their nation.

LOOKING IN, LOOKING OUT

Soon after World War II, a difference emerged between the United States' inward and outward views of the world. When Americans looked inwardly at their nation, absent concerns of what was happening on the outside, the picture that emerged was often positive and confidently aspirational. It was a picture of a triumphant way of life and values that seemed destined to define humankind's future. When Americans looked outside to the rest of the world, however, what increasingly was seen was the threat of a mysterious and ominous enemy, embodied in the growing Communist empire of the Soviet Union. And when this enemy on the outside seemed poised to threaten the United States internally and existentially, it shook the confidence that otherwise characterized the United States' view of itself. This anxious feeling was evident throughout the cultural landscape.

Thus, while Americans were outwardly confident, questions remained below surface appearances. For a time, the mainstream United States frowned on even asking such questions, as if to doubt any aspect of the nation's makeup or character was tantamount to betrayal. Yet the world was never as simple as the telling of the American story often suggested. The real situation, domestically and internationally, was complex. Social and political forces were in motion at home and abroad, sometimes creating new complications and unpredictable situations. Reconciling these real-world scenarios with the idealized story that Americans told themselves about their nation was occasionally difficult, generating a sense of unease and doubt. And such cases provided a context for the rise of the darker, alternate picture of the United States—a vision of the United States' potential doom.

Hollywood would be quick to reflect this new way of envisioning the world, and in coming months films about threats emanating from outside of the United States would begin to appear regularly in theaters across the country. Expressing outlooks that were similar to the increasing apprehension with Americans perceived the dangers of global communism, many of these films would suggest nightmarish, sometimes catastrophic consequences if the United States were to let down its guard.

The years of the Great Depression had, in some sense, helped prime Americans to see things in terms of morality and immorality. The moral climate in those years in some ways reverted to a more traditional nature than had been the case just a few years earlier in the Roaring Twenties. World War II presented the nation with a frightening, existential threat. The nation's enemies seemed to have global ambitions that would crush all who stood in their way. These background elements helped frame American experience (and Hollywood's subsequent reflection of it) in ways that emphasized stark choices of good versus evil. And they helped pave the way for imagining that there might be dire consequences if the United States were to succumb to either the internal threat of immorality or the external dangers of communism.

But in 1945, these apprehensions still seemed far away, as the United States basked in the glory of winning the war and contemplated a new world of seemingly endless possibility. Political culture reveled in this self-perception of the United States in the postwar world. Popular culture—and Hollywood, in particular—similarly repeated these views. But despite widespread acceptance, there was caution. And soon the telling of the American story, both in Washington and in Hollywood, would reveal cracks in the gleaming surface.

CHAPTER 3

A Dangerous World

The great victory achieved in World War II had propelled the United States to the forefront of world powers, but within that victory were the seeds of doubt and anxiety. U.S. politics and popular culture often reflected and amplified the positive aspects of the United States' new position and prestige, but the darker potential inherent in the new realities of the world was always nearby. After the war, then, a vision of the United States on the brink of disaster began to take shape in American politics and popular culture. Sometimes this was very obvious, but at other times it was subtly hidden in narratives that seemed to be about something else.

Overcoming the Great Depression and the challenges of World War II had been possible only at great cost and sacrifice. But as difficult as they were, the hard years of the 1930s and first half of the 1940s were transformational for the United States. Upon meeting these enormous challenges, the nation found itself standing at the head of what it called the "free world." It had attained a level of power and influence that was unmatched in modern times.

Yet, if the United States was now viewing the world from the top of a mighty mountain, it was a view that was not altogether comforting. Powerful enemies had been decisively vanquished in World War II, but new enemies stood ready to test the United States' might and values. Almost immediately, the USSR was perceived as the primary new foe. It had been an ally of the United States during the war. After the war, however, old suspicions about it came rushing back. The ideological conflict between the two powers in the postwar world soon escalated into a long and costly "Cold War." And as U.S. politics became enmeshed in increasingly heated Cold

War rhetoric in the late 1940s, a sense of anxiety and apprehension was also reflected in popular culture. The high emotion of the new world situation presented enticing thematic possibilities for Hollywood, which it was ready to adapt and exploit.

In some ways, the dangerous new world that emerged from the ashes of World War II was very cinematic, especially as dramatically articulated by American leaders. In political rhetoric of the day, noble heroes and evil villains appeared on the international stage as the world was envisioned in a dichotomous, all-or-nothing way. It was an oversimplified, distinctly nonnuanced way of seeing the world. And it contrasted markedly with the realist, pragmatic way of envisioning American foreign policy, which tended to see more "gray areas" in the international arena. But to leaders at the time, the international scene in the years immediately after 1945 seemed to suggest that in the emerging Cold War, the United States and its allies were engaged in a new existential fight for survival. This struggle was seen as one that was filled with hidden motivations and allegiances and took a path with unpredictable twists and turns.

By the second half of the 1940s, Hollywood was at a crossroads. The world was changing, and so were audiences. As this new world developed after the global war, the American movie business was already searching for fresh themes and new kinds of films that would continue to attract audiences to theaters. The largely escapist stories of the Depression years and the overtly patriotic themes in movies of the war years were losing their appeal. Therefore the film industry looked for new themes and new cinematic experiences that would draw moviegoers. Hollywood aimed to make movies that would be perceived as contemporary, relevant, and modern, in addition to being simply entertaining.

The drama of international politics in the postwar period provided a context that in some ways was well suited to Hollywood. Indeed, the evolving political outlook after 1945 often dovetailed with the narrative inclinations to which the American film business was much accustomed. The dichotomous good-versus-evil, freedom-versus-communism framework that was the hallmark of Washington's view of the world at that time was, like the stories in many Hollywood movies, a world of "good guys" and "bad guys." In both Washington's and Hollywood's worldviews, the contrasts are stark, and the potential for conflict immediately obvious. The emergent political description of the world was thus consistent with Hollywood's usually strong impulse to reduce complex phenomena into easily understood and uncomplicated, oversimplified stories. If one looks at many American film and television productions in the postwar era, there are many productions across many movie genres that replicate this type of narrative framework.

In literal and metaphorical representations, many screen productions repeatedly emphasized the United States' worldview. American thematic ideas—appearing in various guises almost as morality plays—pictured a world that often mirrored some of the confidence and swagger that the United States exhibited in international relations. But even as they portrayed this positive picture, an underlying sense of impending doom was often present as well. The implication of many films—in war, science fiction, Western, and other genres—was that order and justice were precarious. The threat of chaos and destruction was never far away in films of this type.

The contrasting narrative strands of triumph and ruin that developed in postwar Hollywood were deeply connected to the broader political environment. To understand the narrative strand in Hollywood's output, it is therefore instructive to examine the anxious political contexts that burst onto the American scene after World War II.

AN END AND A BEGINNING

The circumstances of history tell much about the anxious underside of American life that emerged even as the United States was reveling in newfound power and success in the years following World War II. It is in such details that the sources for persistent political and cultural themes of decay and devastation can be found.

The defeat of Germany and Japan in 1945 brought not only peace but a sense of triumph and satisfaction that was felt throughout American society. In some ways, the euphoria that winning the war evoked continued for a long time, melding with the already existing, but still evolving, American Dream narrative strand in U.S. culture. To that way of seeing things, the war was something akin to a test of the United States' mettle, and victory sealed the nation's place as the rightful leader of the world's nations. The interpretation of the war as not only a military victory but also a victory of the American way of life and system of government added a powerful moral dimension to the story.

Even as this positive, optimistic narrative strand to the American experience took hold, a countervailing story began to unfold. This parallel narrative was considerably bleaker and more anxious. In it, victory in World War II was still evidence that the United States had passed a moral test. But postwar conditions indicated that the war had been only one test, and as time passed it seemed that perhaps it had not even been the strongest challenge that the United States would face. In the years immediately following the war, threats from outside forces and outside influence seemed the most ominous dangers for the United States. In time, unforeseen consequences from changes in

American living—which in this era seemed to herald nothing but positive possibilities—would also come to be seen as a source of threat and potential doom. But that realization was in the future. In the late 1940s, Americans and their leaders worried about enemies at the gate, not dangers from the world they were creating.

The tumultuous conclusion of World War II set up much of the context that would be important in the era that followed. After Germany's surrender, for example, the Allies occupied Germany, dividing it into four zones. Each of the four major allied powers—the United States, Great Britain, France, and the USSR—controlled one of the zones. (Berlin, in the heart of the Soviet zone, had special symbolic meaning and therefore was also divided among the allied powers.) But although it was divided into four sections administratively, the partitioning of Germany on ideological grounds was really only a two-way split. On one side was the U.S.-led world of democratic societies. On the other was the Communist world represented by the USSR. The division of Germany in many ways suggested what was to come: a polarized world in which there was a monumental struggle between two superpowers, each desiring to bring as many nations under their influence as possible.

In the months following Germany's surrender, the Soviet Union came to dominate most of Eastern Europe. This spread of communism in Europe was an anxiety-provoking development for the United States. American possession of nuclear weaponry provided a limited sense of relief for Americans, since at the time only the United States had harnessed the power of the atom for its arsenal. But still, the expansion of Soviets influence and ideology seemed an increasing threat.

By the late 1940s, rapidly changing circumstances elevated American anxieties, setting off ripples in American politics that soon became powerful waves. Indeed, the fears that fueled the anti-Communist zeal of McCarthyism several years later did not arise overnight or without reasons. The years of the late 1940s were a cauldron into which events and crises from around the world mixed to generate a powerful force that shaped American political culture for years to come. The perceived crises and challenges to the United States seemed ever increasing. The effects of this mounting sense of danger were palpable.

Although the zealous anti-Communist hysteria and investigations of the early 1950s are probably among the most well-known events in the Cold War, in fact these feelings developed over a period of several years. And far from quelling emerging anxiety in the late 1940s, President Harry Truman played an important part in creating a politically anxious climate that others would later exploit.

As early as 1947, for example, Truman ordered the Department of Justice to compile a list of "totalitarian, fascist, communist or subversive" groups. Within a few years, a wide variety of organizations were so listed, ranging from the Ku Klux Klan to the Committee for the Negro in Arts to the Washington Bookshop Association and more.[1] Yet none seems to have been seen as representing as significant a threat as did groups with Communist or socialist ties. In fact, the administration carried out a large number of investigations of American citizens at this time. As Douglas Miller and Marion Nowack report, "Between the launching of his security program in March 1947 and December 1952, some 6.6 million persons were investigated. . . . All of this was conducted with secret evidence, secret and often paid informers, and neither judge nor jury."[2]

Also in 1947, the president articulated what came to be known as the Truman Doctrine. It defined the American outlook in global politics for many years. The vision laid out a grand way of conceiving the United States' place in the international sphere.

The background to the Truman Doctrine can be found in diplomatic communications in 1946. Reports prepared by George F. Kennan, an American diplomat stationed in the Soviet capital, outlined the rudiments of a new strategy that was highly influential in setting new American foreign policy regarding the USSR. In a document from that year that has come to be known as the "Long Telegram," Kennan argued that the best way to cope with potential Soviet expansion was to develop a policy of containment. Said differently, Kennan argued that the main goal of the United States regarding the USSR should be to keep the Soviets' influence from spreading.

Kennan's proposed strategy was based on his reading of the USSR's behavior, which at times perplexed American leaders. It was Kennan's belief that the USSR did "not take unnecessary risks" and that it was "impervious to the logic of reason." But he also believed that Soviet leaders were "highly sensitive to logic of force," which implied that American might should be prominently and constantly on display in dealing with this foe. Faced with a show of military strength, Kennan wrote, "[the USSR] can easily withdraw—and usually does when strong resistance is encountered at any point. Thus, if the adversary has sufficient force and makes clear his readiness to use it, he rarely has to do so. If situations are properly handled there need be no prestige-engaging showdowns."[3]

Working from this analysis, Kennan outlined a five-point strategy to deal with the Soviet threat. First, he believed the United States should study and understand the true nature of the adversary in the same way that a "doctor studies unruly and unreasonable individual." Second, he argued, "We must see that our public is educated to realities of Russian situation." (This task, he said, should be undertaken "mainly by Government.") Third, he argued that for the United States, "every courageous and incisive measure to solve internal problems of our own society, to improve self-confidence, discipline, morale and community spirit of our own people, is a diplomatic victory over Moscow." Fourth, he stated, "We must formulate and put forward for other nations a much more positive and constructive picture of sort of world we would like to see." And finally, he wrote that the United States "must have courage and self-confidence to cling to our own methods and conceptions of human society. After all, the greatest danger that can befall us in coping with this problem of Soviet communism, is that we shall allow ourselves to become like those with whom we are coping."[4] Kennan thus saw the Soviets as dangerous, even somewhat irrational adversaries. But he was confident that taking steps such as those he proposed would allow the United States and its allies to limit Soviet influence over time.

Kennan's telegram did not have an immediate effect. In 1947, however, a political crisis in Greece (which emerged just as the United States became concerned about developments in Turkey) provided Truman with a context in which he could build upon Kennan's ideas. In a speech to a joint session of Congress in 1947, the president outlined the Truman Doctrine. In his remarks, Truman declared that Americans were standing at a pivotal juncture. He said:

At the present moment in world history nearly every nation must choose between alternative ways of life. The choice is too often not a free one.

One way of life is based upon the will of the majority, and is distinguished by free institutions, representative government, free elections, guarantees of individual liberty, freedom of speech and religion, and freedom from political oppression.

The second way of life is based upon the will of a minority forcibly imposed upon the majority. It relies upon terror and oppression, a controlled press and radio, fixed elections, and the suppression of personal freedoms.

I believe that it must be the policy of the United States to support free peoples who are resisting attempted subjugation by armed minorities or by outside pressures.

I believe that we must assist free peoples to work out their own destinies in their own way.

I believe that our help should be primarily through economic and financial aid which is essential to economic stability and orderly political processes.[5]

Truman further argued, "The free peoples of the world look to us for support in maintaining their freedoms. If we falter in our leadership, we may endanger the peace of the world—and we shall surely endanger the welfare of our own nation."[6]

The Truman Doctrine thus painted a picture of a world of stark moral and political contrasts. Its articulation of the world situation suggested that one path of American action would lead to success and continued freedom. By implication, the other path would lead to the nation's doom. It was, therefore, the role of the United States, Truman said, to stand up for "freedom" everywhere in the world. The United States had no real choice in this view but to oppose communism wherever it might be found. Thus the Truman Doctrine laid out a rationale for forceful intervention when it was deemed necessary to halt Soviet expansion. In fact, the Truman Doctrine established the rationale for American military interventions in far-flung places for many years to come. And it helped reinforce the notion that the United States was involved in a titanic struggle with an evil enemy, the Soviet Union. The implication was that this was a fight for the very survival of the American way of life that the sacrifices of World War II had delivered to the American people. To lose such a battle might bring unimaginable and catastrophic results because this was not a fight only or even mainly about territory. It was about maintaining freedom.

As part of its overall strategy to combat the perceived evils of communism, the Truman Doctrine also promoted economic and development assistance as a means to spread American influence. This more peaceful strand of thinking led to the Marshall Plan, which sought to rescue the economies of Europe. Its goal was stabilizing those societies and presumably bolstering their resistance to the lure of communism. An additional benefit was that stable democracies could also prove to be valuable markets for American goods.

In a commencement address to the graduates of Harvard University in 1947, Secretary of State George Marshall explained some of the reasoning behind the plan bearing his name:

It is logical that the United States should do whatever it is able to do to assist in the return of normal economic health to the world, without which there can be no political stability and no assured peace. Our policy is not directed against any country, but against hunger, poverty, desperation and chaos. Any government that is willing to assist in recovery will find full co-operation on the part of the U.S.A. Its purpose should be the revival of a working economy in the world so as to permit the emergence of political and social conditions in which free institutions can exist.[7]

There were soon many opportunities to test Truman's policies. In the years immediately following, many international crises erupted, each providing challenges to the United States' desire to slow the spread of communism.

Importantly, in the late 1940s these developments helped establish a world-view that was highly dichotomous. Ideologically, the world was divided into the "good" camp—that of the United States and its sphere of influence—and the "evil" camp—dominated by the forces of communism. It was a black-and-white world with negligible middle ground in the eyes of the superpowers. Nonaligned nations scarcely mattered, except insofar as they could be recruited to one camp or the other.

Since there were really only two perceived sides to the situation, the stakes were viewed as very high. Loss, though feared, was too terrible to contemplate, at least very directly or very openly. Yet the culture did acknowledge such fears less overtly, processing nightmarish possibilities in other ways, and especially in storytelling on film and in print.

THE HOUSE UN-AMERICAN ACTIVITIES COMMITTEE AND HOLLYWOOD

By the late 1940s, the threat of communism was a major concern in Congress. Soon, the House Un-American Activities Committee (HUAC) searched for enemies and traitors within American borders, sometimes in unexpected places.

Originally established in 1938 as a temporary arm of the House of Representatives, HUAC had become a permanent committee in 1945. And although its activities during the war were largely focused on individuals and groups who could undermine the war effort—especially Nazi sympathizers or agents—after the war HUAC turned its focus to the perceived threat of communism. This attention to communism was not entirely new. Having been created in the final years of the Great Depression—in an era when many Americans were attracted, however briefly, to Socialist and Communist ideas—Communist influence in American life had been a major focus of HUAC activities before U.S. entry into World War II.

It was clear from the 1947 investigations that members of HUAC were deeply suspicious of Hollywood. The film industry was a "Red propaganda center," according to Rep. J. Parnell Thomas, an ardent anti-Communist Republican and then chair of the committee.[8]

This attitude was a continuation of mistrust about the movie business that had started years earlier. For example, in 1940 the HUAC convened high-profile hearings in which actor Humphrey Bogart and Hollywood writer John Howard Lawson were called to testify. At that time, committee members wanted to know about Communist connections that witnesses might have or might know about. Bogart distanced himself from any involvement in or knowledge of Communist activities and seems largely to have escaped with little damage to his reputation.[9] Lawson less successfully diverted suspicion, but for the time being not much more came of it.

Suspicion about the glittery and apparently decadent life of Hollywood had long been in the background. In an effort to appease criticism, the movie industry had already established self-censorship practices, which it formalized in the Production Code, in order to stave off congressional interference.

In reality, the politics of most Hollywood movies were relatively pedestrian, replicating mainstream American social and political attitudes. But some films strayed from this tendency, which sometimes brought negative attention to the film industry as a whole. One example was *Grapes of Wrath*, a 1940 screen adaptation of John Steinbeck's novel that was directed by John Ford and featured American everyman actor Henry Fonda in the lead role. The film shows how an Oklahoma family loses their farm and livelihood and then journeys west, in search of a new beginning. They end up as migrant workers in California, suffering indignities and hardships as they struggle to make ends meet.

To some viewers, the portrayal of American life in this movie had disturbing leftist overtones. (Similar complaints had been leveled against the book on which it was based.) Moreover, the film's portrayal of businesses as cold and heartless and the depiction of social institutions as failing needy Americans met with disapproval by many conservative political leaders. Such negative portrayals of American life and institutions often fueled disapproval of much about the film industry.

The perceived intrusion of leftist ideas into Hollywood films, coupled with already nagging suspicions about immorality that were already part of the Hollywood myth, were in the background as HUAC launched its postwar investigations. The deep-seated suspicions that many lawmakers felt about Hollywood well before the war thus resurfaced after it.

In this context, some of Hollywood's output in the war years, which previously had not been seen as controversial, was revisited. In hindsight, some people wondered if Hollywood had been sufficiently and consistently patriotic after all. Of specific concern to some observers was the fact that several wartime Hollywood movies had portrayed the Soviet Union, perceived as the United States' primary enemy in the late 1940s, in a favorable light. Popular actor Gregory Peck, for example, had starred as a heroic Russian fighter in *Days of Glory* (1944), and actress Ginger Rogers had appeared in a film called *Tender Comrade* (1943), the title alone of which was sufficient to raise eyebrows in the Cold War environment. And other movies had also shown the Soviet Union in a favorable light, including *Miss V. from Moscow* (1942), *North Star* (1943), and *Counter Attack* (1945).

From one vantage point, this was not a very mysterious development since, during the later war years, the USSR had sided with the Allies. After the war was over, however, that seemed less important to those whose concern now focused on the perceived Communist threat. Accordingly, when HUAC began in earnest to consider the possible infiltration of Communists into American society, Hollywood studios, especially those that had sometimes portrayed the Soviets in a sympathetic light, were obvious targets of attention.

In 1947, many Hollywood representatives were called to testify before the committee. The leaders of the movie business were eager to avoid difficulties. Their industry had already endured major disruption in the previous two years. Members of two major Hollywood craft unions—the Conference of Studio Unions and International Alliance of Theatrical Stage Employees—had become embroiled in a major labor action, involving both a strike and a lockout. That situation had been very contentious and occasionally boiled over. In October 1945, for example, angry union members were involved in a violent protest at the entrance to the Warner Brothers Studios.

Some people called to testify at the 1947 HUAC hearings were so-called friendly witnesses. These were people who were willing to testify against suspected Communist influence in the movie industry. This group of witnesses, which included prominent studio executives such as Louis B. Mayer and Jack Warner, was eager to show Hollywood in a good light. They therefore promoted the notion that the movie business was zealously anti-Communist and overtly patriotic. Other "friendly" witnesses before HUAC included the actors Gary Cooper, Robert Montgomery, and Robert Taylor, who were then some of Hollywood's most prominent leading men.

HUAC's interest in Robert Taylor largely was the result of his appearance in a movie called *Song of Russia* (1944). The script for that film had been written by Paul Jarrico and Richard Collins, both of whom had been associated with the Communist Party. Although Collins later said the writers had not conspired to work on the project but were "just assigned to it, as a team" by MGM studios, their prior leftist associations were troubling to HUAC members.[10]

As might be expected for a movie about an ally that was produced during a major war, much of *Song of Russia*'s portrayal of the Soviet Union was favorable. The film glossed over many of the more negative aspects of Soviet life and policy. Instead, it portrayed the USSR as a dependable partner in the war against Nazi Germany. By the late 1940s, when the war was over and the Soviets had come to be seen as a major threat, however, this somewhat fawning depiction seemed much less innocuous to some HUAC members than it probably had during the war years.

Some of the most interesting testimony in the 1947 hearings can be found in remarks of the Russian-born writer Ayn Rand. An ardent anti-Communist with a harsh view of Hollywood, Rand was a formidable witness. At one point, she was asked to define the word "propaganda." Rand replied, "I use the term to mean that Communist propaganda is anything which gives a good impression of communism as a way of life. Anything that sells people the idea that life in Russia is good and that people are free and happy would be Communist propaganda."[11]

Much of Rand's testimony specifically condemned the movie *Song of Russia*. Her attitude about whether its depiction of Russia amounted to pro-Communist propaganda was immediately obvious:

> Now, here is what the picture *Song of Russia* contains. It starts with an American conductor, played by Robert Taylor, giving a concert in America for Russian war relief. He starts playing the American national anthem and the national anthem dissolves into a Russian mob, with the sickle and hammer on a red flag very prominent above their heads. I am sorry, but that made me sick. . . . As a writer, I can tell you just exactly what it suggests to the people. It suggests literally and technically that it is quite all right for the American national anthem to dissolve into the Soviet. The term here is more than just technical. It really was symbolically intended, and it worked out that way.[12]

Later in her testimony, Rand and committee members discussed whether the film might be forgiven for having obscured a true picture of Russian life because at the time the Soviets were allied with the United States in the struggle against Germany. On this point, Rand was clear; she saw no justification for Hollywood's flattering portrait of Russia, no matter when the film was made or under what circumstances. As she said, "I don't believe that the morale of anybody can be built up by a lie. If there was nothing good that we could truthfully say about Russia, then it would have been better not to say anything at all."[13]

Rand's testimony reflected the postwar political climate in the United States, where disdain and fear of the Soviet Union was commonplace. In just a few years, the USSR had become not only *an* enemy; it was *the* enemy—an enemy that was not only increasingly despised but one that was also feared.

In the days after Ayn Rand's appearance, other "friendly" witnesses testified before HUAC. These included Ronald Reagan, who was a fervent anti-Communist. The future U.S. president was then a popular actor and officer in the Screen Actors Guild, one of the most powerful unions in Hollywood. (Reagan was elevated to the presidency of the Screen Actors Guild in November of that year.)

Yet another "friendly witness" was Walt Disney, who was also a vocal critic of Communist influence in the film business. Several years earlier, there had been a bitter strike at Disney studios involving the animators, the outcome of which left Disney resentful. He felt so strongly, in fact, that he had taken out an antiunion advertisement in the July 2, 1941, edition of the trade newspaper *Variety*, in which he bluntly stated, "I am positively convinced that communistic agitation, leadership and activities have brought about this strike."[14] His views had not softened by the time of the 1947 HUAC hearings, where he continued to speak out against what he regarded as Communist infiltration into the ranks of Hollywood.

THE HOLLYWOOD TEN

But despite the appearance of "friendly" Hollywood luminaries before HUAC, the 1947 hearings are better known for their subsequent focus on alleged Communists and Communist sympathizers. This was as expected. Before the hearings had started, many people in the industry were fearful the committee intended to target specific individuals, singling them out for special scorn and possible repercussions. The realization that HUAC was anxious to discover the identities of such individuals with alleged Communist associations, and to make these names known, was troubling to many people working in the industry.

In an effort to counter the accusatory tone of the HUAC, a group called the Committee for the First Amendment was formed just a few weeks before the 1947 hearings. (Among its leaders were such well-known Hollywood personalities as Humphrey Bogart, who had been called to testify earlier in the decade, as well as Lauren Bacall and Danny Kaye.) But even before the hearings commenced, it was evident that the tide was against them. Despite traveling to Washington with the hope of making their case as the October hearings transpired, the group was largely ineffective in blunting the effects of HUAC investigations.

Indeed, HUAC was about to shine a harsh light on so-called unfriendly witnesses. HUAC paid special attention to a group of writers and directors who came to be known as the Hollywood Ten. The group consisted of Alvah Bessie, Herbert Biberman, Lester Cole, Edward Dmytryk, Ring Lardner Jr., John Howard Lawson, Albert Maltz, Samuel Ornitz, Adrian Scott, and Dalton Trumbo.

Bertolt Brecht, the famous German writer, was originally considered part of this group. (He would have been the 11th member.) But unlike the others, he agreed to testify. Brecht told the HUAC that he had never been a member of the Communist Party, but the following day he fled to East Berlin, the Soviet-controlled zone of the city. He lived there under Communist rule until his death in 1956.

The Hollywood Ten, meanwhile, were thought to be deeply involved in Communist activities in Hollywood, or at least knowledgeable about such "un-American" activities. Regarded with deep suspicion by HUAC, the individuals in the group seemingly were determined to avoid incriminating themselves or informing on others. The members of this group refused to cooperate with HUAC's questioning, which they justified by citing the U.S. Constitution. Unsurprisingly, HUAC was not impressed with this defense for refusing to testify. The committee took the matter to the full House of Representatives, where, in 1948, the Hollywood Ten were convicted of charges of contempt of Congress. They were sentenced to prison terms of up to a year.

Imprisonment was not the only trouble faced by the Hollywood Ten, however. Soon after their appearance before the HUAC, they were blacklisted, becoming instant pariahs throughout the industry in which they had previously earned a living. Even after serving jail time, they found themselves unable to work in a business that was anxious to distance itself from anything or anyone having Communist associations. Although some of the men found work under assumed names and aliases after their ordeal, their refusal to testify had a devastating effect on their careers for many years

But the HUAC hearings affected more than the careers of these 10 individuals. Indeed, the fate of the Hollywood Ten sent a profoundly chilling message to all of Hollywood. Within a few weeks of the hearings, a secret meeting of Hollywood leaders was held at the Waldorf-Astoria Hotel in New York City. The purpose of the gathering was to devise an industry-wide response that would help repair Hollywood's damaged reputation. The result was a document called the "Waldorf Statement," which declared Hollywood's intention to be proactively vigilant in the face of the presumed threat of Communist influence in the film business. Major studio executives participated in the meeting, including Louis B. Mayer (of Metro-Goldwyn-Mayer), Samuel Goldwyn (of Samuel Goldwyn Company), and Harry Cohn (of Columbia Pictures). Dozens of other prominent people in or close to the business were also in attendance.

On December 3, 1947, immediately after the conclusion of the meeting, Eric Johnston, then serving as president of the MPAA, issued a press release on behalf of the industry leaders. This "Waldorf Statement" explained Hollywood's view of the situation and what it intended to do in the future. The document said, in part:

> We will not knowingly employ a Communist or a member of any party or group which advocates the overthrow of the government of the United States by force or by any illegal or unconstitutional methods. In pursuing this policy, we are not going to be swayed by hysteria or intimidation from any source. We are frank to recognize that such a policy involves danger and risks. There is the danger of hurting innocent people. There is the risk of creating an atmosphere of fear. Creative work at its best cannot be carried on in an atmosphere of fear. We will guard against this danger, this risk, this fear. To this end we will invite the Hollywood talent guilds to work with us to eliminate any subversives, to protect the innocent; and to safeguard free speech and a free screen wherever threatened.[15]

Thus several years before the height of anti-Communist hysteria in the early 1950s, HUAC had already set the tone for future congressional action. HUAC's Hollywood investigations provided a sobering example for workers in the entertainment industry and beyond that current or past associations with communism could have severe consequences. Undoubtedly, HUAC investigations into the high-profile movie business helped fuel the anxious political climate that was growing ever more fearful.

The HUAC hearings and other political developments of the period amply demonstrate how fearful the United States had become of Communist intrusion into the life and affairs of the United States. Such a possibility was regarded as an extremely serious danger, with grave implications for continued American success and for the hard-won life of the American Dream that otherwise captured the country's imagination.

THE DEADLY ENEMY BECOMES DEADLIER

This anxious political climate showed few signs of letting up as the 1940s progressed. In 1948, for example, the Soviets began a yearlong blockade of roadways leading from the western zones to isolated West Berlin. This led to the Berlin Airlift, a massive American-led project in which supplies were flown by military transport from to West Berlin. The standoff continued until the Soviets again permitted overland traffic a year later.

Tensions between the United States and Soviet Union dramatically increased the following year when, on August 29, 1949, the USSR detonated its own atomic bomb. This was a frightening, unthinkable development in the eyes of Americans, and the powerful explosion immediately changed the dynamic of international politics. The sense of security that American control of the atom had provided to the United States evaporated. A full-fledged nuclear war was now possible, even if the thought of it was too terrible to contemplate.

It is difficult to overstate the deeply disturbing effects the revelation of Soviet nuclear weaponry had on the United States. The shock prompted nagging questions and suspicion. One response to the new multinational nuclear reality was the search for answers. How, it was asked, could it be that the Soviets had so quickly mastered the secrets of the atom? Was it possible that they had help, possibly in the form of stolen American secrets? Such questions jumped to the forefront of the American political response to the Soviet Union's attainment of the atom bomb. The search to unravel what had happened soon was under way.

One possibility, of course, was that the Soviet bomb had been developed without access to American nuclear secrets. The USSR had long been focusing on its military, and it would have been reasonable, even for ordinary American citizens, to surmise that the Soviets had been working on advanced weaponry in earnest. But many people, including officials, were skeptical. They wondered if the Soviets really could have replicated American efforts so quickly unaided by access to classified American research.

Indeed, the United States had achieved nuclear weaponry as the result of a truly massive and covert effort. The American military nuclear research program had been organized around the Manhattan Project, an ultrasecret effort that was enhanced by assistance from emigrant European atomic scientists. In 1939, a secret letter to President Roosevelt from physicist Albert Einstein was instrumental in instigating the project. Einstein's letter was a dire report to the president. "Some recent work by E. Fermi and L. Szilard," he wrote, "... leads me to expect that the element uranium may be turned into a new and important source of energy in the immediate future. Certain aspects of the situation . . . seem to call for watchfulness and, if necessary quick action on the part of the Administration." Einstein further warned, "It may become possible to set up a nuclear chain reaction in uranium," the massive power of which could be the basis for a new kind of bomb. "A single bomb of this type," he wrote, "carried in a boat and exploded in a port, might very well destroy the whole port together with some of the surrounding territory." Of special concern, more-over, was the observation that "Germany has actually stopped the sale of ura-nium from Czechoslovakia mines which she [sic] has taken over" and that "the son of the German Under-Secretary of State, von Weizsäcker, is attached to the Kaiser-Wilhelm-Institut in Berlin where some of the American work on Uranium is now being repeated."[16]

The circumstances surrounding American and subsequent Soviet develop-ment of nuclear weaponry provide a window into the world of secrecy, dread, and anxiety that would later come to characterize the Cold War. This aston-ishing achievement in military technology on the part of both powers was filled with murky events and moral ambiguities.

The basic details of the Manhattan Project are well known. Beginning as a small program, it eventually grew into a massive effort involving over 125,000 people and an expense of over \$2 billion. The project was coordi-nated at a complex located in remote Los Alamos, New Mexico. By the final months of the war, research and development efforts had proved successful, and the atomic bomb had gone from being a theoretical possibility to an awe-somely powerful reality. Yet this had been accomplished with almost total secrecy. Many high-ranking government officials were kept in the dark about it. It was only after he assumed the presidency, for example, that even Harry Truman was finally briefed on what the work of the Manhattan Project actually had been.

Throughout these developments, American officials believed that the Soviet Union was unaware of the Manhattan Project's progress. Unknown to American officials, however, the Soviets had gained some awareness of the U.S. nuclear program as it developed during the war years.[17] In fact, senior Soviet officials had suspected American advances in nuclear weaponry for some time. As early as 1942, Georgi N. Flerov, a young scientist then serving as a Soviet military officer, had written to Stalin about suspicions of secret Allied atomic research. Flerov had noticed a small but important detail as he scanned the research literature in the field: many leading nuclear scientists, who were known to be experts on nuclear fission, were no longer publishing their findings. Thinking it was unlikely that they all had simply stopped con-ducting research for no reason, Flerov speculated that their work had gone underground. He correctly surmised that these scientists might be working on a secret project of some sort outside the Soviet sphere of influence.[18]

A military-oriented nuclear research agenda was subsequently established in the USSR as early as 1942. And once the Soviet effort started, it benefited not only from the Soviet scientific establishment but also from aggressive espionage efforts, as would become apparent in the following decade.

For the moment, however, the realization that the Soviet Union now possessed nuclear weapons, regardless of how they had been obtained, was a development of truly nightmarish proportions with apocalyptic overtones. All-out nuclear warfare, which had the potential to level cities and destroy all that the United States had built, now seemed to be a real possibility.

HOLLYWOOD AT THE END OF THE 1940s

By the time the Soviets showed the world that they also possessed atomic weapons in 1949, Hollywood had already begun producing anti-Communist entertainments. A wave of these films was released in that year. Again, many had titles that left little doubt about what the films would portray. Among the 1949 films in this group were such productions as *Conspirator* and *I Married a Communist.*

Another entry in this group of movies was *The Red Danube* (1949), directed by George Sidney and starring Hollywood notables Walter Pidgeon, Ethel Barrymore, Angela Lansbury, Janet Leigh, and Peter Lawford. The story follows a British military officer, Col. Michael "Hooky" Nicobar (played by Walter Pidgeon), who is on assignment in the British sector of post–World War II Vienna. Nicobar has been given the task of assisting with the repatriation of Soviet citizens then living in Austria and slated for return to their homeland. He gradually comes to see this activity as wrong and unfair to the people being returned to the Soviet Union. This realization is accelerated when he becomes friendly with a Russian ballerina (played by Janet Leigh), who is trying to avoid being sent back to the USSR. A pivotal point in the story occurs when the ballerina commits suicide rather than being forced to return to the Soviet Union. Throughout the story, the Catholic Church plays a prominent role by shining a light on the apparent evils of the godless Soviet Communists.

One review of this movie concluded that *The Red Danube* is "a propaganda film designed to make you hate Russia and recognize the Vatican as the true champion of freedom. This may be laudable, but so one-sided in the view, so all-black versus all-white, that it reminds you of nothing so much as the wartime propaganda in which the Soviets were all virtuous, the enemy totally evil and cowardly."[19] Such words show that even in this period, some people recognized how Cold War rhetoric was at times over-heated. But the film's portrayal of starkly contrasting sides in the new Cold War was, of course, thoroughly consistent with the mindset of the era. More than that, it was consistent with the determination of Hollywood studios to avoid the appearance that they were sympathizing with the Communists. As such, *The Red Danube* was a movie in the spirit of the indus-try's "Waldorf Statement" some months earlier.

Another 1949 film in this vein was *The Red Menace*, directed by R. G. Springsteen. It was an especially sinister portrayal of domestic American communism. Exhibiting a theme that would resonate in future years across American culture, communism is portrayed as a significant danger to young Americans, who might succumb to its superficial appearance of idealism. The film's plot involves a young man and woman who had been associated with a Communist group. However, they have come to see communism as evil. And indeed, the movie portrays the Communist group as particularly dastardly, though somewhat lacking in competence. A review in *Time* maga-zine noted that the Communists in the movie exhibited "sheer indiscretion and moral decay [that] would surprise even the FBI."[20]

At the end of the story, the young man and woman successfully escape the influence of communism and are so overcome with renewed patriotism that they surrender to a police officer they encounter. But the officer decides that these young people have seen the light, and he therefore sends them on their way in the film's stereotypical happy conclusion. In the end, then, moral order consistent with American ideals is restored, and the danger is avoided.

In the same year that many new anti-Communist movies, which had been in production for some months, were released to theaters, the Soviet Union demonstrated its arrival as a nuclear power. This startling and frightening new development erased any remaining doubt that a dangerous new context had altered many basic perceptions about the world. The world seemed more dangerous than ever before. This was a bold and frightening assessment. It was probably true.

As the 1940s closed, therefore, two distinctly different sides of the United States were well under development. One side was that of the United States, the victor in war and the new superpower that proudly proclaimed the virtues of freedom and democracy and the good life. But on the other side was the beginning of a darker, more insecure and suspicious cultural streak, an out-growth of anxieties in the newly bipolar, nuclear world, in which creeping communism seemed poised to threaten all of the successes of the hard-fought war. In some ways this darker side—a potentially nightmarish vision that threatened to turn the United States into a veritable wasteland—was often suppressed, hidden beneath a more happy and mundane exterior that appealed to many Americans.

It would be a mistake to presume that external pressure from Washington was the sole, or arguably even the main, reason that Hollywood soon began producing films with anti-Communist themes. In fact, Hollywood already had a long history of producing entertainments that reflected popular sentiments. Its enormous success primarily had come not from challenging status quo thinking, but from mirroring popular attitudes and prejudices and by interacting with their audience's dreams, and sometimes nightmares. World War II had provided Hollywood with a ready-made theme that was filled with possibilities for conflict, heroism, and moralism. Since the USSR was now constructed in the public mind as a dark and malevolent force, it offered similar possibilities to Hollywood. In other words, the Cold War presented seemingly endless dramatic possibilities, in many ways ideally suited to the types of storytelling that the American film business was well accustomed to providing.

A NEW THREAT IN THE SKIES

A different kind of phenomenon, which at first seems unrelated and puzzling, came to public attention in 1947, and whatever else it may signal, it illustrates the anxieties that were creeping over the cultural landscape in that era. There had long been accounts of unexplained aerial phenomena, arguably dating back centuries. But the sighting of an unidentified flying object (UFO) in 1947 captured the American imagination in a way that previous accounts had not. To many people, reports of UFOs suggested that the United States was potentially the target of an attack from an unknown source, perhaps the Russians, or perhaps even from somewhere beyond earth.

A pilot and businessman named Kenneth Arnold reported a strange object in the skies over the American West during an otherwise routine flight in June 1947. His account of an unknown, saucer-shaped craft racing across the skies was quickly picked up by the news services and subsequently reported around the country. Arnold's description of a mysterious aircraft that was "saucer-like" or "like a big flat disk" captured headlines across the nation. Adopting Arnold's description, the press came to use the term "flying saucers" to describe these objects.

Arnold's account marked the beginning of the modern UFO era in the United States. Almost immediately, speculation began that these unknown and unverified crafts came from another planet. Talk of "space men" and "aliens"—the kind of talk that previously had been restricted to popular fiction—soon became a topic of conversation across American society.

In retrospect, the appearance of the UFO phenomenon appears closely linked to other developments in American politics and culture at that time. Carl Jung, the esteemed psychologist, was almost immediately struck by the sheer number of reports of such observations, which became increasingly numerous in the late 1940s. In a later essay about the subject, he speculated that the sightings might be examples of psychological projection. As Jung wrote, "One can hardly suppose that anything of such worldwide incidence as the UFO legend is purely fortuitous and of no importance whatsoever. The many thousands of individual testimonies must have an equally extensive causal basis."[21]

According to Jung's reasoning, the cause of the widespread UFO phenomenon could be found in "an emotional tension having its cause in in a situation of collective distress or danger, or in a vital psychic need. This condition undoubtedly exists today, in so far as the whole world is suffering under the strain of Russian policies and their still unpredictable consequences."[22]

Indeed, in an era just after the development of nuclear weapons and at a time when rocketry was emerging as a powerful new technology with military applications, the abrupt appearance of UFO sightings seemed more than a simple coincidence. Implying unknown danger—or potential danger—and possibly a herald of invasion, the sightings closely paralleled the sense of heightening political anxieties in the United States in the late 1940s. The theme of UFOs would be a recurring one that crossed over to popular culture in coming decades.

THE END OF THE DECADE

The 1940s had been a transformational time. The United States entered the decade in the late throes of the Great Depression, only to become embroiled in a global conflict of immense scale. And no sooner was the war over than a dangerous new reality, the Cold War, redefined international relations in the new atomic age.

By the late 1940s, events in far-flung places gave American leaders reason to pause. Czechoslovakia was absorbed into the Communist sphere in 1948. In the same year, the Soviet imposed a blockade on West Berlin, challenging the United States and its Western allies. Meanwhile, far from Europe, the Communist state of the Democratic People's Republic of Korea was created in 1948. And a year later in neighboring China, Mao Zedong's forces successfully drove the government of Chiang Kai-shek out of power and offshore. The Communist People's Republic of China was declared on October 1, 1949.

In the comfort of their homes, Americans at the end of the decade could largely feel good about the life they were creating in the postwar world. But when they looked beyond, it was hard to escape the feeling that the status quo was precarious. The Soviet Union seemed menacing, especially now that it was armed with nuclear weapons. Another world war did not seem outside the realm of possibility.

American popular culture continued to absorb and reflect these broader developments. It would continue to do so in the years that would follow, as an apocalyptic strand of the American narrative developed more overtly.

CHAPTER 4

Above and Below
the Shiny Surface

The external dangers inherent in the new, unpredictable age of the atom were obvious almost immediately after World War II. In this rapidly changing world, the perceived threat of communism from the outside led to an undercurrent of uneasiness that permeated much of American culture at that time. But life within American borders was also changing rapidly. For a time, such changes seemed mostly positive, especially for the middle-class, white United States, which was poised to benefit substantially from the transformation that was under way.

In later years, some of what had seemed quite positive and forward looking to many Americans in the years immediately after the war would start to appear more double-edged. In fact, within the span of a few decades, much of what Americans originally regarded as signs of progress would take on negative overtones. Many of the apparently beneficial aspects of postwar American life would, over time, come to be seen as having hidden costs— social, economic, and environmental costs that would eventually threaten the United States' sense of well-being.

Hollywood, meanwhile, produced films that were related to the new way of life that was developing in the United States. It mostly depicted life in an approving and positive way. Yet even in these years, some American films reflected less desirable currents. Such movies revealed stresses and strains that were emerging in the quickly changing social world and also suggested the beginnings of growing fears that the positive potential of American life could fall into ruin. A review of some aspects of postwar domestic life reveals a picture of the conditions that would later prompt new worries and fear in the United States.

AMERICAN LIFE AFTER THE WAR

The war experience transformed the United States. No sooner had the war ended than Americans set out remaking their world. Within a few years, their efforts created an astonishing life of material bounty. So, life did not simply return to what had been considered normal before the war or the Great Depression that preceded it. Instead, many aspects of the postwar United States seemed radically new. And it was within this newly created world that a new sense of normalcy emerged.

In the early 1940s, the large-scale mobilization of the population for global war had caused multiple effects on society in both large and small ways. The huge number of people involved directly and indirectly was one major factor. More than 1.5 million Americans served in the armed forces during the war, which significantly drained the civilian workforce. During the war, the nonmilitary parts of the American economy needed to replenish a workforce that was now without the services of many young men—as well as the approximately 2 percent of service personnel who were women—now in military service. The war prompted an urgent need for more civilian workers in industry, business, and agriculture. These were important components of the war effort, as well as essential for the continuation of everyday civilian life, which was now strained.

The war had generated a massive new demand for trucks, tanks, planes, ammunition, equipment, and all manner of goods and services from American industry. To fill the ranks of workers needed for wartime production, American industry increasingly called on members of the society who had previously been excluded from jobs in factories and offices. There was much work to be done, and women, African Americans, and other Americans who had previously been shut out of these jobs were now, if not always overtly welcomed, at least tolerated. During the war, this change had come about as the result of necessity. Not surprisingly, after the war the wartime taste of more steady, lucrative employment was enough for many people in those groups to wish to stay on their jobs. Most were probably not eager to return to either unemployment or lesser employment opportunities just because a generation of mostly young, mostly white men were now coming home. Such feelings would grow and contribute to social unrest in later years.

The relatively few but stressful years of war deprivation ended abruptly in the United States. The war had a very high social cost for the nation, with hundreds of thousands dead and millions of families disrupted. But the social fabric was for the most part not destroyed. American families, although battered, were mostly not broken. No advancing armies had marauded over American soil. No aerial bombardments had scattered families across a wide area.

Americans had suffered and paid a steep price for victory, but many communities were probably strengthened in the years of shared sacrifice. There were, unfortunately, some tragic exceptions to this generalization. The forced relocation of Japanese Americans to detention centers in the American West was probably the worst case. But for the most part, returning soldiers recognized their home communities and found many familiar faces. The people they became reacquainted with may have been changed somewhat by the war experience, but for the most part, soldiers had a place to which they could return. Home remained home.

On a broader level, American institutions largely emerged from the war years in a strong position. The federal government had expanded its authority and the scope of its reach in order to maintain the war effort. It had inserted itself into industrial production, for example, diverting some material and production to war-specific uses. The government had also overseen rationing of many everyday goods to be sure its armed forces were well equipped and well fed.

Even before the war was over, American officials began to think about life afterward. With the anticipated demobilization of the American military at the war's approaching end, government officials recognized that the economy would need to remain vigorous if a new wave of unemployment was to be avoided. Given the huge number of soldiers who would soon return to civilian life in need of jobs and homes, it was a daunting prospect. Though a strong defense budget would still be needed, much economic capacity would be freed from military ties. The economy could be kept in high gear, it was envisioned, by realigning it with civilian life's needs and desires. Factories that made jeeps could return to making cars, for example. Raw materials that were used in armaments could be made into toasters and washing machines. Building techniques honed for military housing could be applied to residential communities.

But all of this presupposed that there would be strong consumer demand for products and services. Realizing this even as the war progressed, government and business leaders drew upon the nascent consumerist impulses, which had already started to emerge in the latter years of the Great Depression.[1] Even before the war had ended, then, government officials started thinking about what life after the war might look like. And they were eager to make sure that it did not look anything like the Great Depression, from which the nation had emerged only at about the time the war started. They realized they would need to ensure that there would be ample buyers when wartime industrial production shifted primarily to civilian purchasers in a postwar world. This was not something they left to chance.

The generation that had won World War II presumed that the steady march of progress and a higher standard of living would be widespread. It was, after all, a core part of American life and therefore one of the things people thought the war had been about. The potential of improved standards of living and a consumer-based society could be achieved only if Americans stayed productive after the urgent needs of wartime production ended.

A potential unemployment problem was already a topic of concern by 1945. Most Americans well remembered that just a decade earlier, at the height of the Great Depression, it had been a major source of distress. To stave off that problem, a plan was devised that would divert a significant segment of discharged soldiers for a period of time, so that their huge numbers would not flood the employment market all at once. The Servicemen's Readjustment Act, popularly known as the GI Bill, provided an incentive for many discharged soldiers to further their education prior to entering the workforce. And indeed, the percentage of men going on to college or university education rose dramatically after the war.

Still, some predictions suggested that unemployment could rise dramatically.[2] Fearful of a return to the days of widespread joblessness that had characterized the Depression years, Congress passed the Employment Act of 1946. This legislation gave the federal government the responsibility of maintaining high employment levels, while also securing overall price stability in order to thwart high inflation rates.

In the end, despite such fears, employment did not return as a major problem. Between 1945 and 1948, unemployment remained below 4.5 percent. Nevertheless, some labor issues did erupt. The so-called Great Strike Wave of 1946 involved millions of American workers across many states and industries.[3] For example, workers in packinghouses across the United States went on strike. Also in that year, strikes gripped oil refineries in 20 states.

The strikes appear to have panicked much of the American public. This probably contributed to huge Republican successes in the congressional elections of November 1946. As Irving Richter and David Montgomery explain, many voters appear to have "acted on the belief that the giant postwar strike wave was politically motivated, the product of 'communist' and 'subversive' influences."[4] Republican candidates, who were typically staunchly anti-

Communist and anti-Socialist, thus represented something of a defense against the encroachment of presumed leftist influence in American life.

Emerging Consumerism

With the high levels of employment during the war, Americans had generally earned more than they had in years. But with wartime-induced scarcity of consumer goods, American workers saved for the future, more by necessity than by choice. They saw shortages and a limited selection of goods as a temporary state of affairs and envisioned a life of more abundance when the war was over. They largely came to envision a postwar world and imagined a new, prosperous life as more than a luxury. It seemed a truly American way. The prospect of buying shiny new toasters or refrigerators or cars was perceived as a patriotic aspiration that showed a commitment to the way of life that the global war was defending.[5]

The vision of postwar abundance was sometimes colorfully made by American industry, which began to advertise to the consumer market months before the conflict ended. Industry's message built upon ideals of the American Dream, which was already part of the American consciousness, and was now presented as something akin to a just reward for the many sacrifices of the war.

A wartime magazine advertisement from General Electric made the point. It stated:

> That little home sketched there in the sand is a symbol of faith and hope and courage. A promise of the gloriously happy days . . . when Victory is come.
>
> Victory Homes of tomorrow will make up in part at least for all the sacrifices of today . . . and that's a promise!
>
> They will have better living built in . . . Electric living with new comforts, new conveniences, new economies to make every day an adventure in happiness.[6]

The New Suburbia

As personnel poured out of the military and into civilian life, they joined other Americans in the creation of a new, postwar world modeled after the ideals of the American Dream. Housing construction had been slow for many years, but the influx of demobilized personnel from the armed forces fueled new growth.

Soon after the war ended, a firm called Levitt & Sons devised a plan to build on a massive scale using new, more efficient building procedures that they had learned while fulfilling a contract to construct housing for navy families in Virginia during the war.[7] Acquiring a tract of land in Nassau County, Long Island, in the state of New York, Levitt & Sons went about planning a tightly packed community in what was farmland. Applying methods borrowed from mass-production industries, their technique allowed for speedy construction. A community of over 17,000 houses quickly appeared on a landscape that had been open fields just a few years earlier.

The Levittown houses were small, with the original design restricted to kitchen, bath, living room, two bedrooms, and a crawl space. But the houses had one big selling point: they were inexpensive. When the first units were announced, the rental price was advertised at $52 per month for veterans. Units were offered for sale with $60 monthly mortgage payments.[8] The new houses in Levittown soon proved to be much in demand, and the Levittown experience provided a template for the home construction business that would be repeated for decades to follow.

The emphasis on owning homes at Levittown and elsewhere in the emerging suburban world soon overshadowed the allure of inexpensive rental housing. Even with new strategies to keep the cost of home ownership low, however, that still left the open question of how people would be able to afford to move into the new homes. Few people had the means to pay for a house with money they had managed to save already. Especially for younger families—and the new homes were squarely aimed at young, traditional families—there had not yet been a long period in which to save, and peak earning years were likely decades in the future. So how were they to have the means to move to the suburbs? The answer to this question came with increased access to credit. The relocation of families from urban to suburban setting was done with borrowed money, with home mortgages that allowed people to buy now and pay later. It was a highly optimistic enterprise, built on the hopeful outlook of the American Dream, in which the future would always be better and more prosperous than the past.

Home mortgages made it possible to bet on the future, which at the time seemed to be a safe bet. Of course, the darker side to mortgage loan practices was never far from the surface, even though it was not widely acknowledged for many years. Indeed, there were built-in inequities, making it nearly impossible for people falling into certain demographic groups to obtain loans that were made readily available to others. The practice of "redlining," in which many banks automatically refused mortgage applications from people who lived in certain disadvantaged neighborhoods, was just one prominent example of outright discrimination.[9]

As people—especially middle- and upper-working-class white people—moved to the new world of suburbia, a cascading series of needs was created. Not all of these were actual needs, of course, but much of modern life in the postwar decades was built on the idea that vast arrays of items and services are required to make ordinary life into the "good life." Acquiring the stuff of "the good life" had both a cultural as well as material-comfort appeal. In the four years after the war, for example, Americans bought 5 million stoves, 20 million automobiles, and 20 million refrigerators.[10] The advertising industry, which rose to new heights during this era, created demand for a wide variety of new consumer products such as these, successfully convincing Americans that these were not luxuries but necessities.

And the social impulses at work in suburbia, in which residents compared their standard of living to those around them—the "keeping up with the Joneses" phenomenon—helped a culture of consumerism develop and flourish. Along with this new emphasis on convenience, ease, and comfort came more processed foods, disposable items, and thousands and thousands of other things to make life seem easier and better. The stress produced by constantly trying to "keep up" was one of the few undersides of the American Dream to be noticed. But still, the consumer culture took hold and in many ways transformed American life.

The Coming of the "Baby Boom"

Within months after the war, the so-called baby boom began to alter American life in ways that would last decades. With significantly raised expectations for a prosperous future, the birthrate in the United States soon rose dramatically. Already by early 1948, the National Industrial Conference Board noted that rapidly increasingly population had "significance ... to businessmen [that] can hardly be overstated."[11] Indeed, as *Time* magazine noted, "the U.S. added 2,800,000 more consumers to its population in 1947."[12]

It was clear that American business well understood the implications of a population boom. A report that year concluded: "Manufacturers of children's clothing and toys, obstetricians and hospitals are affected immediately. . . . Actually, the effects of the population bulge ... will spread to every corner of the economy."[13]

The Open Road

The creation of a new version of suburbia required more than an ample supply of affordable houses. The relocation of vibrant elements of the workforce into single-family homes outside of American cities was possible on a large scale only with changes in social and physical infrastructure. Suburbia created the modern commuter, the widespread phenomenon in which employees were increasingly unbound from the geographical restrictions resulting from where they were employed. In many ways, the immediate postwar decades were the height of American car culture, an era in which people and their automobiles on the open highway were a potent symbol of personal freedom, exemplifying seemingly everything that was good about the United States.

The continued and explosive growth in automobile ownership, which had commenced before the war, was a main factor in this. And this phenomenon meant that new roads, highways, and superhighways were necessary. A critical point in the development of the sprawling superhighways that crisscross the nation was the Federal-Aid Highway Act of 1956, which created the modern interstate highway system. Building on ideas that had been generated in 1939 and 1944, this legislation spurred rapid growth and modernization of roadways, enhancing the older infrastructure, which was poorly equipped to handle the growing volume of traffic in the postwar era.[14]

Simple facts that might have made a person think twice about building a society around the automobile were not given much thought in the early years. That this lifestyle was predicated on cheap and abundant oil that might not last, or that cars could become a major source of air pollution, to name just two examples, were not initially viewed as serious concerns. Within several decades, however, concerns about oil dependency, pollution, and endless traffic would come to be seen as major headaches in everyday American life.

Such was the new world that was created in the postwar United States. Optimistic and forward looking, it was built on the idea that the future would be a bright world. But it was a world that was also based on essentially traditional foundations that had evolved from very American ideas, none more powerful than that of the American Dream in shaping the society at mid-century.

Yet the positive, aspirational nature of this new world was more fragile than it may have appeared on the surface. This new life was new, not yet secure. Indeed, society was in flux across many dimensions, with the pace and direction of change sometimes hard to predict and even harder to manage. And so despite the shiny, new surface appearance of life in the United

States, there was much opportunity for anxiety, even if that feeling was often hidden beneath the surface.

HOLLYWOOD AND THE NEW PATTERNS OF AMERICAN LIVING

The movie business had emerged from World War II relatively unscathed, but it soon faced many challenges. As it tried to adapt to the rapidly changing social world, Hollywood was, if not struggling, then earnestly searching for a direction in the postwar world.

Going to the movies had remained a popular pastime in the prewar years of the Great Depression. Although ticket sales lagged somewhat in the late 1930s, movies remained a common facet of American life throughout that decade and into the war years. But the end of the war was a major change in many ways. How Hollywood movies would remain relevant and continue to hold American attention was, in the latter half of the 1940s, a question of some concern on the part of the film industry. The challenges were on multiple fronts.

For one thing, there was new competition. Television emerged as a growing mass medium. The technology behind television was not new and had been in development since the 1920s. And even before the United States was drawn into the war, an early version of the television was displayed in New York to great public interest at the World's Fair in 1939, the same year that NBC (National Broadcasting Company) began regularly scheduled network broadcasts.[15] Within a few years of the end of World War II, television was regarded as a viable enough technology to prompt the launching of commercial broadcasting in the medium. With programs such as *Texaco Star Theater*—a popular radio show that moved to television in 1948—television soon reached a wide audience. It was largely the same audience that Hollywood had relied upon for a half century.

In 1948, the film industry faced another challenge with the U.S. Supreme Court decision in the *United States v. Paramount Pictures* case. In the ruling, the Court concurred with the Department of Justice claim that the studios were violating antitrust law because they controlled both production and exhibition of films. As a result of the decision, the major studios were compelled to divest their ownership of theater chains, which eroded cash flow and profits.

Audience tastes and interests were also changing. In the postwar years, Hollywood searched for commercially and culturally relevant themes and forms. Many movies produced during the war had used that global conflict as the basis for their stories. With the war now over and Americans eager to move on, however, new ideas were needed. It was a forward-looking time culturally, aiming to the future. It is hard to imagine that moviegoers would indefinitely have maintained enthusiasm for a continuing string of movies about a conflict just ended. Hollywood needed something new.

During this time, many movies reproduced prevailing attitudes about the positive and aspirational nature of postwar American life. Such ideas were reinforced in a wide variety of productions. A popular film that coincided with the emergence of suburbia, for example, was *Mr. Blandings Builds His Dream House*. The popular 1948 comedy, directed by H. C. Potter and starring Cary Grant and Myrna Loy, illustrates some of the American mind-set about domestic life in the postwar years.

According to the film's narrative, a well-to-do New York family decides to relocate from their city apartment to a more spacious community in Connecticut. Jim Blandings (Cary Grant) and his wife, Muriel (Myrna Loy), decide to buy an old farmhouse that they can "fix up" to meet their contemporary needs. As they set out to remodel and modernize the home, everything goes wrong. The house becomes more of a financial sinkhole than a "dream house," and eventually it is torn down so that a new one can be built. It is all played for comic effect.

In a revealing moment of exasperation, Blandings says,

> It's a conspiracy, I tell you. The minute you start they put you on the all-American sucker list. You start out to build a home and wind up in the poorhouse. And if it can happen to me, what about the guys who aren't making $15,000 a year? The ones who want a home of their own. It's a conspiracy, I tell you, against every boy and girl who were ever in love.

The film reflects an urge to escape city life that was common in the early days of the United States' suburbanization. The implicit yearning to escape the less positive aspects of city life is obvious. But more than that, the characters in the film display an attitude about the importance of being "new" in that era.

Jim and Muriel Blandings set out to restore an old house, but then realize that only a brand new structure can serve their needs. As in the case of real-life Levittown, shiny, new homes are shown to be the answer. In the idealized picture of modern suburbia that was emerging, all a family had to do was take the keys, fill the home with appliances and other modern conveniences, and they were ready to partake in the good life, the modern life.

The struggles of the fictitious Blandings family against a tide of mishaps as they attempt to modernize their quaint older home serve to reinforce the decision that they ultimately make: new is better. The context of late 1940s American life, therefore, adds a substantial, though perhaps unintended, dimension to the message underlying the pleasant comedy of the film.

Westerns

The American film industry had never stopped producing genre movies of many types, even at the height of the war. With the new realities of the post-war world, producers continued to tap into these strands of movie making as they also searched for new ideas. Some genres continued to be as popular as they had been before the war. Holiday fare, comedies, love stories, and Westerns appeared in theaters with regularity. The latter of these, Westerns, were arguably about to enter their heyday.

Indeed, the myth of the American Old West was a powerful narrative strand in popular culture—one that could be recast and reshaped to serve as something of an explanatory and metaphorical myth. The idea of frontier, for example, resonated throughout the Cold War period and fit nicely with American political rhetoric about a society on the cusp of a new world. More than that, Westerns typically presented a world of clear-cut morality.[16] Good guys were unambiguously good, steeped in traditional American values, as they were understood at that time. Villains, meanwhile, were evil, deserving of their predictable demises.

One example is John Ford's movie *My Darling Clementine*, which was released to American theaters in 1946, just months after the war's end. By this time, it had been seven years since Ford's great success with the Western film *Stagecoach*. That movie had transformed actor John Wayne into one of Hollywood's most successful stars. Now, Ford issued a new Western saga with another well-known and beloved actor, Henry Fonda, in a leading role. Fonda was cast as the legendary Wyatt Earp, a historical figure who is best known for his participation in an 1881 gunfight at the O.K. Corral in Tombstone, Arizona. A well-crafted and largely fictionalized film, the story nonetheless remains essentially a familiar Western. *My Darling Clementine* displays unambiguous heroes and clear-cut villains. One reviewer was impressed by the way the movie depicted the "beauty of rugged people and a rugged world." It was, as were most Westerns, a way of showing the way that heroic Americans had imposed order on a chaotic world.

The manner in which *My Darling Clementine*'s script treated the underlying historical episode on which it was loosely based is telling. In fact, the true story of the incident at the O.K. Corral has much less moral clarity than the film portrays. Indeed, in its time the brief gun battle was a murky event. The gunfight left Wyatt Earp, his brothers Morgan and Virgil Earp (an assistant U.S. marshal), and their compatriot Doc Holliday immersed in controversy about whether it had been a justified fight or simply a case of murder. One of the men killed by the Earp party at the O.K. Corral appears not to have been armed, and aspects of the story are quite cloudy. But *My Darling Clementine* mostly glosses over these reservations. Of course, this is not unexpected for the era in which Hollywood was still quite reluctant to confront such ambiguities very directly. Yet the transformation of a morally confusing historical event into a clear and unambiguous movie story illuminates a strong cultural inclination in the early years of the postwar United States that in some ways continues into the twenty-first century.

Another popular Western of the era was *Red River*, a 1948 film from director Howard Hawks. It is a typical Old West saga played against spectacular scenery depicting the American frontier. John Wayne and Montgomery Clift star as two cattlemen leading a herd from Texas to Kansas. For most of the film, the main point of conflict centers on whether they should follow the usual trail or take a chance on an alternate one as yet untried. In other words, it is largely a morality play about whether to play it safe or take a chance to get a better outcome. This message fit squarely within postwar American themes and mirrored the thought that the modern United States required modern thinking and new ways of doing things, even as it honored the traditions of the past. The balance of tradition and innovation was, after all, one of the questions visible in many aspects of postwar culture. (It can be found, for example, in the seeming modernity of Levittown that nonetheless paid homage to traditional American communities of the past.)

Later in the story of *Red River*, the cattlemen encounter a wagon train of easterners heading west that is under attack from Native Americans. From that point on, the movie veers into traditional Hollywood stereotyping and formula. But although this may detract from the overall effect of the film, it nonetheless provides a clue into what was taken for granted by both audiences and filmmakers of that day: that whatever tensions there were between old and young in the American story, these would not slow down American progress.

Indeed, nearly all Westerns prior to the 1960s told some variant of an American triumphalist story. As metaphors for the United States of the mid-twentieth century, the genre was highly successful. Forces of chaos and lawlessness might cause trouble, according to this way of envisioning the era, but they would not succeed in thwarting the progress of the United

States. The implication was that the American way of life would push forward and that it would master the frontier.

Yet another example is the 1949 film *She Wore a Yellow Ribbon*, directed by John Ford and again starring John Wayne, who by this time was almost universally associated with the Western genre. A rousing and admiring portrait of the U.S. Cavalry, this film contains many hallmarks of the Hollywood Western. Ford, a masterful director with a command of filmmaking's possibilities, achieves the triumphal effect of *She Wore a Yellow Ribbon* visually. As a review in the *New York Times* observed, "No one could make a troop of soldiers riding across the western plains look more exciting and romantic than this great director does. No one could get more emotion out of a thundering cavalry charge or an old soldier's farewell departure from the ranks of his comrades than he."[17]

Against the backdrop of the stunning visual grandeur of the American Old West, Ford tells the story of Americans subduing natural and human obstacles. The film both exemplifies and perpetuates a grand, mythic version of U.S. history, in which the triumph of the United States and its ideals are seen as the inevitable course of events. Indeed, many Westerns of this era say much the same thing. The good characters are so good, and the other characters are either so bad, in the moral sense, or else backward that these films imply that no outcome other than American triumph is possible. Custer's defeat at Little Big Horn—one of the low points in the traditional telling of American military history—is here in the background, but there is little doubt that the story of the movie will reveal Custer's demise as an aberration.

Ominous Cinematic Visions

Even as it was producing movies that enthusiastically embraced and reinforced themes of American morality and success, Hollywood also continued to issue films that pictured a more negative and sometimes ominous vision of American life. One such category of filmmaking was the genre known as film noir. This genre of film, which remains loosely defined to this day, arguably had begun in the 1930s but reached its zenith in the following two decades, though important works in the genre continued to appear occasionally long after.

Typically, the films that have been labeled "film noir" are, as the name implies dark, filled with a strong element of cynicism and reveal a sordid undercurrent to everyday life. Coexisting with polite and proper society, many of the main characters in these films have lurid secrets, criminal tendencies, and an inability to control their darker impulses. In many ways, the narratives of the films work as almost deadpan, dark parodies of polite society, which in the films appears oblivious to its own seamier elements.

Although there had been less successful versions of this theme earlier, it was the appearance of films such as the 1941 version of *The Maltese Falcon* that attracted attention to the then as-yet-unnamed genre. The film was directed by John Huston and featured a stellar cast that included Humphrey Bogart, Mary Astor, and Peter Lorre. Based on a gritty detective novel by Dashiell Hammett, Huston's film was very popular with audiences. Similar films followed, and even during the war, movies with this darker, more cynical outlook were produced by Hollywood. Among these were director Otto Preminger's *Laura* (1944), Edward Dmytryk's *Murder, My Sweet* (1944), and Billy Wilder's *Double Indemnity* (1944).

The latter of these, *Double Indemnity*, presents a brilliant and witty interpretation of the underside of American morals of the era. The main male character, Walter Neff (played by Fred MacMurray), is a typical, big-city insurance salesperson, keen to make his quota and succeed in his business life. When he visits an upscale Los Angeles home to sell accident insurance, however, his life takes a fateful turn. Although Neff's potential customer is not interested in buying a policy, it turns out that this man's unhappy wife is quite interested in something far more sinister. After inquiring about whether she could secretly buy life insurance on her husband, she soon schemes with Neff to kill her husband in a way that appears to be suicide so that she can collect on the insurance.

Especially for its time, *Double Indemnity* was a lurid story of moral corruption hiding, almost out in the open, in the mundaneness of routine life. Indeed, the film's major scenes are in very blasé settings. The major action occurs in places such as a corporate office, an upscale living room, a commuter train, and a neighborhood grocery store. Similarly, a major aspect of the film's story is the suggestion of moral decay and corruption in a guise that appears very ordinary. In *Double Indemnity*, as is common in many film noir productions, the tawdry world represented attracts so little attention that it can be almost unnoticed by so-called polite society.

With outlooks such as that evident in *Double Indemnity*, movies in the film noir genre provided an already-existing strand of storytelling that Hollywood could tap into amid the social restructuring of the late 1940s and into the 1950s. This type of filmmaking played into anxieties, sometimes culturally repressed, that coincided with what appeared to be more positive developments throughout the decade of the 1940s. The darker themes of film noir suggested that perhaps everything was not as rosy as it appeared. These films cautioned that human shortcomings—greed, lust, hubris—did not disappear simply because the standard of living was improving for many Americans.

The film noir genre remained a staple in American theaters after the war, as well, and its persistence over the next few years added a counterpoint to the lighter and more positive fare that Hollywood issued in the same era. The story of *The Postman Always Rings Twice* (1946), for example, is one of lust, murder, and betrayal. Based on a novel by James M. Cain (who had also written the story on which *Double Indemnity* was based), it tells the story of a young drifter who becomes intimately involved with a young married woman he meets. The two hatch a plot to murder the woman's husband, which they soon carry out.

In some ways, the underlying story in the novel on which the film was based stretched the limits of accepted morality as interpreted in the mid-1940s. The plot of the book was regarded as sufficiently immoral and potentially outside the bounds of acceptability that there was some question as to whether it could be produced and released without running afoul of the Production Code, which strictly limited what could be depicted on-screen in American theaters. But by the time Cain's novel was adapted for director Tay Garnett's movie version, the story was muted and tailored to meet production Code standards. As the *New York Times*'s Bosley Crowther noted, *The Postman Always Rings Twice* came to screen "without illustrating any of the bluntly carnal scenes of the book."[18] Instead, this treatment of the story transformed the plot into a more or less traditional tale of crime and punishment that emphasized traditional morality by showing the dire consequences of disobeying it. As Crowther also astutely observed, the film reveals "a sincere apprehension of American tragedy. For the yearning of weak and clumsy people for something better than the stagnant lives they live is revealed as the core of the dilemma, and sin is shown to be no way to happiness."[19]

The Postman Always Rings Twice, like most movies in that genre, appealed to two opposite impulses among viewers. On the one hand, and very overtly, it showed how yielding to temptation led to only short-term gratification. The ultimate result is almost certain punishment and anguish in the moral universe of 1940s American cinema. In that way, the film continued to reinforce prevailing social attitudes about the importance of obeying social laws and rules. Yet the film also appeals to the opposite impulse. It plays on audience curiosity about the perceived excitement and exhilaration of giving in to strong emotions such as lust. The forbidden nature of the main characters' actions adds a compelling dimension that in some ways undercuts the traditional morality on the surface. Clearly, it was this second facet of the story, which had been minimized when adapted for the screen, that initially worried censors.

The darker and in some ways primitive human impulses that are central to this film and others in the film noir genre were kept in check in the 1940s. But such stories, in which mostly ordinary people give in to weakness at key moments, with distressing results, also suggest a nagging worry that the private and inner lives of common people might not live up to the staid and traditionally moral exteriors that were visible to the outside world. Indeed, as a genre film noir emphasized that hidden motivations, petty behaviors, uncontrollable lust, and violent impulses could be close to the surface anywhere in the United States. In this way, many of movies in the genre represented an underside of life that Americans knew existed, to some extent, but wished to keep at bay for fear of potentially ruinous results.

Indeed, a hallmark of the film noir genre is the disturbing picture it painted of what American life could be like just below an otherwise pleasant surface veneer. In 1949, one compelling example of the genre was *The Third Man*, from British director Carol Reed. Starring Orson Welles, who had starred and directed *Citizen Kane* several years earlier, and Joseph Cotten, who also had a major role in *Citizen Kane*, Reed's movie featured a script by Graham Greene that told a brooding story about black-market dealings, violence, and deception in postwar Vienna. With its dark and moody lighting, the overall tone of the film is unmistakably seedy and sinister. An important scene near the end of the film features a shootout in subterranean sewers, which is hardly subtle in the unsavory view of the world it presents.

Along with narrative-style film noir that appeared throughout the late 1940s, a parallel series of films with similar themes, but told in a quasi-documentary style, appeared in American theaters. *Kiss of Death* (directed by Henry Hathaway), for example, starred Victor Mature and Richard Widmark as career criminals with a sadistic streak. Another well-known film, director Jules Dassin's 1948 movie *The Naked City*, followed an intense murder investigation. That same year, *Canon City* was director Crane Wilbur's version of a Colorado prison escape. Also in 1948, *The T-Men*, director Anthony Mann's tale of federal agents working undercover in a counterfeit ring, featured a grisly scene in which one of the agents is executed in front of his horrified colleague. Other movies, such as Joseph Newman's *Abandoned* (1949) and Alfred Werker's *He Walked by Night* (1948), similarly featured cold-hearted criminals and shocking misdeeds.

Taken together, the film noir films and other lurid crime movies of the era presented a stark contrast to the forward-looking and largely idyllic picture of postwar life that was emerging in other parts of the culture. Their bleak narratives are far from the almost silly and, by comparison, inconsequential problems encountered by the protagonists of *Mr. Blandings Builds His Dream House*, for example. Instead, these were stories of individuals ensnared in unexpected webs of violence and depravity. These bleaker films embody a nagging feeling of fear and anxiety beneath the surface of the happiness and promise that were tirelessly promoted by advertisers, businesses, and many cultural institutions of the era.

Hollywood Looks at Race

The United States had always been a multiracial society, though its history with successfully and equitably dealing with that fact has frequently been marked by troubles and inequities. The first wave of the Great Migration, in which more than a million and a half African Americans moved from the South to the North and West, was a significant demographic change to which the nation had not yet fully adjusted. By the 1940s, a second wave of migration was under way. Such changes were the source of some anxiety.

Hollywood addressed the so-called race issue with several films in the late 1940s. The topic was certainly current and relevant, though it was at times controversial. For example, director Alfred Werker's *Lost Boundaries*, a 1949 film starring Mel Ferrer, told the revealing of story an African American man and his family, who for years had "passed" as white residents in a quaint New England town. When the racial identity of the man and his children is revealed, however, the underlying prejudices in the community, despite their previous acceptance, become painfully evident. As a *Time* magazine review concluded, "The children, unaware of their antecedents, were normal, happy-go-lucky American school kids—until the their father, whose secret had been exposed . . . told them the truth. From there on, they became in their own minds pariahs in a nightmare world of shrieking suspicions and shrinking fears."[20] The language of *Time* magazine's review seems to acknowledge the harshness of racial separation in the United States in the late 1940s: "Out of these contacts emerge some fresh insights into Negro viewpoints, and into the intricate network of etiquette and anguish separating those [African Americans] who can 'pass' from those who cannot."[21]

One of the better-remembered films in the late 1940s trend that *Time* magazine called "Negro-problem films" was *Pinky*. A big-budget 20th Century Fox release from producer Darryl Zanuck and director Elia Kazan, this movie stressed entertainment along with a social agenda.[22] The main character is a young woman, Pinky (Jeanne Crain), who returns to the South after several years studying to be a nurse in the North. As with

Lost Boundaries, the complicating factor in the story is that Pinky is another African American character passing as white. In the film's narrative, Pinky is constantly subjected to prejudice and danger. But the morality of the movie's characters avoids simple racial dichotomies. A *Time* magazine article assessed that the movie was about "the sorry plight of the U.S. Negro" and would "doubtless irritate both professional Southerners and professional champions of racial equality."[23] The *Time* reviewer, like others of that day, regarded Pinky as a cut above some of the other movies dealing with American social dilemmas of the era, stating, "But Pinky is the most skillful type of propaganda: in avoiding crude and conventional labeling, it leaves a strong impression that racial discrimination is not only unreasonable but evil."[24]

A similar perspective was forthcoming from the *New York Times*. Its review of the film noted, "The hopeless discomfort of poor housing, the ignominy of police abuse, the humiliations of Jim Crowism and the sting of epithets are sharply sized. Likewise, the mean antagonisms of certain bigoted elements in the South are vividly caught."[25] Yet the ultimate effect according to this review was somewhat muted. The film was, after all, a product of its era, and it surely reflected some attitudes that persisted even as social attitudes in some quarters were changing. As the *New York Times* review also said, "Its observation of Negroes, as well as whites, is largely limited to types that are nowadays far from average ... No genuinely constructive thinking of relations between blacks and whites is offered."[26]

Still, such films openly and squarely addressed the topic of race in a way that was largely new in the history of the American cinema. And in this respect, Hollywood's attention to the subject shone light on a subject that would become a major challenge to American society in the coming decades.

THE END OF A DECADE

By the time the 1940s came to a close, it was clear that parallel and contrasting narratives had emerged in postwar American culture. Hollywood exemplified these differing pictures of American life, probably exaggerating the underlying truth in many of its productions. In their visions of the postwar United States, one version of life was happy, safe, prosperous, and comfortable; the other was dark, unpredictable, and plagued with problems that threatened the very existence of the life pictured in the other version. This dichotomous portrait of the United States that was depicted in the movie world may have tended to oversimplify the world as it really was, but the impulses that Hollywood depicted were real. The great fear emerging in an era of seeming promise and prosperity was, in fact, that the darker world that actually was, in some ways, just beyond what many Americans wished to see would spill over into real life. In the following decade, the feeling of dread and anxiety would continue to develop, shaped in new and even bigger ways by powerful fears emanating from the dangerous world of international politics.

CHAPTER 5

Rising Paranoia

Life was good at the midpoint of the twentieth century for many Americans. The nation had not only survived a war five years earlier; it had also achieved a decisive victory that yielded an emerging new life of convenience and bounty. But there was a flip side to this story with a much darker and more foreboding nature. The world seemed safe from the threat of fascism, but whether it would remain secure in the face of communism was an open question.

There were lurking dangers beyond the nation's shores. These, and emerging perceptions of threats embedded in life closer to home, were a nagging presence in the American psyche. Such dissonant feelings found expression in a variety of cultural forms and contexts. At times, they collectively fed a profoundly anxious subtext in American life. Indeed, a dark and sometimes nightmarish counterpart to the American Dream became increasingly common in political rhetoric and popular-culture forms of expression.

American cinema was one of the most prominent arenas in which insecurities resulting from the tumultuous political world were played out in the era. Sometimes such fears were evident in films. At other times, it was Hollywood itself that aroused suspicion, as had been the case in previous years. A new wrinkle in the latter came when the Supreme Court controversially reversed an earlier decision, the 1915 *Mutual Film Corporation v. Industrial Commission* case, which had denied films' First Amendment protection of free speech. Now that this legal restraint was removed, critics of the film business wondered whether Hollywood could be trusted to produce works that would reflect the traditional morality they deemed essential to the United States' strength and virtue.

Hollywood produced many works that were not directly connected to the political turbulence of the era, of course, but a significant number of its productions were reflective of the fearful cultural climate. Some of these films told stories in which narrative connections to unfolding real-world political events were unambiguous. Films with stories of espionage, conspiracy, and betrayal are obvious examples of this impulse. Other films reacted to political drama and intrigue more indirectly than this. Many genre pictures (including science fiction and Western movies) allowed filmmakers to treat themes of apprehension and paranoia in creative ways, sometimes amplifying themes from the political realm. At the same time, the growth of the television medium, which in many (though not all) ways was an outgrowth of cinematic traditions, provided new outlets in which political concerns were sometimes disseminated on screen.

It is widely recognized that many films—as varied as the John Wayne vehicle *Big Jim McLain* (1952), about a Communist plot in Hawaii, or *Invasion of the Body Snatchers* (1956), about menacing alien life forms—are deeply connected to the political environment in which they were created. But to gain a deep appreciation for just how much the anxious political culture is infused in Hollywood's output of the era, a closer look at that background is revealing.

PERCEPTIONS OF DANGER AND A RISING CULTURE OF FEAR

The picture of ordinary life that the United States often presented to itself, in popular-culture forms ranging from magazines to movies and television, was often more positive and optimistic than might be expected given the perception of a looming existential threat from the outside. But more anxiety-prone aspects of American life in the 1950s, which largely, but not exclusively emanated from the fear of communism, were frequently on display.

At the dawn of the 1950s, the dangers of the "Red Menace"—a period reference to the threat posed by the Soviet Union—seemed more ominous than ever. As many Americans, especially middle- and working-class white Americans, were settling into lives of relative comfort with a rising standard of living, the threat from the outside seemed very real. Over the coming decade, Americans would seek ways to cope with the ongoing danger.

Events in January 1950 confirmed this alarming political climate. On January 14, Chinese Communists assaulted the American consular offices in

Beijing. The following week, a State Department official named Alger Hiss—who in 1944 had helped plan the United Nations—was convicted in a scandalous trial related to accusations that he had been a Communist. And on the last day of the month, the Truman administration revealed that it had ordered the development of the hydrogen bomb, a nuclear device many times more powerful than the atomic weapon used at Hiroshima.

In this climate, many Americans were increasingly suspicious that the Communist menace had already arrived on American shores and that the enemy was now living among them in the form of Communist agents and sympathizers. Much of domestic culture and politics turned inward to this perceived threat. The heightened anxieties caused by fear of an invisible, internal danger erupted into a powerful, paranoid cultural climate.

The Alger Hiss case illuminates the increasing sense of insecurity in American culture. In HUAC hearings of 1948, a man named Whittaker Chambers had accused Hiss of being a Communist agent. It was a shocking allegation since Hiss had worked within government for more than a decade, including time as an official in the State Department. The accusation was all the more sensational since Hiss was on good terms with both Dean Acheson and John Foster Dulles, two powerful political figures beyond reproach.

With apparently little evidence to support Chambers's charges, however, Hiss sued Chambers for libel, seeking damages of $75,000.[1] But during those court proceedings, Chambers upped the stakes: he not only accused Hiss of having been a Communist; he also claimed Hiss had been involved in outright espionage. To back up his accusations, Chambers led the FBI to a cache of microfilmed State Department documents, which he claimed Hiss had provided him illegally in 1938. And according to subsequent FBI analysis, the microfilmed material was produced on a typewriter that had been issued to Hiss at the time.[2] Since the crimes that Hiss was accused of committing had taken place beyond the statute of limitations, he was charged with perjury rather than espionage. A first trial ended with no decision, but in a retrial he was convicted.

The Hiss trial proved to be an opening salvo in the decade's domestic political war against Communist influence in American life. In coming months, increasing attention was directed to this perceived threat, as U.S. political culture was overwhelmed by an increasing mood of fear and outrage.

In February 1950, Joseph McCarthy, a Republican senator from Wisconsin, capitalized on this mood in the otherwise unlikely setting of a Women's Republican Club meeting in Wheeling, West Virginia. In a speech he delivered there, McCarthy laid out his view of the dangerous postwar world. His remarks were apocalyptic in tone. He warned, "Today we are engaged in a final, all-out battle between communistic atheism and Christianity. The modern champions of communism have selected this as the time, and ladies and gentlemen, the chips are down—they are truly down."[3] McCarthy cautioned that the situation was getting worse, adding, "Six years ago, . . . there was within the Soviet orbit, 180,000,000 people. . . . Today, only six years later, there are 800,000,000 people under the absolute domination of Soviet Russia—an increase of over 400 percent."[4]

Already in early 1950, then, the tone was set for much of the decade. Eager to defend the homeland against anything that could threaten the postwar bounty of American life, attention focused on the external threat of the Soviet Union and the evils that nation symbolized to Americans. The zeal of Joseph McCarthy's anti-Communist campaign was therefore part of a larger and generally accepted view of the world that stressed vigilance and rapid response to communism. This attitude was widely felt throughout American political culture. The underlying fear and loathing with regard to communism crossed party lines in Washington and throughout the nation.

Meanwhile, unfolding developments in Asia further fueled American anxieties. Communist leader Mao Zedong had founded the People's Republic of China in 1949, which instantly brought an enormous portion of the world's population under Communist control. In Vietnam, the Communist forces of Ho Chi Minh fought to wrest control of that nation from France.

Then in 1950, a major crisis materialized as the struggle for control of the Korean Peninsula ignited into full-fledged war. The conflict pitted Communists in the north against the pro-Western government in the south. In June of that year, the armed forces of North Korea (Democratic People's Republic of Korea) crossed the 38th parallel, which had divided the peninsula since the end of World War II, and invaded South Korea (Republic of Korea), which was an American ally. The United States quickly organized a UN-backed military response, and for a time the American-led forces were successful. By autumn, U.S. forces arrived at Pyongyang, the North Korean capital.

This development, however, alarmed Chinese leaders, who were not content to simply watch the approaching American-led forces. In response, the Chinese joined the fight. With the situation getting out of control, Truman said, in a press conference of November 30, 1950, that the United States was considering the possibility of using the atomic bomb. Soon afterward, on December 15, the president declared a national emergency. In just about six months then, the world seemed to be on the brink of chaos.

The conflict continued into 1951. In March of that year, General MacArthur took matters into his own hands and directly threatened China with dire consequences if it did not withdraw from the war. But MacArthur's ultimatum had come without authorization from Truman. Angered at MacArthur's initiative, the president summarily—and controversially—fired the general on April 5.

The war continued. But by the summer of 1951, the situation essentially reached a stalemate. An armistice was signed in 1953, though the conflict was not fully resolved.

The fight against communism continued within the United States. In the early months of the Korean conflict, a controversial piece of legislation, the Internal Security Act of 1950, became law. It focused on investigating and controlling Communist activity in the United States. Meanwhile, Truman had secretly approved another important document, which had been prepared under the auspices of the National Security Council. Known as NSC-68, the covert document offered advice about how the United States should deal with the looming Communist threat.

Additional domestic events continued to reinforce the idea that the dangers were far closer than battles in foreign lands. In 1951, the sensational trial of Julius and Ethel Rosenberg highlighted the anti-Communist climate of the era. The government alleged that the Rosenbergs had been key players in a spy ring that had passed American atomic secrets from the Manhattan Project to the USSR. A conspiracy of this sort was something that many Americans had feared since the Soviets exploded an atomic bomb in 1949. The trial was front-page news and the guilty verdict not surprising. Others implicated in the Manhattan Project espionage plot received severe punishment, but not the death penalty. The Rosenbergs, however, were not to be beneficiaries of any leniency. Upon conviction, they were promptly sentenced to death. Their punishment was carried out in 1953.

By the time the Rosenbergs were brought to trial, the political climate of the United States was in a dire, paranoid-like state. Although there were some people who believed the Rosenbergs had been treated unfairly and were paying the price for American society's state of fear, for the most part the public accepted—and may have been relieved—that the culprits had been found.

In 1952 Dwight Eisenhower, the World War II hero, was elected president. This returned a Republican to the White House for the first time in two decades. Joseph McCarthy was reelected that same year and subsequently was assigned to the Senate Committee on Government Operations, of which the Senate Permanent Subcommittee on Investigations was a subsidiary. This assignment provided McCarthy with a platform from which he could launch further explorations of what he presumed were Communist infiltrations into positions of power in Washington.

In autumn of 1953, McCarthy turned his attention to the U.S. Army. He was convinced Communists lurked in the American military, but his investigation initially met with little success. The senator was undaunted, however, and pressed forward, eventually summoning Brigadier General Ralph Zwicker. By this time, McCarthy was a media star and his actions were heavily covered in American news reports. Despite his fame, however, his interrogations of an army general gave many people pause. In his dogged questioning of a respected military leader, many Americans thought McCarthy was going too far. The senator's zealous anti-Communist stance initially had been perceived as a political positive, but it now appeared to be a potential liability, not only for the senator but also for the whole party. Support for McCarthy began to weaken.

In March 1954, CBS reporter Edward R. Murrow's popular television news program, *See It Now*, brought additional attention to McCarthy and his tactics. Murrow's reports amounted to an exposé, presenting a portrait of the senator that was far from flattering. Already McCarthy had extended himself by making accusations based on flimsy evidence and in the process making enemies of powerful people. Now, he began to look like a bully.

In the months between January and June 1954, McCarthy's public approval ratings plummeted. Many Americans—though not all—came to believe that McCarthy's way had become too extreme. As Congressman George H. Bender concluded, "McCarthyism has become a synonym for witch-hunting, Star Chamber methods, and the denial of . . . civil liberties."[5]

It is difficult to say with certainty how much the United States' fears eased by the middle of the 1950s. But by this time, the new world that had been created from the ashes of World War II was a decade old and no longer a new threat. And some things had changed. Soviet leader Joseph Stalin had died in 1953, removing the face of Soviet despotism. In some ways, Americans were becoming accustomed to the perils of the outside world and to the idea that the Soviets were likely to be a threat for some time to come. Still, Americans continued to worry about "creeping" communism. Political leaders spoke of the "domino theory"—the idea that communism might eventually surround the United States incrementally, establishing itself one country at a time.

Over the coming few years, the anti-Communist fervor, though still present, lessened. But just as Americans seemed to be adjusting somewhat to the dangers of the bipolar, Cold War world, they faced unexpected news—the 1957 launch of the Soviet Union's tiny *Sputnik 1* satellite. This shocked Americans. *Sputnik* showcased a technology that could easily be converted for military use. Panicked by the Soviet Union's apparent success with a potentially deadly new military technology, the United States redoubled its efforts to shore up the national defense. It poured money and attention into existing and new programs that aimed to increase security.[6]

Crises continued to emerge with some regularity after Americans started to recover from the initial shock of *Sputnik*. But in many ways, by the late 1950s the years of worry about Communist barbarians at the gates of the United States were largely absorbed into the cultural life of the nation. Domestic life was relatively calm on the surface. Americans were adjusting to the more or less permanent threat emanating from beyond their borders. Meanwhile, the near-hysteria that had sometimes been prompted by Cold War fears that the enemy had deeply infiltrated the United States and its institutions had largely faded to manageable levels. Americans were starting to come to terms with the admittedly dangerously divided world.

HOLLYWOOD AND THE EXTERNAL THREAT

By the 1950s, postwar realities had made a substantial impact in the kinds of productions that Hollywood issued. Although many types of films were released, with many types of narratives, in the late 1940s and early 1950s a number of films had undercurrents of paranoia and dread in their story lines, suggesting potential American ruin in ways that often lacked subtlety. As the decade wore on, many productions treated similar themes, some more artfully than others, evoking a more generalized sense of anxiety, even though more blatant treatments of these themes continued to be released. But the feelings of fear and unease, as symbolized in stories suggesting doom and destruction, continued to be an important narrative element in many screen productions.

The anti-Communist anxieties of the early Cold War were deeply emotional and revealed a society that, at some level, feared the worst. Most Americans did not doubt that the Soviet Union was determined to extend its empire throughout the world, using whatever means of force and duplicity that would be necessary to achieve that end. Not surprisingly, Hollywood quickly picked up the theme.

As with much of Hollywood's output over the years, however, the consistency of the industry's enthusiasm for the subject was not always matched by consistency in quality. Some Cold War movies were first-rate and immensely popular. Others were mediocre at best and scarcely made an impression. Still, on balance, from the late 1940s until the late 1950s, the Cold War was a popular subject with Hollywood. This meant that American audiences were exposed to a series of productions in which the American Dream was portrayed as under siege by Communist powers aiming to impose a totalitarian version of their ideology across the globe.

In the late 1940s, movies such as *Conspirator*, *The Red Menace*, and *I Married a Communist* provided audiences with a heavy dose of anti-Communist stories. This strand of movie making continued in the 1950s with a long line of films that were mostly variations on this theme. These included *The Whip Hand* (1951), *Arctic Flight* (1952), *The Atomic City* (1952), *Diplomatic Courier* (1952), *Red Snow* (1952), *The Thief* (1952), *My Son John* (1952), *Never Let Me Go* (1953), *Man on a Tightrope* (1953), *Night People* (1954), and *Trial* (1955).

One representative example of this type of production was the 1951 movie *I Was a Communist for the FBI*. Directed by Gordon Douglas, it tells the story of Matt Cvetic, a real-life government informant, though on-screen Cvetic's experiences are fictionalized to the point that, as one writer later described, the story has "little to do with real history."[7] As portrayed in the film, however, Cvetic is a valiant hero who endures estrangement and enmity from his family and friends as he pretends to be a Communist in order to gather information.

Though it captured some of the anxious political climate of the times, the film's initial reception was not altogether positive. *New York Times* critic Bosley Crowther wrote that the movie contained "dangerous innuendos" and "suggestions—always from the villains' oily tongues—that people who embrace liberal causes, such as the Scottsboro trial defense, are Communist dupes."[8] Such shortcomings aside, the narrative of *I Was a Communist for the FBI* fit comfortably within the way the perceived Communist threat in the United States was routinely and frequently being portrayed in political rhetoric and in the news media of the time.

A film the following year was somewhat more artful and commanded greater public attention. This was *Big Jim McLain* (1952), which was directed by Edward Ludwig. Unlike many other "Red Scare" movies, this was a major production. It starred the popular actor John Wayne, who, in addition to being a vocal anti-Communist, was also one of the film's producers.

The movie's story plays out against the backdrop of the Korean War. In the narrative, HUAC, which is portrayed in a highly flattering manner, has dispatched two government agents (played by Wayne and James Arness) to Hawaii. The agents' mission is to investigate and thwart a Communist plot involving a longshoremen's union. As the story unfolds, Jim McLain (Wayne's character) is presented as a no-nonsense patriot, who bristles at the way alleged Communist infiltrators have manipulated their legal rights—by "hiding behind the Constitution," as the character says—to scheme against the United States.[9]

Big Jim McLain was a financially successful film, earning roughly $2.4 million, or about triple its production costs.[10] It success was an indication that the public was ready and willing to hear the movie's unambiguous, and perhaps somewhat heavy-handed, anti-Communist message.

Fear of communism and nuclear danger were the topics of another film that year, *The Atomic City* (1952). This suspenseful movie, which was directed by Jerry Hopper, was described in one review as a "low-budget, high-voltage film,"[11] but in many respects it was an effective vehicle in conveying the apprehensive political climate of the time.

The story of *The Atomic City* follows efforts to rescue an American scientist's son. Soviet spies who are seeking American hydrogen-bomb secrets have kidnapped the boy. Frantic to return his son to safety and resolved not to hand over U.S. nuclear secrets to the enemy, the scientist, Dr. Frank Addison (played by Gene Barry, who was also the lead actor in *The War of the Worlds* the following year), desperately turns to the FBI for help.

Although the boy is returned to safety by the end of the story, the film has by then reinforced the notion of the Soviet Union and the communism it represented as an evil force that would respect no civilized boundaries in its quest for world domination. *The Atomic City* also reinforces the general idea that American citizens were in grave danger in the nuclear world. Only the strength of American institutions (in this case, the FBI) could save them—and by extension, their way of life—from a deadly fate.

Invasion U.S.A. is another 1952 film depicting similar themes. The movie defies easy categorization and is a political film with a dark fantasy element. Much less subtle than most other anti-Communist movies of the time, *Invasion U.S.A.* is also arguably the most apocalyptic of the era's Cold War movies in terms of tone and narrative. The film's story begins in a New York City bar, where customers watching television learn that the "enemy"—unspecified, but surely intended to be the Soviet Union—has overrun Alaska in what appears to be the first step in an all-out assault on the United States. Almost immediately upon hearing this news, it is revealed that widespread attacks throughout the United States are under way. The Boulder Dam is destroyed. Major urban centers, and even Washington, DC, are soon targets of enemy action that includes the use of atomic bombs. The situation looks bleak for the United States, and efforts to counter the invasion appear doomed to failure.

By the end of the story, the United States is apparently about to fall. But then the film's focus abruptly returns to the New York bar where the story started. It is then revealed that the terrible events were an illusion. It turns out that one of the people at the bar had hypnotized the others in the group, causing them to imagine his cautionary tale as if it had been a real event. His purpose was apparently to demonstrate to the group how easily an unprepared United States could fall to hostile forces in a malevolent world. His message was therefore one of perpetual vigilance, since that, in his view, is all that can ultimately save the United States from the real dangers posed by its enemies.

A movie lacking in subtlety, actual atomic bomb film clips were edited into *Invasion U.S.A.* in order to add to its visual impact. Even in its day, the film was recognized as purveying an alarmist message. A review in *Variety*, for example, noted that the movie was "a potent exploitation release" that was "conducive to a 'scare' promotional campaign for good returns in the general and exploitation markets."[12] Although featuring a little known cast, *Variety* concluded that the "idea is spectacularly presented, and Alfred E. Green's direction makes the most of the potential offered in lending credence to the theme."[13] More generally, the story of *Invasion U.S.A.*, like others with its general theme, demonstrates Cynthia Hendershot's observation that "the pervasiveness of the nuclear threat is what these films metaphorically represent. In the Atomic Age, there is no place to hide."[14]

Danger from the Skies

Reports of flying saucers and potentially alien spacecrafts had emerged in the late 1940s, becoming a subject of widespread speculation. In retrospect, the appearance of the UFO phenomenon appears closely linked to other developments in American politics and culture at that time. More precisely, the theme of invasion by a powerful and mysterious enemy closely parallels the sense of anxiety that had developed in the United States at mid-century. Science fiction conventions allowed such fears to be presented indirectly, at a psychological distance from what may have been very real (or perceived as very real) earthly threats of the time.

The United States' fear of nuclear attack created an anxious mood that permeated much of the 1950s and early 1960s, and science fiction movies about invaders from space provided one way of telling stories about invasion, destruction, and domination. Hollywood had long realized that like amusement park visitors flocking to thrill rides and haunted houses, movie audiences were often attracted to productions in which they confront fear and even terror, as long as these feelings were contained and presented in an entertaining way. Science fiction therefore provided one way of dealing with ready-made political and cultural fears in a relatively benign way.

Hollywood had already experimented with stories about astronauts and people and creatures from other worlds before the late 1940s. Often in stories developed for youth audiences, this type of fare had been seen, for example, in serialized films such as *Flash Gordon* (1936). Science fiction stories that made their way to film had often seemed somewhat like standard adventure stories that were simply set in outer space. The locales were exotic and the creatures literally otherworldly, but for the most part the plots replicated the same kind of stories that moviegoers might see in Westerns or other genre pictures.

Several years later, however, the increasingly frightening era of nuclear weapons, rocket experiments, and threat of international communism significantly altered the context in which science fiction films were produced and consumed. Although they may have continued to mostly be geared toward a youth audience, the postwar science fiction films responded to many of the very real and serious concerns of the times. On the one hand, these movies sometimes reflected a sense of wonder and speculation about space flight and even life on other worlds. But on the other hand, they often were thinly veiled nightmares, presented in futuristic tales that played on the growing fears and anxieties of danger in the nuclear-tinged Cold War.

One of the earliest, and also the best, movies about extraterrestrial aliens visiting earth was director Robert Wise's acclaimed *The Day the Earth Stood Still*. Wise, a major Hollywood talent who had gained notice editing *Citizen Kane*, directed a wide range of movies, from film noir productions such as *Born to Kill* (1947) to the 1965 classic *The Sound of Music* and many more. His approach to the science fiction theme in *The Day the Earth Stood Still* was informed by his interest in telling believable stories, even if the premises were sometimes unusual.

The narrative of *The Day the Earth Stood Still*, which was adapted from a short story by Harry Bates entitled "Farewell to the Master," is about a solitary alien visitor named Klaatu (played by Michael Rennie), who lands a huge saucer-shaped spacecraft in the middle of Washington, DC. Upon landing, Klaatu emerges from the craft with a message for humanity. Almost immediately, however, a nervous soldier shoots Klaatu and seriously wounds him. The alien is then whisked off to a hospital where, under guard, government officials seek to question him.

Klaatu recovers quickly, but his arrival has already set off a panic. Some people fear Klaatu's arrival signals an invasion from Mars, while some fear that it is a trick of the United States' earthly rival, presumably the USSR.

Following his rapid recovery, Klaatu then slips away, unnoticed, from the hospital to explore life among the ordinary people of earth. Assuming the identity of Mr. Carpenter, he befriends a widow, Helen Benson (played by Patricia Neal), and her young son, Bobby. In conversations with the mother and her son, Klaatu sees a friendlier and more open-minded point of view. He eventually reveals his identity to them.

As he explores earth's ways, Klaatu arranges a dramatic demonstration of alien powers. For a half hour, power is cut everywhere on the planet, stopping ordinary life in its tracks. This turn of events causes fear and panic around the globe. But soon Klaatu's identity is discovered, and before he can complete his mission of meeting with world leaders he is shot again, this time apparently fatally.

With Klaatu seemingly dead, Helen Benson rushes to the alien's spacecraft and utters the famous line "Klaatu barada nikto," which awakens the alien's huge and seemingly invulnerable robot, Gort. The robot then retrieves Klaatu and brings him back to life. Then, in the climax of the film, Klaatu emerges from his spaceship and issues a stern warning to all of humanity:

> It is no concern of ours how you run your own planet, but if you threaten to extend your violence, this Earth of yours will be reduced to a burned-out cinder. Your choice is simple: join us and live in peace, or pursue your present course and face obliteration. We shall be waiting for your answer. The decision rests with you.

As the story draws to a close, Klaatu returns to the ship and leaves earth to ponder his dire warning.

In many ways, *The Day the Earth Stood Still* stands out among the science fiction films of the 1950s because of its focus on "moral issues instead of explosions,"[15] as one writer has suggested. And in some respects, the film appeals to noble intentions of harmony and universal understanding. Yet it is difficult to miss that the alien's plea for peace and responsible use of nuclear weapons is cloaked in the threat of earth's total destruction. The choice given to humankind—whether to live peacefully or not—is not really a choice after all. It is a dictum that must be obeyed. So the movie is not only, as has been described, the story of "Klaatu, a visitor whose mission is to put an end to the petty hostilities of the Earthlings before they wipe themselves out."[16] It is also the story of an ultimatum delivered by an elegant stranger. The story seems to caution that humans have limited control over their own destiny and should be careful if they are to survive.

Another film that expressed a viewpoint that would become common in the era's science fiction movies with an alien invasion theme was the ominously titled *The Thing from Another World*, which was also released in

1951. In this film, the story involves a seven-foot-tall, humanoid-looking alien that feeds on blood, which is a plot element that is rich with metaphorical implications. Set in the arctic north, the narrative involves an American team that is sent to investigate what appears to be a mysterious crash. Eventually, they discover a saucer-shaped craft with a seemingly lifeless body encased in the ice. The body, still frozen, is then taken back to the team's base for further examination. As the team's next steps are debated, however, the alien is inadvertently reanimated. The hulking creature (played by future television star James Arness) then begins what amounts to a rampage on the base.

In the end, the creature is killed. The movie ends with a more serious warning, however. In melodramatic fashion, a voice emanating from a radio broadcast declares, "Watch the skies everywhere! Keep watching the skies!"

Beneath the surface of the narrative, largely hidden by sometimes far-fetched plot elements, then, are themes that did relate more closely to the anxiety-ridden political culture of the era. The caution to "Watch the skies," although playing on the public's fascination with UFOs at the time, parallels the more real and immediate potential danger from the skies that was not alien spacecrafts but an incoming attack from a worldly foreign enemy. Indeed, taken out of context, this message—which at that time would almost certainly have been interpreted as a warning to beware of a Soviet attack—can be lost.

Although Hollywood movies are multilayered and their makers are usually focused on making entertaining and financially successful products, films seemingly as fantastic and unreal as *The Thing from Another World* often do portray, perhaps inadvertently, the mind-set and mood of an era. And science fiction, which reached new heights as a popular movie genre during the 1950s, was not only a way to cash in on the UFO craze but also a way to tell stories that played to the anxious political climate of the era.

In 1953, the alien invasion theme returned unambiguously to American movie screens with *Invaders from Mars*. Director William Cameron Menzies, a Hollywood veteran, was well suited for work on this film. His previous credits included directing the 1936 movie *Things to Come*, a futuristic tale written by science fiction legend H. G. Wells.

Invaders from Mars, which became one of the most popular movies in the genre, centers on the story of a young boy named David (played by Jimmy Hunt), who witnesses a strange object crash from the sky not far from his house. After the boy alerts his parents, David's father heads off to investigate. When the father returns a while later, however, David notices that he is behaving in a strange, almost hostile way. As the story progresses, David notices that many other townspeople are also behaving oddly. They appear to be under the control of some outside force. When David tries to report his concern to authorities, however, few take him seriously. But two people, a family doctor and a local astronomer, soon take interest in the events. Upon further investigation and knowledge already in his possession, the astronomer concludes that the object is a spacecraft from Mars, probably carrying aliens planning an invasion. The U.S. military is then summoned to the scene.

The narrative moves along briskly thanks to a number of contrivances and coincidences that, in a more realistic production, might have been crippling to the story. Despite many plot inconsistencies that strain credulity, however, *Invaders from Mars* was an enormously influential film in the science fiction genre and dealt with important cultural themes of its era. An evil alien turning ordinary Americans into zombie-like slaves is a theme highly consistent with the political culture of fear and, in some cases, hysterical-like reactions to it that typified the height of the McCarthy era. Like the political climate in the real world of the time, the fictional world of *Invaders from Mars* presupposes that what is alien is also evil and intent on destroying the United States. And to be sure, while movies with this theme often spoke of earth's destruction or enslavement as a whole, the narratives of these films consider things only from an American point of view. Such is the single-minded presumption that the American way is the pinnacle of human achievement that it is as if to say, if the United States is destroyed, then the world is destroyed.

Many of the themes explored in *Invaders from Mars* are revisited in the more serious cinematic effort, *The Invasion of the Body Snatchers*, arguably among the best films of its kind from that era. The 1956 production from director Don Siegel tells the story of a small-town physician, Miles Bennell (played by Kevin McCarthy), who is mystified by local residents exhibiting behavior so bizarre that they appear to be imposters. As additional reports are forthcoming, Bennell consults with a psychiatrist, who believes the reports are little more than a mostly harmless form of "mass hysteria." Bennell remains concerned.

Later, as more and more townspeople continue to succumb to the odd behavior, Bennell and the few friends who take him seriously make an ominous discovery. Human-size pods, which have apparently "drifted through space for years," have crashed to the earth's surface. The pods are one by one destroying the humans who come in contact with them and replacing the humans with exact but emotionless replicas.

Eventually, as the pod beings attempt to destroy Bennell and his friends in an effort to eradicate all humans in the area, Bennell makes an escape to a nearby town. At his first encounter with the outside world, he is overcome with emotion, shouting, "They're here already! You're next! You're next!"

Bennell is taken to a hospital for medical examination. And although at first his story seems too incredible to be taken seriously, the report of an accident involving giant pods nearby convinces the authorities in this other community to listen. But as they attempt to report the apparent danger to higher authorities, the film ends, leaving open the question of whether humanity will realize and respond to the silent invasion in time to save itself.

Certainly, *Invasion of the Body Snatchers* captures the mood of anxiety and fear that had developed in the United States in the decade prior to its release. But although there is little doubt about that general aspect of its perspective, it is more complex than many viewers may realize at first. Indeed, more than one reading of it is possible once the film is examined closely.

The most obvious way to interpret the pods and pod beings is, of course, within the anti-Communist context that characterized that era. The emotionless, automaton pod creatures are impenetrable in their motives and seemingly devoid of any of the human qualities that Americans might think make life worth living. Although exaggerated, this gray, colorless, and listless life was nonetheless quite similar to the way in which life in Communist societies was metaphorically regarded in the United States in the 1950s. Viewing the Soviet Union as a monolithic authoritarian regime, life there struck Americans as cold and deadening.

But whether from a remote part of the universe or simply from the Soviet Union an ocean and a continent away, however, the point was the same: that ordinary Americans stood in danger of losing their vibrancy, individuality, and free will. Only caution and vigilance stood between the wonder of American life—in the film typified by a small, idyllic community seemingly devoid of real problems—and ruin. The problem, as portrayed both in the film and by many mainstream politicians of the era, was in encouraging and motivating people to stay alert at all times.

Yet, as compelling as this reading of the film may be, the narrative is sufficiently ambiguous to allow alternate—or perhaps, additional—interpretations. Such perspectives again are based on the portrayal of the pod people as essentially barely conscious beings apparently lacking in free will and untouched by any moral concerns. As enemies of humanity, the pod creatures might also be seen as a negative consequence of certain facets of modernity. In a way, they might symbolize the strong tendency for conformity that was sometimes noticed in this era, seemingly suggesting a dull, deadening loss of individuality in the increasingly bureaucratized corporate world. From one perspective, this could cause American society to corrode from within.[17]

Evidence of this reading can be found, for example, in dialogue uttered by Bennell at a point during the story in which he and his female companion are trying to avoid detection by the pod people. Bennell says, "In my practice, I see how people have allowed their humanity to drain away, only it happens slowly instead of all at once. They didn't seem to mind—all of us, a little bit. We harden our hearts, grow callous. Only when we have to fight to stay human do we realize how precious it is."[18]

Other movies from the era also touched on the outer space theme, although in different ways. They are revealing, however, for the pictures they show of life, presumably American life, when faced with new challenges and dangers resulting from the space-age era.

The 1951 film *When Worlds Collide*, directed by Rudolph Maté and produced by George Pal, which in some ways could be categorized in the disaster movie genre, has a story in which a rogue star is discovered to be on a course that will intersect the earth's orbit in just eight months. The planet is seemingly doomed. In addition to scenes of catastrophe, chaos, and melodrama in the process of bringing the plan to realization, the film somberly shows how the project leaders select the few people who will make the journey to safety—in other words, who will survive and who will die.

Producer George Pal was also behind another film from the era with an older story but a similar theme. This was the 1953 film adaptation of H. G. Wells's science fiction classic, *War of the Worlds*. Directed by Byron Haskin and starring Gene Barry and Ann Robinson, the familiar story involved a terrifying invasion of earth from aliens in huge spaceships. Seemingly uninterested in negotiating with humans or explaining their motives, the aliens proceed to destroy cities and hunt down and kill humans. Earthly defenses appear to be of little use, and there seems little hope that successful opposition can be mounted. As the landscape is increasingly reduced to rubble and littered with slaughtered humans, the plot follows the main characters as they attempt to stay a step ahead of the aliens.

Like *When Worlds Collide* and other movies with similar plots, the story in *War of the Worlds* shows an attack from the outside. Humans in both films are victims whose existence is threatened by unexplainable forces. Although it may appear as though this sort of film is quite different from the more typical alien invasion movies of the same era—sharing only the fact that they all have something to do with outer space—in fact, they do share with the more typical alien invasion films a sense that human life—American life—is precarious and not something that can be taken for granted. All these films exude a moral sense in which American values such as piety, individual responsibility, and achievement either are important as the outright solutions to the varied external threats or are instrumental in at least enhancing the individual's ability to achieve a better outcome and survive frightening uncertainties. In other words, though life around a person (usually the film's hero or main character) may descend into immense danger and chaos, core American values—as perceived by mainstream U.S. society in the 1950s—are shown as the best defense.

Thus many of the science fiction movies of this era were predicated on the idea that ordinary American life—which is almost always portrayed as serene and harmonious—was in jeopardy. In a way, they metaphorically suggest that the American Dream, which was poised to come to fruition after the struggles of the Great Depression and the enormous sacrifices of World War II, was not secure and that it could not be taken for granted. Did it really matter whether the enemy was in Moscow or on Mars? Lack of vigilance or drifting from the things that made the United States great would lead to the same result: the destruction of a way of life that seemed to be on the brink of even greater success. It was American values—faith in God, faith in technology, faith in the individual, and faith in American social institutions—that would spell the difference between a furthering of the American Dream or a descent into an American wasteland.

"Cold War" Movies

Other films also dealt with the anxious Cold War political climate, sometimes directly and sometimes indirectly. Alfred Hitchcock's *Rear Window* (1954), for example, is a film in the latter category. Although its plot has nothing to do with spies and the world of international communism, it is a film in which the psychological state of anxiety and dread is a central feature. A wheelchair-bound man, who is confined to his urban apartment while he recuperates, witnesses what appears to be a brutal murder in an apartment across the street. Yet when he reports the crime, there is no sign of foul play. The story then revolves around the man's desperate attempts to get someone to believe his account.

Not long after, in 1956, Hitchcock remade his own film *The Man Who Knew Too Much*, further enhancing his reputation as a director who "builds terror in the unlikeliest places."[19] Starring Jimmy Stewart and Doris Day, the film was a high-profile production and won critical praise. The story involves a family that inadvertently becomes embroiled in an assassination plot. The main character is an American physician named Benjamin McKenna (played by Jimmy Stewart), who is traveling in Morocco with his wife (played by Doris Day) and their young son. After a chance encounter with a dying man, Dr. McKenna is not sure what he has stumbled upon and initially presumes he has become entangled in a series of misunderstandings. Yet the plotters presume McKenna knows more than he does, and they kidnap the couple's son to ensure co-operation until the scheme is carried out. Eventually, the action switches to London and a series of dangerous episodes leading up to the planned assassination, which is thwarted only at the last minute. As with many other films of the era, Americans are portrayed as innocent victims, caught in dangerous events beyond their control or understanding.

Like *The Man Who Knew Too Much*, Hitchcock's *North by Northwest* (1959) also revealed a world dominated by intrigue. Yet, although Hitchcock's formidable wit is evident in both films, the tone of *North by Northwest* is decidedly different from the earlier movie. The suspense aspect of *North by Northwest* is fully on display, but the story itself seems lighter and almost tongue-in-cheek.

The narrative involves Roger Thornhill, an advertising executive (played by Cary Grant) who is presumed by the enemy (apparently the Soviets) to be a spy. Soon immersed in intrigues between American and enemy spies that he does not fully understand, Thornhill's life appears to be in grave danger. More than that, the American spymaster (played by Leo G. Carroll) who is overseeing the case appears willing to let the innocent and unsuspecting Thornhill become a casualty of the Cold War espionage in which he has inadvertently become enmeshed. Only at the last minute, in fact, does the spymaster intervene to extricate Thornhill from danger.

Unlike the more dire and perhaps hysterical portrayals of international danger in most American spy and conspiracy movies from the early Cold War, *North by Northwest* anticipates a mood, which would be more fully developed in the 1960s, in which the madness and absurdity of the Cold War is presented. In a way, the film portrays the world of danger and intrigue, which had been depicted in a very dark manner in earlier films, with something approaching comic resignation.

A film with more overtly apocalyptic treatment of this type of theme was *On the Beach* (1959). It depicts the slow, apparently certain end of human life that results when huge clouds of radiation drift over one continent after another. This production, directed by Stanley Kramer and adapted from a novel by Nevil Shute, stars Gregory Peck, Ava Gardner, and Fred Astaire. The decidedly fatalistic narrative shows the last remaining human civilization, in Australia, as it carries on while awaiting its fate. The fearful, depressing story is highly consistent with the very real nuclear anxieties of the era. It was a critical hit, dealing with themes in a straightforward drama that had often been addressed only when cloaked in science fiction narratives.[20] But as Terry Christensen and Peter Haas have observed, "it left audiences feeling helpless because it gave no clue as to what could be done to prevent the atomic holocaust."[21]

The dire and depressing story presented in *On the Beach* reflects a more despondent mood than the much lighter, if suspenseful, espionage drama of *North by Northwest* that was released in the same year. These are two sides of the same coin, however, since the gloomier *On the Beach* is really nothing more than a possible end game in deadly nuclear-era spy exploits depicted in *North by Northwest*. Interestingly, the potentially disastrous consequences of nuclear confrontation, which *On the Beach* so starkly depicts, often were not approached directly in other productions of the era, at least not in a serious vein. The portrait of humankind's ruin in that film was perhaps a subject the filmmakers, and maybe audiences, preferred to see from the relative comfort of some psychological distance, through allegory or satire or other indirect means.

DOMESTIC LIFE IN THE UNITED STATES OF THE 1950s

As menacing political winds threatened from the outside, in the United States of the mid-twentieth century the nation nonetheless still appeared capable of withstanding the throes of fear and anxiety that global communism elicited. With only a few wrinkles, the American economy remained reasonably robust in the years after the war. Unemployment never materialized into the major problem that economic planners had feared just a few years earlier. In fact, by the end of the 1940s Americans seemed to be doing increasingly well economically.

Material wealth, vigorous employment and spending, and a positive outlook toward the future accompanied the increasingly suburbanized world of the 1950s. The everyday life that middle-class and upwardly mobile working-class Americans, especially white Americans, were building in some ways projected a surface appearance that seemed idyllic. (Many Americans who were not in the racial majority continued to struggle after the war.) For these people, it often seemed as though the American Dream was coming true, at least in many conceptions of it that appeared and were reinforced in popular culture that portrayed a common, and often positive, way that middle-class Americans wished to think about their lives. Problems existed but were being solved, or so was a common message. Indeed, it was an era in which faith in technologies of all sorts was prevalent.

Yet beneath the surface, the picture varied. Indeed, as the 1950s progressed, cracks in the positive outward picture of domestic American culture began to appear. It was these cracks that would be the forerunners of full-blown crises of confidence in coming years that would be perceived as grave threats to the American Dream. But in the 1950s, the full extent of what would unfold in future years remained unknown and largely unsuspected.

Some problems were becoming quite noticeable and already a viewed as a cause for concern, however. In the recognition of such problems, there lurked the fear that these represented a dangerous break from the traditions and values that Americans regarded as cornerstones to their way of life. These issues therefore were powerfully symbolic of the nation's precariousness, seemingly having the potential to undermine all that had been achieved.

Many facets of life can be two-edged, with both positive and negative implications. In the years after World War II many Americans, eager to put the previous years of scarcity and sacrifice behind them, enthusiastically embraced many of the changes that were sweeping across the social and cultural landscape. New housing patterns, new material comforts, new jobs, new knowledge—at first glance, these all seemed to be the harbingers of a new golden era.

Yet if the United States was achieving social and technological progress, these were not without cost. And while it may not have been fully appreciated at the time, there was more to this cost than the financial aspects. In many ways, there were now significant ruptures with past ways of understanding the world and going about life. Sometimes, in the enthusiasm for new things that seemed to herald the good life, the social cost exacted by these ruptures was not immediately evident. But over time, such costs would be widely recognized. Within several decades, as examples, the downsides of suburbanization and automobile dependence, the health consequences of "fast food," and the negative effects of overextended credit would be widely recognized. Although a full accounting of the costs of 1950s-era "progress" was years away, some people noticed signs of potential trouble and discord in the 1950s, at a time when few Americans—especially in the upwardly mobile, white middle class—questioned the innovations that came rapidly their way.

At first, postwar suburbia was largely viewed as an innovation that represented the future. More than simply new and inexpensive mass housing, the suburbs were essentially new communities established beyond the cities, with their perceived problems, crowds, and aging and sometimes decaying edifices. The suburbs were not simply a solution to a housing demand, then, but also a means of escape. And not coincidentally, the suburbs provided working- and middle-class white city dwellers a way to remove themselves from the increasingly multicultural and multiracial city populations. Indeed, the new suburbs tended to have mostly white populations, which was also no coincidence since exclusionary lending and selling practices, coupled with social pressures, often made it difficult for nonwhites to purchase homes in the suburbs.[22]

As people moved to the new world of suburbia, a cascading series of perceived needs was created. And the conformist social impulses at work in suburbia, in which residents compared their standard of living to those around them, helped a culture of consumerism develop and flourish.[23] The stress produced by constantly trying to "keep up" was one of the undersides of the American Dream to be noticed. But still, the consumer culture took hold and in many ways transformed American life.

Increasingly after World War II, the world of employment came to be dominated by huge, much admired corporations, the number and scale of which had not been previously seen. As a practical matter, upward economic—and hence, social—mobility was often symbolized by success in a corporate setting. And as corporations grew in size and prominence, the influence of their bureaucratic features and organizational culture was significant.

Other important changes were also under way in American society. Civil rights issues commanded much attention. For example in 1954, in a case known as *Brown v. Board of Education*, the Supreme Court declared that school segregation based on race was unconstitutional. The following year, an African American woman named Rosa Parks refused to give up her seat on a public bus to a white passenger, as was still required by Alabama law. Her subsequent arrest eventually led to a widespread boycott of buses in Montgomery, Alabama. The highly publicized protest lasted more than a year. Then, in 1957 court-ordered school desegregation in Little Rock, Arkansas, led to a tense confrontation between federal and state authorities. President Eisenhower sent troops to protect the nine African American students who had been assigned to the previously all-white Little Rock Central High School.

Now regarded as among the most important events in the early history of the civil rights movement, such developments were greeted with apprehension by many Americans, especially those in the majority. They were alarmed at what appeared from their perspective to be rapidly changing social norms and practices with regard to race. The perceived swiftness of change, however, was clearly in the eye of the beholder. The Civil War and slavery had ended nine decades earlier, but African Americans still were not regarded as social or legal equals in much of the United States.

The era also saw shifting attitudes about sexuality. In a decade with an outward emphasis on conformity to traditional American norms, many Americans were both concerned and fascinated by changing adult behaviors.

Already, there was more public discussion of American sexual behavior than had previously been the case. Dr. Alfred Kinsey and associates, for example, had published *Sexual Behavior in the Human Male* in 1948 to much public attention. (The sequel, *Sexual Behavior in the Human Female*, was published five years later.)

This new frankness—at least in terms of that era—in discussing the topic of sexual behavior also was apparent in American popular fiction of the day. *Peyton Place*, a popular novel that was published in 1956, was emblematic of both the allure and anxieties caused by shifting social attitudes. The book was publicized as "an extraordinary new novel that lifts the lid off a small New England town." Indeed, though on the surface the setting was a typical, all-American community, the story has been described as "a scorching tale of lust, rape, incest, adultery, murder, alcoholism, and hypocrisy."[24] Twentieth Century Fox Studio rushed a movie version, directed by Mark Robson, to American theaters the following year.

Still other problems, such as crime and youthful rebellion, appeared to be clear manifestations of potential social breakdown. In some ways, concerns about rebellious youth coincided with American society's "discovery" of teenagers in the 1950s. By then, many Americans worried about the generation that had been born in the years of the Great Depression and World War II. More specifically, anxious adults were afraid that the youth of the nation were losing their way amid the complicated realities of the postwar world. The fear that American teenagers would fall into a moral abyss of crime or drugs or illicit sex was a constant concern. These anxieties were not entirely a new development. Juvenile delinquency was already recognized as a major social concern by the time the war had ended. A 1946 issue of the magazine *The Rotarian*, for example, focused on the question "Who is to blame for juvenile crime?" Included in the discussion was a brief article by Attorney General Tom Clark, who wrote, "This is what the scoreboard says on juvenile delinquency: 15 percent of all the murders in America are committed by persons under 21 years of age. Twenty-one percent of all crime is committed by this same age group."[25]

Father Edward J. Flanagan, a prominent figure who had founded the Boys Town orphanage in Omaha, Nebraska,[26] speculated about the reasons for the rise in juvenile crime. Flanagan cited both parental and societal responsibility for this turn of events, but he also pointed an accusing finger at Hollywood. "Let's be honest with our boys and girls," he wrote. "Every time we step up to the box office, we put a stamp of approval on the kind of movie that is showing."[27]

This unease about the nation's youth, which in some respects resembled anxieties in previous eras, continued to hold a place in the American consciousness even as the postwar consumerist culture of plenty often took center stage. By the mid-1950s, however, many Americans worried that the situation was taking a turn for the worse. Congress investigated juvenile delinquency in earnest. In well-publicized hearings, legislators searched for the causes and possible answers to the problem. And again, entertainment media were held to be major culprits. The movie industry was regarded with special suspicion.[28]

A witness before the Senate Subcommittee to Investigate Juvenile Delinquency reported:

Criminal violence, human brutality, sadism, and other manifestations of psychopathic disorder, have increased noticeably in motion pictures and on television within the past 2 years.... Concurrently and in many instances coincidentally, the treatment of sex in motion pictures and on television has been less restrained.[29]

The supposed relationship between movies and delinquent behavior was clear in the eyes of this witness, who explained:

Motion pictures dealing with social disorders within the American system ... must be said to likewise impress the minds of spectators wherever they are seen. Indeed, since evil has for many persons a stronger fascination than good, the impact of films featuring criminal violence, brutality and sexual immorality must be said to exercise correspondingly greater influence upon human behavior.... For youths especially, the personal element in pictures calls for consideration. A film projecting violence and antisocial rebellion among youthful characters may present greater dangers of exciting imitative behavior among the young when it is played out by a movie.[30]

According to testimony, technological advances in the film business made "dramatized images ... far more powerful in their effect upon the human mind and imagination than the printed word." And although the witness admitted "no precautions in presenting crime in motion pictures can guarantee that imitative behavior will not result," he nonetheless recounted an incident that occurred after the movie *Johnny Belinda* (which he called "an excellent motion picture"), which was reportedly "shown at a children's matinee" at a California theater in May 1951. As he explained:

In the film there occurred, with perfect dramatic validity, a scene of sexual attack against a deaf and dumb girl. This scene was filmed with the utmost restraint: it was essential to the story.

Yet on that afternoon . . . within a short time after this attack was witnessed on screen, a young man . . . followed a little girl out of the audience, lured her to his rooms, attacked and murdered her.[31]

Hollywood and Teenage Rebellion

A trio of films in the mid-1950s, and the public's reaction to them, serve to emphasize how much Americans worried about youthful rebellion and the potential threat it posed to American domestic life. These were not cheaply made and thoughtlessly produced exploitation movies (of which there were many), however, but rather prominent films issued by major studios.

Columbia Pictures released the first of these, *The Wild One*, in 1953. It was produced by Stanley Kramer and directed by László Benedek, who had won the Golden Globe Best Director award for the 1951 screen version of *Death of a Salesman*. More noteworthy still was *The Wild One*'s star, the electrifying young actor Marlon Brando. By this time, Brando had won critical praise and a large following on the basis of his work in the movies *A Streetcar Named Desire* (1951) and *Viva Zapata!* (1952).

These solid Hollywood credentials did little to mute anxieties prompted by the film's narrative. Even a generally positive review in the *New York Times* noted that the movie was a look beneath the surface of American life that revealed "an ugly, debauched and frightening view of a small but peculiarly significant and menacing element of modern youth" and a story about "a swarm of youthful motorcyclists who ride through the country in wolf-pack fashion and terrorize people in a small town."[32]

The outcry about young rebels in American society was nothing new. Even the movie's narrative, when stripped of the then-modern setting and motorcycle gang associations, was not especially innovative. In fact, as Darragh O'Donoghue has observed, "*The Wild One* is a transposed Western: a band of black-clad outlaws descends on a dusty one-street town with a 'saloon'; a weak lawman is unable to prevent a prisoner being sprung from jail; the bikers-as-Red-Indians circle a young virgin; one of the boys even wears a Davy Crockett-like hat."[33]

But it is perhaps because *The Wild One* told a familiar story—a story that paralleled the traditional mythic narrative in which Americans had confronted and tamed chaos and evil deeds in the American West—that the film resonated with audiences in a way that heightened anxieties. Motorcycle gangs were a potent symbol of deviance from society's norms. And the main characters and their actions emphasize this point. Brando's iconic character Johnny is described as "vicious and relentless" in one review; another main character, a member of the motorcycle gang called Chino (played by Lee Marvin), is described as "a glandular 'psycho' or dope-fiend or something fantastically mad."[34]

As the very title of *The Wild One* implied, the film depicted a world in danger of coming apart at the seams. Motorcycles and rebellious youths stood out as symbols in a society that appeared to be dissolving into chaos, a world in which traditional values—especially respect for authority and American institutions—was in danger of being lost.

Metro-Goldwyn-Mayer released a different kind of film about rebellious youth soon after, in spring 1955. *Blackboard Jungle*, directed by Richard Brooks, was a movie adaptation of a novel by Evan Hunter, which involved troubles at an urban high school. In the story, rogue students show utter disrespect for authority and frequently vent their frustrations with displays of violence. An undercurrent of racial and ethnic conflict runs throughout the narrative.

Blackboard Jungle, which starred Hollywood veteran actor Glenn Ford as the heroic teacher and brought Sidney Poitier, playing a troubled teenager, to prominence, told a disturbing story. It confirmed widespread anxieties about urban strife, which sharply contrasted with the supposedly safer "new" world that was being created in American suburbs.

The film was a product of this cultural mood, and its opening reception reflected unease about the possibilities of young people running amok. As Douglas L. Rathgeb has observed:

> *Blackboard Jungle* opened in a charged atmosphere that bordered on moral hysteria. The same civic, educational and religious leaders who had protested Evan Hunter's sensational novel a year earlier now attacked the film on the same grounds: it glorified hoodlums, insulted the teaching profession, and it suggested that anarchy was the norm among America's teenagers. The day the film opened in New York City, a teacher was stabbed and thrown off a roof.[35]

A review in the *New York Times* asserted that the film addressed "a contemporary subject that is social dynamite" and was "a full-throated, all-out testimonial to the lurid headlines that appear from time to time, reporting acts of terrorism and violence by uncontrolled urban youths."[36]

Blackboard Jungle attracted much press attention. The popular weekly publication *Life* magazine ran a two-page spread about the movie entitled

"Bad Boys in the Schoolroom: In 'Blackboard Jungle' Hollywood Gives Exciting If Overdrawn Picture of a Growing Problem."[37] The accompanying photographs (still images taken from the film) had captions such as "Rape attempt is made by a vocational student on a pretty teacher in the school library"[38] and "The sadistic mastermind of the school gang pulls knife for showdown with [the new teacher]."[39]

At Senate hearings about juvenile delinquency, which were held shortly after the film was released, one witness submitted testimony that stated: "Among the large number of youths attending *Blackboard Jungle*, some of the theater managements reported unusually loud, noisy, belligerent behavior."[40] Indeed, fear that the films about youthful rebellion would spark imitative behavior was a central concern. And so, when this witness also stated, "I believe youths already involved in crime and violence will immediately identify themselves with the ringleaders in *Blackboard Jungle*,"[41] the worry was that Hollywood's treatment of the subject would have the presumably unintended effect of amplifying the very problems that the films portrayed.

Perhaps the most famous of the youth rebellion films, however, is *Rebel Without a Cause*. It sparked controversy before it even opened. Indeed, prior to its release the Warner Brothers studio head was confronted by the Senator Estes Kefauve, who said, "We have had some calls saying this [*Rebel Without a Cause*] is not a good picture, from the viewpoint of influence on young people."[42]

Although *Rebel Without a Cause* surely fits into the category of a teenage rebellion movie, the story only mildly challenges the status quo conformism of the 1950s. The unease with which many Americans originally greeted the film is therefore noteworthy and suggestive of the insecurities lurking beneath the surface of 1950s American culture.

In the film, the iconic star James Dean plays Jim Stark, a troubled teenage boy whose family has relocated to a new community. The narrative reveals the teenager's broken relationship with his parents, his encounters with bullies, and his efforts to impress a teenage girl (played by Natalie Wood). The story suggests that Stark's dysfunctional family, and especially his emasculated father (played by Jim Backus) and overbearing mother, have contributed to his plight as a "good boy" who is now well on the way to self-destruction.

Beyond showing the story of one teenager, however, *Rebel Without a Cause* paints an unflattering portrait not only of teenagers in the mid-1950s but also of the adult culture, which is portrayed as unable to cope with the demands of changing society. The teenagers in the film are largely aimless and untethered to the adult world. Meanwhile, major social institutions—especially school, law enforcement, and family—are shown to be if not dysfunctional, then at least ill-equipped to manage the problems facing the drifting youths at the center of the story. As J. David Slocum has written:

> Crucially, as a 1950s melodrama, *Rebel Without a Cause* calls attention to the instability of conventional gender and social relations. Its critique of society is biting because it targets exactly those institutions of mass social or bourgeois life—family, home, school—meant to be uplifting, stable, and safe but that can turn out to be alienating and victimizing.[43]

The 1950s was the heyday of teenage exploitation films. The titles of some of the movies suggest the reason behind skepticism about Hollywood's aims with such films. Among these are *So Young, So Bad* (1950), *Girls in the Night* (1953), *Girl Gang* (1954), *Teenage Crime Wave* (1955), *Rumble on the Docks* (1956), *Teenage Bad Girl* (1956), *Untamed Youth* (1957), and *Four Boys and a Gun* (1957).

Films with youth rebellion as the subject matter were dependable in producing box office returns. But the difference in tastes and attitudes between American older and younger viewers was becoming increasingly pronounced. It was, after all, in this same era that the singer Elvis Presley, now regarded as a relic of mainstream tastes and sensibilities, was seen by some adults as a powerful symbol of moral decay and corruption among American youth.

UNINTENDED CONSEQUENCES IN THE TECHNOLOGICAL AGE

To average Americans in the 1950s, modern technologies seemed to be wonders that made an ever-improving life of comfort and convenience possible. The potential downside to such technologies—side effects such as pollution, possibility for misuse, and so forth—was seldom given much consideration. Technology and large-scale industrial production in the 1950s provided Americans with an astonishing array of consumer goods. There were mass-produced houses and shiny automobiles. The latter of these were essential to the new suburban lifestyle and were dependent on an endlessly flowing supply of inexpensive oil. But there were also televisions, refrigerators, electrical appliances, household gadgets, lawnmowers, and more. All of these were the result of new scientific and technological advances.

Many movies in the science fiction genre were directly related to the emergence of this modern technological age. These focused on the theme that in tampering with nature, humans were playing with forces with unknown consequences. A number of science fiction movies in the 1950s had stories in which human experimentation results in frightening, sometimes apocalyptic results. Many feature stories in which monstrous creatures are unwittingly unleashed in situations that seem destined to wipe out humankind. Some of these featured enormous monsters of various kinds. These were in some ways a throwback to earlier monster movies such as *King Kong* (1933), but now with a decidedly 1950s aura in which science has run amok. Still others update ideas that can be traced back to Mary Shelley's novel *Frankenstein*, which had been adapted for screen in a widely known 1931 movie of the same name that was directed by James Whale and featured the actor Boris Karloff. One of the early sound films, it tapped into the already established cinematic tradition of horror movies and spawned several sequels. Its story had centered on the idea that humans tempted fate when they tried to interfere or manipulate the natural order of things.

Among the most well known of the 1950s "creature" films is *Them!* (1954). The movie was a cut above some others in the genre. A review in the trade publication *Variety* described it as "a well-plotted story, expertly directed and acted in a matter-of-fact style to rate a chiller payoff and thoroughly satisfy the fans of hackle-raising melodrama."[44] The movie shows the story of immense radioactive ants that attack a town in the American Southwest. As one character says at the conclusion of the story, "When man entered the atomic age, he opened the door to a new world. What we may eventually find in that new world, nobody can predict."

More famous still is the Japanese movie *Gojira*, released in Japan in 1954 and in the following year in the United States with an Americanized title. Originally produced by Toho studios for a domestic Japanese audience, the story involves a gigantic, dinosaur-like monster that has been reawakened by nuclear testing and that subsequently wreaks havoc on Japan. The U.S. distributor added new scenes with actor Raymond Burr to provide an American angle to the story. The revised film, which combined the new scenes with most of the original material, was retitled *Godzilla* for distribution in the United States.[45]

In Japan, the film was an obvious reminder of the misery that had been inflicted by use of atomic weapons in the world conflict a decade earlier. The film clearly casts atomic weapons as a dangerous affront to nature. As writer David Kalat notes, "Nuclear testing is clearly the villain of the movie, even in the sanitized American version, but responsibility for the testing is displaced to some anonymous off-screen party."[46] But it is not so much a negative representation of Cold War nuclear politics as it is an indictment of humanity's frequent inability to use nature's forces for good. In the context of movies of the 1950s, *Godzilla* was another entry that suggested humans experimented with the power of nature at their peril. The implication might have been that unless great care was taken, humankind's arrogance could prove to be its undoing.

Like most science fiction movie making in the 1950s, however, *Godzilla* was aimed at a youthful audience and not taken seriously by mainstream reviewers. One newspaper reported, "If the kiddies come home thumping their chests, smoking sticks of red fire and shouting 'Everybody out or else!' You'll understand."[47] The *New York Times* began its review with the words, "As though there are not enough monsters coming from Hollywood," and concluded that the film was "incredibly awful."[48] Yet despite being widely regarded as almost disposable, throwaway entertainments of little consequence, the airing of themes in such films provides evidence that the anxious climate in the United States in the 1950s had deeply penetrated American popular culture.

Other types of science fiction films explored similar themes from a smaller scale, with stories focusing on the plight of a solitary individual who by extension represents the potentially dire fate of humankind more generally. The story of *The Incredible Shrinking Man* (1957), from prolific director Jack Arnold and scriptwriter Richard Matheson, follows a man named Scott Carey (played by Grant Williams) who is exposed to a drifting cloud of radioactivity while boating off the California coast. Initially, the radiation appears to have little effect. But over the coming months, Carey starts to notice that he is physically shrinking, a development that eventually results in his disappearance into the microscopic world, where he will presumably shrink away to his doom.

As Cynthia Hendershot observed, *The Incredible Shrinking Man* was a film that portrayed "the potential eclipsing of the human species" as a result of the atomic age. More than simply a reflection of Cold War fears—though it was also that—this movie was an outgrowth of the troubling realization that humankind's mastery of the atom "could lead postwar society to a utopian existence," or, conversely, might "plunge the world into a horrific dystopia."[49]

Another well-known example is *The Fly*, a 1958 movie directed by Kurt Neumann. The story follows the fate of a scientist (played by David Hedison[50]), whose atoms become mingled with a fly. This turns him into a half-human, half-insect monster. The famous and much parodied scene at the end of the film shows the human-headed fly crying out the words, "Help me! Help me!" Although absurd and melodramatic, *The Fly* reinforced reservations about the pace of scientific and technological change in the era. Its message about science gone wrong was a warning of sorts about the ill effects of human overconfidence and about human hubris in attempting to disturb the universe's natural order.

These are a few of the 1950s movies with stories in which monsters and experiments gone wrong threaten not only American life but also the very survival of humanity. Exaggerated and alarmist in tone, the underlying message can be obscured by the melodrama and, for contemporary audiences, limited visual effects. But the general warning was not without substance. In the following decades, it would become increasingly apparent that some modern technologies had inherent dangers that were not, at first, fully realized. Environmental damage, genetic side effects, and other threats that were hidden in modern technological and scientific advances would prove to be public concerns and the sources of some controversy.

THE RISE OF TELEVISION CULTURE

Television had started to come to prominence in the late 1940s. But it was in the 1950s that it became a widespread phenomenon, taking hold as a central feature in American life, for better or worse. It significantly altered both mainstream American culture, generally, and Hollywood, more specifically.

Americans purchased televisions in massive numbers. Between 1950 and 1955, the number of American households with a television rose from 3.9 million to 30.7 million.[51] These consoles were imposing pieces of furniture, featuring small, bulky video tube technology that created pictures that were primitive by the standards of just a few years later. But in many ways televisions were the new American hearths, and families gathered around them to watch favorite shows and to share experiences in more or less real time across a continent in a way that only radio had previously approached.

The popular culture that television generated was based partially in the wide dispersal of television across the nation. But it was also a product of what modern viewers probably would have seen as a drawback: limited viewing choices. With a scant handful of networks, viewing was concentrated among a limited selection of shows. It was far from the very fragmented landscape of television viewing that resulted from the spread of cable television several decades later.

Many of the most popular television shows of the 1950s reflected the new lifestyles and attitudes of Americans. Some shows portrayed city life. These included the durable comedies *I Love Lucy* (1951–57) and *The Honeymooners* (1955–56). But many popular shows were set in smaller communities. Series such as *The Adventures of Ozzie and Harriet* (1952–66), *Father Knows Best* (1954–60), *Leave It to Beaver* (1957–63), and *The Donna Reed Show* (1958–66) comically portrayed stereotypical family life and its problems. Significantly, one characteristic of these largely formulaic shows was that the problems in a given story (the "situation" implied in the label "situation comedy") were solved by the end of the episode.

Televised dramas were also popular. These long-form shows were significant competition for theatrical movies. So-called anthology series offered direct competition, for example. Series such as *Pulitzer Prize Playhouse* (1950–52), *Fireside Theater* (1949–58), *Studio One* (1948–58), *Robert Montgomery Presents* (1950–57), and *Kraft Television Theatre* (1947–58) offered high-quality viewing, featuring thoughtful scripts that were well directed and well acted.

Other dramas—series that featured the same characters from week to week—also provided strong competition that lured movie audiences away from theaters. Series such as *Dragnet* (1951–59), *Wagon Train* (1957–65), *Gunsmoke* (1955–75), *Maverick* (1957–62), *Have Gun, Will Travel* (1957–63), and *Perry Mason* (1957–66) increasingly joined the ranks of the most viewed television programming as the 1950s wore on.

At the same time, variety shows and news programming also offered a steady slate of viewing options. The upshot was that despite the few television networks, in the context of the era viewers were presented with an array of television programming that could be enjoyed from the comfort of the home.

One net effect of television's meteoric rise was a huge drop in weekly movie theater attendance. About 60 percent of the American population attended movie theaters in 1946. A decade later, in 1956, that number had dropped by half, to about 30 percent.[52] This was an alarming trend for Hollywood and one from which it would never fully recover. Though the industry found ways to keep theatrical films a mainstay of American popular culture, never again would movie houses be able to match the huge proportion of American viewers' attention in the same way that had been the case in previous decades.

One way the movie side of the studios fought back was by becoming increasingly active in the production of shows for television. Columbia, for example, established Screen Gems for the purposes of producing television programming in 1951. Other studios also became deeply involved in developing material for television.

Another trend in Hollywood's efforts to slow audience erosion was by pushing the limits of the technology. The use of color film became more common, and the size of movie screens was sometimes increased dramatically in an effort to provide viewers in theaters with sensory experiences that 1950s television could not match. Technological innovations included widescreen formats such as Cinerama, CinemaScope, as well as 3-D processes to give viewers the illusion that people were jumping off the screen. Yet none of these would seriously slow the inroads that television continued to make in the competition for audience attention. Television would soon eclipse movies as the main screen medium in the United States. The film business slowly adjusted and learned new ways to remain viable, but it never again attained the stratospheric attendance statistics it had garnered in earlier decades.

A DECADE OF CHANGES

The heightened American anxieties of the early 1950s had not completely evaporated as the decade drew to a close, but American life had largely absorbed them and internalized their effects. Nuclear fears remained, as did apprehension about international communism. Life in the United States marched forward, however.

In some respects, and especially for those who had fled to suburbia and adopted its lifestyle, the nation seemed to be making steady progress. Others, who had less access or opportunity to join the ranks of the upwardly mobile middle class, may have been more skeptical, but their voices were not easily heard.

In film and popular entertainments, fears of the nation's doom and destruction had been incarnated in a wide range of offerings. In such fare, the American Dream sometimes seemed under attack. Yet such a perspective was not necessarily pervasive and was more of an undercurrent in popular culture than a dominant lens through which Americans viewed their society.

But still largely hidden from recognition were signs that, if they had been more noticed, would have been potentially troubling. Society was developing in ways in which there were hidden inequities, and advances in living standards had long-term costs and ramifications that largely remained obscured. And the international situation was far from settled. The United States would soon become embroiled in a conflict in Southeast Asia that would have profoundly unsettling consequences.

So, while the intense feelings of anxiety that were evident in the early 1950s had become somewhat muted, conditions were still ripe for challenges to the American Dream and the life it envisioned. And new threats would become apparent, presenting contexts in which the nation's ruin sometimes seemed to be ominously on the horizon.

CHAPTER 6

Eruption

As the 1960s began, the cultural climate of fear and anxiety that had been evident a decade earlier had lessened to some extent, though a series of crises and reasons for concern continued to influence the national mind-set. But if Americans were more accustomed to the dangers in the world created since World War II, in fact, the world was not necessarily less dangerous. Events that were soon to develop would amply demonstrate that point. Still, the United States' capacity to adapt to changing social environments, even when filled with risk, was also evident.

In a few years, the challenges to American life that had seemed so threatening in the 1950s would be replaced by new challenges. For at the dawn of the 1960s, the United States was on the precipice of enormous social and political change, even if at first the nature of the coming upheaval was not fully realized. The transformation of American society that would begin in the 1960s would not erase the apocalyptic vision of failure in American culture. Rather, that subtext of the American narrative would evolve and grow, taking on a new appearance in the process.

The decade would be equally tumultuous for Hollywood. Just as traditional attitudes and ways of doing things were to be challenged in the wider culture, filmmaking in the United States faced significant pressures to change. And again, as would be the case in the society at large, some changes came from within Hollywood's system, but some were the result of pressure from the outside, as the industry continued to reflect the influences of world in which it was situated.

CRISES AND OPTIMISM

The final years of Dwight Eisenhower's second term had been filled with a series of crises. Despite their gravity, the United States was mostly able to navigate around them. In Cuba, rebels under the leadership of Fidel Castro overthrew strongman leader Fulgencio Batista, a man viewed as an irritant by U.S. officials. Washington seemed ill-prepared when Castro's forces drove Batista into exile in 1959, and at first Americans did not fully understand Castro's Socialist inclinations. But soon Castro orchestrated the confiscation of an increasing number of foreign-controlled assets, slowly raising concerns among American leaders. With Castro's anti-American rhetoric and his apparently close relationship with the USSR, Eisenhower approved planning to topple Castro's regime. But action would have to wait. The plan was not ready to put into action until after Eisenhower left office.

A more direct confrontation with the USSR came about in May 1960, when an American U-2 high-altitude aircraft, on a surveillance mission over Soviet territory, crashed. At first, not knowing details and thinking it possible that the pilot had died, U.S. officials issued a story about a missing plane that was on a routine weather research mission for NASA. In reality, the plane was controlled by the Central Intelligence Agency (CIA) and had nothing to do with NASA, and the cover story was an attempt to keep as much of the mission as secret as possible and protect against embarrassing revelations about the American espionage program.

Only four days after the flight was lost, however, the Soviets confirmed that an aircraft had been shot down. At that point, it still seemed to American officials as though the downed U-2 pilot, Francis Gary Powers, was dead, and so Washington officials continued to promote their cover story about an innocent research mission gone astray. But then Soviet leader Nikita Khrushchev revealed that not only had the plane been shot down by Soviet forces, but its pilot had been captured alive and was now a prisoner of the USSR. This turn of events was deeply embarrassing to the United States.[1]

Throughout this era, the United States and the Soviet Union were engaged in many spy efforts, as they sought to gauge the power of each other and calibrate their assessment of the evolving strategic competition between the two superpowers. But the U-2 incident cast a new light on American-Soviet relations, which appeared headed in a troubling direction.

Yet despite ongoing concerns arising from the continuation of the Cold War and a shifting domestic culture, the 1960s began with a sense of optimism. Many Americans seemed to be looking for a new direction when they elected, by a narrow margin, the youthful John F. Kennedy to the presidency in November of 1960. His victory ushered in what appeared to be something akin to a fresh start for the United States. As time passed, many people even referred to the dashing Kennedy years as the United States' "Camelot," a reference to the golden era of Arthurian legend.

There were nagging concerns in the background, however. In Dwight Eisenhower's farewell address to the nation, he not only spoke of the necessity for the United States to maintain military preparedness. He also had a warning. Eisenhower said,

> Our military organization today bears little relation to that known by any of my predecessors in peacetime, or indeed by the fighting men of World War II or Korea.
>
> Until the latest of our world conflicts, the United States had no armaments industry. American makers of plowshares could, with time and as required, make swords as well. But now we can no longer risk emergency improvisation of national defense; we have been compelled to create a permanent armaments industry of vast proportions. Added to this, three and a half million men and women are directly engaged in the defense establishment. We annually spend on military security more than the net income of all United States corporations.
>
> This conjunction of an immense military establishment and a large arms industry is new in the American experience. The total influence—economic, political, even spiritual—is felt in every city, every State House, every office of the Federal government. We recognize the imperative need for this development. Yet we must not fail to comprehend its grave implications. Our toil, resources and livelihood are all involved; so is the very structure of our society.
>
> In the councils of government, we must guard against the acquisition of unwarranted influence, whether sought or unsought, by the military-industrial complex. The potential for the disastrous rise of misplaced power exists and will persist.
>
> We must never let the weight of this combination endanger our liberties or democratic processes. We should take nothing for granted. Only an alert and knowledgeable citizenry can compel the proper meshing of the huge industrial and military machinery of defense with our peaceful methods and goals, so that security and liberty may prosper together.[2]

Indeed, as the Cold War had come to be regarded as a more or less permanent state of affairs, the military implications, as they had developed in the years since 1945, had become increasingly institutionalized—that is, taken for granted. It was interesting that Eisenhower, the military man, both noticed and commented on this change, which even by 1961 had largely permeated society. Eisenhower had been part of that change, of course, and no doubt regarded many aspects of mid-century American military policy as necessary safeguards in the global struggle against communism. Yet the president was clearly aware that some of the changes created in the climate of Cold War politics could have troubling implications if left unchecked. It would not be until later that the implications of Eisenhower's comments were fully realized.

A NEW FRONTIER

If the previous 15 years had seen American unease largely directed at dangers on the outside, the decade of the 1960s was a time when internal strife and tensions boiled over to generate a new kind of fear—that American society would be destroyed from the inside. This was to be a radical change in the cultural climate, and it took several years to fully materialize.

Although John F. Kennedy's lofty and positively framed rhetoric sought to establish a new direction for the United States as he assumed office in January 1961, there were still many uncertainties. And while the language of a "new frontier" seemed to capture a forward-looking mood on the home front, in foreign policy matters things were hardly becoming clearer or more in line with American desires. In the Far East, the situation in former French Indo-China, which had been deteriorating for 15 years, was starting a long downward spiral, as least as judged by American objectives.

Vietnam had been divided into two separate, hostile regions since the end of World War II. By 1961, conditions in Vietnam remained troublesome, and Kennedy approved the deployment of a contingent of military advisors to help stabilize the situation. Although not fully realized at the time, it was the start of a protracted conflict in which the United States would be increasingly drawn into a proxy war against international communism.

Elsewhere, new crises emerged. In 1961, the United States was already determined to see Fidel Castro deposed. In the Bay of Pigs operation, which had initially been planned under the Eisenhower administration, anti-Communist Cuban nationals were trained in the United States and sent back to Cuba to topple Castro's regime. But the intended invasion was a disaster for the United States and a humiliating defeat for the then-new Kennedy administration.

Tensions with the Soviet sphere of influence continued. A few months later, troubles in Europe led to the building of the Berlin Wall, which literally as well as symbolically created an imposing barrier between the Soviet and

Western zones of the partitioned German city. Back in Cuba, Fidel Castro secretly agreed that his nation would provide a base for Soviet nuclear missiles. This precipitated one of the most dangerous confrontations in all of the Cold War, the Cuban missile crisis. The United States became aware of the missiles only after film from a routine U-2 surveillance flight was developed. The discovery set off a flurry of activity and an intense 11-day crisis in October 1962.

The United States immediately instituted a naval blockade of Cuba. Kennedy demanded that the Soviets remove the missiles at once. Tense exchanges continued, with each side apparently willing to call the other's bluff. The American public, meanwhile, was sent into a panic. It seemed that the brink of nuclear war, which had been feared for so long, had now been reached. Eventually, the Soviets backed down and agreed to remove the missiles, and the crisis ended. But it was a disturbing and unnerving episode that rattled American confidence. If Americans had thought the Cold War had reached a tense but tolerable stasis, then the Cuban missile crisis largely shattered these illusions.

There had been many tense moments in the decade so far, but nothing had prepared Americans for the shock of John F. Kennedy's assassination on November 22, 1963. The president's murder horrified Americans, and the assassination became an emblematic beginning to a new era of unease and unrest in the United States. It appeared that gunman Lee Harvey Oswald had acted alone in carrying out the assassination. This was the official explanation endorsed by the Warren Commission, a blue-ribbon body appointed by Kennedy's successor, Lyndon B. Johnson. But questions remained, and in the minds of many people, the matter was never fully resolved.

HOLLYWOOD CYNICISM IN THE EARLY 1960s

Several mainstream Hollywood movies of the early 1960s demonstrated shifting perceptions of the still-dangerous Cold War world. These films, while differing in tone and content, each reveal nagging concerns about the apparently uncertain abilities of American political and military institutions to solve the complex problems of the nuclear world. More than that, such films suggest that it is not just lack of ability or knowledge that contributes to this state of affairs. Rather, the films portray leaders who are seduced by power and vanity and who lack the moral character and clear-headedness to fend off corrupting influences. Their narratives portray central institutions in the United States in a harsh light, far removed from the lofty visions of the American Dream, in which the U.S. system solved problems and was an example for the rest of the world.

One such film was *The Manchurian Candidate*, director John Frankenheimer's 1962 production that was based on a popular 1959 novel of the same name by Richard Condon. The movie starred Frank Sinatra, already a legendary entertainment figure, along with Laurence Harvey, Janet Leigh, and Angela Lansbury. The fictional story recounted in both the novel and the film involves a group of American soldiers who had been captured, and then released, during the Korean War. However, during their captivity, the soldiers were subjected to mass hypnosis, which was so effective that none of them remembered even having been a prisoner. More than that, the hypnosis was part of a brainwashing technique aimed at converting one of the soldiers into a future assassin. This unfortunate victim, who along with the others had no knowledge or recollection of what had happened, would be later be directed to kill an aspiring candidate in an effort to manipulate U.S. elections and install another man, who would be under Communist control, as the American president.

The film largely follows the efforts of Captain Bennett Marco (Frank Sinatra) to unravel the plot and thwart the planned assassination. In the process, bizarre twists and turns in the narrative invoke issues of motherhood and turn many conventions of traditional American belief upside down.

As a story, *The Manchurian Candidate* closely follows the sort of narrative that had been explored on previous occasions during the 1950s. It was, after all, a story about a Communist plot, involving deception and infiltration, that was about to be foisted on an unsuspecting and unprepared American public. On one level, the hypnotized assassin was not so different from the pod people at the center of *Invasion of the Body Snatchers*, for example. The electric direction and strong performances brought the film much attention.

Another 1960s Cold War film was *Dr. Strangelove or: How I Learned to Stop Worrying and Love the Bomb* (1964). It depicts the anxiety and apparent madness of the Cold War's massive nuclear arms buildup. Directed by Stanley Kubrick, *Dr. Strangelove* featured acclaimed comic actor Peter Sellers in multiple roles, as well as such dependable Hollywood stars as George C. Scott, Sterling Hayden, Keenan Wynn, and Slim Pickens. The film is a dark satire of the apocalyptic possibilities inherent in the race to build weapons that, if actually used, would destroy all involved. Cloaked in absurdity, the film portrayed American and Soviet political and military leaders as comically inept and ill-equipped to safely manage the civilization-ending weapons that they had stockpiled.

In the story, a deranged U.S. general (played by Sterling Hayden) sends an American nuclear-equipped bomber on a mission to attack the Soviet Union. When U.S. leaders are unable to recall this bomber, the president (Peter

Sellers) reluctantly alerts the Soviets, with the hope that the impending crisis can be avoided. But the Soviets have planned for an assault by creating a secret "doomsday device" that will obliterate all life on earth in the event that the Soviet Union is attacked. In the end, the American and Soviet efforts to stop the inadvertent attack are unsuccessful. The H-bomb is dropped over the Soviet target, with an American bombardier riding the weapon, as if it were a bull in a rodeo show, as the bomb hurtles to detonation. The dooms-day device is activated, and the film ends with a montage of global nuclear destruction.

To contemporary eyes, the story of *Dr. Strangelove* may seem absurd, but the absurdity of the nuclear arms race was one of the film's main points. Yet the principal plot element is based on an actual strategy in the era: "mutually assured destruction." What is more, by that time in the Cold War, a dominant frame of thinking with regard to any possible use of the United States' nuclear arsenal was the so-called strategy of launch on warning. The idea behind this way of thinking was that the time between detection of incoming nuclear missiles and their arrival to their intended U.S. targets was so short that there would be no opportunity to think about the ultimate result of a given course of action. Such a scenario would require an immediate response and lead to catastrophic and irreversible consequences.

As Terry Christensen and Peter J. Haas have noted, *Dr. Strangelove* is "relentlessly cynical,"[3] and "derisively" dismisses both "liberal good faith in men" and "conservative faith in the military" as it "attacks technology as well as human folly and fallibility."[4] And as Ray Pratt has observed, the film "pre-figured and anticipated the shattering of public confidence in leading political figures and a declining faith in public institutions."[5] Indeed, *Dr. Strangelove* soon became an important cultural touchstone that was quoted by many members of the younger generation of the era, who "regarded its national leaders as manipulative liars following insane policies."[6]

Also released in 1964 were the Cold War movies *Seven Days in May* and *Fail Safe*, both of which were also focused on the dangers of the nuclear era, though they lacked *Dr. Strangelove*'s biting satire. The story in *Seven Days in May* involves a high-level conspiracy to depose the president and overthrow the American government. Behind the scheme is General James Mattoon Scott (played by Burt Lancaster), a respected military leader. In the story, Scott is the ringleader of a group of government insiders who are furious that the president has not taken a tough enough stand, in their view, against enemy powers. They regard a recently signed treaty as traitorous and become determined to oust the president (played by Fredric March), osten-sibly for national security purposes. As the plot unfolds, the film also follows the efforts of military investigator, Colonel Martin "Jiggs" Casey (played by Kirk Douglas), who is seeking to unravel the meaning behind unusual communications that had been intercepted.

As directed by John Frankenheimer, whose *Manchurian Candidate* covered somewhat similar ground in 1962, *Seven Days in May* is a well-crafted and exciting story of intrigue and a race against time. Yet the narrative, while framed as a thriller and featuring major Hollywood stars, suggests something subversive—a world in which American leaders are not as they seem and where what happens behind closed doors is not as leaders say it is. Washington appears, therefore, as a world of power unto itself, a place where ordinary people are not seriously regarded. In one of the closing moments of the film, which is revealing, even the president—who is otherwise portrayed as an honorable and sympathetic man—decides that news of the thwarted plot should never be made public. He suggests that it is too dangerous for the public to know what really has happened. More than hiding simple corruption or cronyism and more than protecting secrets from the United States' enemies, the president appears to believe that the nation's situation is so delicate that it might not withstand knowing the truth.[7] This is not a picture brimming with confidence in the American way.

Fail Safe, a 1964 release from director Sidney Lumet, stars Henry Fonda, Walter Matthau, Frank Overton, Dan O'Herlihy, and other Hollywood regulars in a story with similarities to *Dr. Strangelove*. Walter Bernstein, who had formerly been blacklisted, wrote the script, which was adapted from a novel by Eugene Burdick and Harvey Wheeler. Like *Dr. Strangelove*, it presents a doomsday outlook of the United States of the 1960s. In this narrative, a squadron of American nuclear bombers is accidentally sent on a mission to bomb the Soviet Union. Unlike the case in *Dr. Strangelove*, however, in which the attack was launched because of an insane commander, in *Fail Safe* the attack is result of human and technological error.[8] When the president (played by Henry Fonda) learns of the mistake and realizes that some of the planes will get through to their target and drop H-bombs on Moscow, he makes a startling proposal to contain this apparently inevitable disaster: the U.S. commander-in-chief contacts Soviet leaders and offers to destroy New York City with a nuclear attack to compensate for the Soviet loss and to prove that the attack on Moscow was a legitimate mistake. The Soviets agree, and although all-out nuclear war is averted, two cities are destroyed and millions of innocent lives are lost.

The theme of potential technological and human error leading to catastrophic results is not inherently a new one. Yet in *Fail Safe*, the stakes are high and the outcome is nearly unthinkable. In this respect, the story does seem to reflect the actual danger that characterized the early 1960s, in which some incidents—most notably the Cuban missile crisis—did possess significant danger. Many people were nervous about the possibilities of nuclear destruction, which had been a much-discussed matter of concern since the 1940s.

Yet other people did not perceive the situation as being so dire. In a *Life* magazine piece, for example, Richard Oulahan expressed skepticism that things could go as wrong in the real world as they had in the movie. His review states, "But I can't agree that anything could become quite so botched up as it is in *Fail Safe*."[9] In fact, Oulahan's complaint was not that the film was poorly done, but rather the opposite. And what concerned him was apparently that people might take the underlying ideas in it seriously. In his view, "the worrisome part in all this is that the picture is so stylishly produced, so well acted and so loaded with suspense that millions of movie-goers will probably believe it all could happen this way."[10] Such remarks may demonstrate the extent to which effective filmmaking, when containing controversial themes, can be greeted with apprehension by some people.

MORAL DECLINE AS A POLITICAL ISSUE

Though Lyndon Johnson had handily won the 1964 presidential election, the campaign, which at times was bitter, had pushed questions of the United States' moral condition into the spotlight of political debate. In fact, the issue had been building for some time. The basic question, according to many of those who were concerned about it, was whether the United States was falling from what was taken to be its previously secure position as a moral beacon, a nation of virtue and righteousness. Such questions, and variations of them, were evidence of growing anxieties that some Americans had about their nation, and of fears that the nation they knew and understood might be in danger of fading into oblivion.

Such questions were not entirely new, of course. They were similar to the type of rhetoric that had accompanied previous eras of moral revival as had been seen, for example, in the Prohibition movement earlier in the century. But coming after the frights of the early Cold War and as significant changes in social behaviors and attitudes—in areas such as racial equality, women's rights, and changing ideas about sexual behavior—were under way, the new discussions about the United States' moral situation reflected the times. And increasingly, there was talk of the United States heading down the wrong path. Many people worried that the end would come unless the course was corrected.

In the view of some people, the entertainment media—and especially television—were at least partially responsible for creeping moral decline in the United States. In spring of 1961, no less a figure than Newton N. Minow, who had been appointed by the new president to chair the Federal Communications Commission, appeared before a gathering of the National Association of Broadcasters and severely criticized the television industry. In his remarks, he said,

> When television is good, nothing—not the theater, not the magazines or newspapers—nothing is better. . . . But when television is bad, nothing is worse. I invite each of you to sit down in front of your own television set when your station goes on the air and stay there, for a day, without a book, without a magazine, without a newspaper, without a profit and loss sheet or a rating book to distract you. Keep your eyes glued to that set until the station signs off. I can assure you that what you will observe is a vast wasteland.[11]

The expression "vast wasteland" was quickly adopted in public condemnations of television and helped perpetuate the image of television as a very poor relation to the film business. Earlier in the 1950s, television already had come to be derisively called the "idiot box" by newspaper columnists and commentators. That the medium was eyed with skepticism and suspicion was a continuation of similar attitudes that had been expressed about the film business for many years. In reality, however, although television was regarded as mostly a separate phenomenon that was largely distinct from the film business—and television networks did air a much wider range of programming than simply narrative entertainments—by this time the Hollywood studios were deeply involved in television production for the lucrative prime-time viewing hours.

Criticism of the United States' moral climate was much broader than a critique of any one industry, however. Not surprisingly, religious organizations and people with strong religious views accounted for much of this discussion early in the decade. In 1961, for example, American Roman Catholic bishops "expressed alarm . . . because of evidence of deepening moral decay in American society."[12] Hollywood was often singled out for scorn. Columnist Hedda Hopper noted "the moral bankruptcy that has resulted in the vicious cycle of pictures dealing with depravity, horror, [and] sex deviation."[13] Looking more broadly across American society, George Romney (then governor of Michigan and the former head of the American Motors Corporation) stated in 1964 that he was "shocked" by the moral decline in the United States.[14]

By the 1964 presidential campaign season, the United States' moral state had become an important issue. Barry Goldwater voiced his concerns frequently. In September of 1964, for example, he said, "The moral fiber of the American people is beset by rot and decay."[15] The remedy to this dangerous path, according to Goldwater and those with similar beliefs, was for Americans to return to traditions of God and country.

In many respects, the concern for the nation's moral standing accelerated in the years that followed the 1964 election. Indeed, many developments seemed, to many people, to be evidence that the United States was losing its way. The war in Vietnam escalated and became an enormously divisive issue throughout the United States, prompting an era of widespread political protests. The civil rights movement continued to press forward, but reaction to the changes it ushered in was often socially contentious. Young people increasingly looked, thought, and behaved in ways that perplexed, and at times infuriated, many members of the older generation. The combined effect raised fears among many Americans—especially those who were devoted to traditional behaviors and values—that their nation was sliding toward ruin.

The nation faced a number of challenges. As the civil rights movement marched forward, for example, there was sometimes violent reaction in the struggle for greater racial equality. Eventually, many reforms were codified in the Civil Rights Act of 1964, but the pace of progress seemed very slow to many people in the African American community. And the level of mistrust remained high.

Racial tensions boiled over in "long, hot summer" of 1967, sparking widespread rioting in cities across the United States. Unrest erupted in major urban centers, including New York City, Detroit, Chicago, Minneapolis, and many others. Altogether, the summer was marred by more than 150 riots, most in June and July. These disturbances were deeply unnerving to a society that was facing increasing strife due to the rising unpopularity of the war in Vietnam. President Johnson appointed a blue-ribbon panel to investigate the causes of the riots and recommend policies that would prevent a recurrence. This panel, the National Advisory Commission on Civil Disorders, issued its findings in March of the following year. Its conclusions were ominous. It stated, "Our nation is moving toward two societies, one black, one white—separate and unequal."[16]

A month after the commission's report was issued, Martin Luther King Jr. was assassinated. And several weeks later, in June, presidential candidate Robert F. Kennedy—who by then openly opposed the Vietnam War—was also assassinated. Given the social rupture caused by disagreement about the Vietnam War, the racial riots that had plagued American cities in previous months, and perceptions that violence and lawlessness were increasing day by day, many Americans thought that their nation was on the brink of complete breakdown. By summer of 1968, reports indicated that a majority of Americans thought their nation had succumbed to moral decline.[17]

Meanwhile, the war in Vietnam was already the source of major controversy. The conflict indisputably inflicted heavy damage on the social fabric of American life. By the mid-1960s, the United States was so deeply involved in it that the military could not keep up with the demand for personnel. This led to a much greater reliance on conscription (the military draft), which soon became unpopular and fueled the growing antiwar movement.

But despite sending half a million American troops to Vietnam, progress was hard to see. Protests became more vocal and widespread, dividing Americans along generational and political lines in a way that appeared to be tearing the nation apart. In 1968, with no end to the war in sight, Lyndon Johnson appeared on television. Looking withdrawn and defeated, he announced that he would not seek a second elected term.

In the fall of that year, Richard Nixon, who had served as Eisenhower's vice president and had built a reputation as a staunch anti-Communist, was elected president. He had appealed to Americans who were worried both about the war and about the direction—in Nixon's view, the negative direction—in which American society was headed. Nixon had promised that he had a secret plan to end the war. But no end to the conflict was forthcoming, and the war, which increasingly lost public support, dragged on.

Changing gender roles also challenged traditional understandings in American life in the 1960s, with the continuing rise of the women's movement. Although there had long been political action aimed at securing greater equality and freedom for women in American society, this era saw heightened activity. Betty Friedan's book *The Feminine Mystique*, published in 1963, spoke with special power to educated, often suburban women, who were dissatisfied with the opportunities and freedoms available to them. In 1966, Friedan and a group of feminists formally established the National Organization of Women to push for comprehensive changes in American society. One of the goals of the women's movement was to raise women's (and men's) awareness about the sexism and discrimination that women faced. Employment was a major issue, with access to jobs and equal pay critical concerns.

Changing ideas about the relative relationship between the sexes also led to questions about traditional understandings of sexuality. Coinciding with these changing gender dynamics was the increasing availability of oral contraception. Many traditionally minded Americans were unhappy with what they thought was the result of widespread use of the birth control pill. "Oral contraceptives are causing a revolution in sex behavior that could shake the foundations of American society,"[18] wrote the popular columnist Jack Anderson in 1965. Thus many people were fearful that oral contraception was yet another factor that was contributing to a breakdown of traditional morality, since for these people, traditional gender roles—both in the workplace and in the home—and traditional sexual behavior were primarily moral issues.

Overall, then, the decade of the 1960s presented the United States with many changes that threatened to undermine traditional ways of thinking about assumptions underlying the American Dream. Such changes therefore symbolized a threat to the continuation of this ideal and, by implication, worries about American decline.

HOLLYWOOD AND THE CHANGING WORLD OF THE 1960s

By 1960, television had come to dominate the American media scene. Many of the studios that had originally been created to make motion pictures had by then added television production to their agendas, and thus to a major extent there was considerable overlap between the theatrical film world and the homebound television world in terms of who was producing the content for each.

Still, movies remained a powerhouse force in American cultural life. And the lure of motion pictures, predicated somewhat on the notion that movies ranked above mere television in the hierarchy of screen entertainment, continued to drive the film-oriented forces in Hollywood to search for continued relevance and films that would attract audiences.

Throughout the decade, many types of films were produced. Some of these continued the changes established over the previous 15 years. But slowly the film industry responded to social change, albeit tentatively. The 1967 film *Guess Who's Coming to Dinner* dealt with interracial marriage, for example. Though quite tentative in its treatment of the subject by later standards, it did broach a subject that was seldom seen in Hollywood films.

Meanwhile, the Vietnam War, which was arguably the decade's greatest controversy, elicited very little response from Hollywood. The primary exception was *The Green Berets* (1968). Staunch anti-Communist actor John Wayne was the driving force behind that film and also starred in it. Harkening back to war films from an earlier era, it unambiguously presented the United States and its military as heroic champions of that which is good. He regarded the movie as a defense of the American position in that war at a time when protests against it were mounting. But for the most part, Hollywood did not address the war as a subject until years later.

Still, American film audiences witnessed a slow shifts over the decade, as changes in social perspectives began to be reflected on-screen and as American society began to rethink many of the traditions and conventions that had been the hallmarks of mainstream life in the nation for more than a generation.

The New Antihero

The very idea of the hero was one such idea that came under scrutiny in the 1960s, for example. A trio of films released in the mid-1960s reenvisioned the Western genre, which had been slowly falling out of favor in theatrical movies. One of the few notable exceptions was director John Ford's *The Man Who Shot Liberty Valance* (1962), a film that featured the iconic star John Wayne as a Western hero, but that began to question some of the mythic elements in Hollywood's traditional treatment of the Old West.

By this time, Westerns had successfully crossed over to television. Series such as *The Lone Ranger*, *Wagon Train*, *The Rifleman*, and *Maverick* were among productions from the genre that were familiar to television viewers across the United States. And series such as *Gunsmoke*, which aired from 1955 to 1975, and *Bonanza*, which aired from 1959 to 1973, were among the most popular series on television for much of their respective runs. Another popular television Western was *Rawhide*, which aired from 1959 to 1965. Its costar, the young actor Clint Eastwood, was selected to play a character with no name by the Italian director Sergio Leone for his Italian-German-Spanish production *Per un pugno di dollari*. It was an Italian director's reinterpretation of American Western films and was released in European markets in 1964.

A few years later, *Per un pugno di dollari* was brought to American screens as *A Fistful of Dollars*. This stylish movie was the first of three Leone films in which Eastwood played the same, unnamed character. (The others were *For a Few Dollars More* and *The Good, the Bad, and the Ugly*.) In the films, Eastwood's character was not so much a hero as an antihero—a violent, seemingly emotionless man operating from an inner sense of what was and was not permissible. Not exactly vengeful, the character operates under his moral code, surviving by his wits and guns. And while seemingly revealing some inner sense of what may or may not deserve punishment, he clearly answers to no one and for the most part seems detached from his actions. Unlike a traditional hero, then, this man with no name seeks to prove nothing—questions of redemption, traditional justice, or heroism appear of little or no concern to him. He instead seems to operate outside any existing moral system. This puts the character at odds with nearly all protagonists in previous film Westerns and with the moral myths they traditionally had embodied. Coming after a cultural era in the United States that had explicitly sought to connect the nation with supposed moral virtue in its mythic past, an era that had even been called "the New Frontier," this new vision of a violent, morally ambiguous past was another signal of the changing cultural landscape.

A European, not Hollywood, production, *A Fistful of Dollars* played an important part in spreading the new, antihero sensibility to mass audiences. Not everyone knew what to make of the film, which to some people seemed cheap and derivative, an impression probably heightened due to the fact it was dubbed, in some parts awkwardly, into English for American distribution. The *New York Times* review said it possessed "just about every Western cliché that went into the old formula of the cool and mysterious gunslinger" and was an "egregiously synthetic but engrossingly morbid, violent film."[19] The most notable aspect of the movie in terms of its contribution to the changing perception of American myth was probably represented by Eastwood's "icy and cynical" character, who is "half gangster, half cowboy" and is "ruthless without seeming cruel."[20]

In fact, the film had an interesting pedigree. *A Fistful of Dollars* is based quite closely on director Akira Kurosawa's 1961 Japanese film *Yojimbo*, in which actor Toshirō Mifune played a ronin (a samurai without a master) in feudal Japan. The story of *Yojimbo* follows Mifune's character as he hastens the self-destruction of two warring crime families, adding his own skill in lethal combat to bring this about. Leone's version of the narrative in *A Fistful of Dollars* transplants the circumstances to a Mexican border town where the Leone's antihero, the man with no name, arrives on the scene.

Although it may seem odd for an Italian director to have made a film that, perhaps inadvertently, influenced American perceptions of the Old West, especially by way of a Japanese samurai film, *A Fistful of Dollars* was more connected to American film traditions than may be obvious. Kurosawa was a strong admirer of Hollywood Westerns and was very knowledgeable about them. As Kurosawa once said, "I have respected John Ford from the beginning. Needless to say, I pay close attention to his productions, and I think I am influenced by them."[21] His widely known 1954 movie *The Seven Samurai* reflected his admiration of the Hollywood Western. That influence had come full circle with the film's adaptation for the American production *The Magnificent Seven*, which was released in 1960. Therefore, in choosing

Kurosawa for source material, Leone had chosen the work of a director who, while not American, had a sophisticated understanding of Hollywood film-making and traditions. Thus Leone's treatment of a very similar story is less unexpected than it might otherwise appear.

Overall, *A Fistful of Dollars* provides an interesting parable that is not only about the nineteenth-century American experience in the Old West. Updated and reflecting the climate of its times, the film also has interesting parallels to the Cold War standoff between superpowers, in which lesser nations are left to either choose up sides or else be relegated to the margins.

Hollywood Revisits Self-Censorship

Another indication of significant change was in the loosening of restrictions on what could be seen and heard in motion pictures. Hollywood's self-censorship program, the Production Code, was fading by 1966. A controversy surrounding the production of *Who's Afraid of Virginia Woolf?* placed the Warner Bros. studio at odds with the Legion of Decency, a powerful Catholic organization that was founded decades earlier to fight immorality in films. The film's script included, as Peter Krämer has noted, "vicious verbal fights with plenty of profanity and obscenity."[22] But the movie was based on a hit play of the era and it starred Elizabeth Taylor and Richard Burton, who were among the most attention-getting stars of that time. Given the changing social attitudes of the time, Warner Bros. opted to push forward with an uncensored version of the film, even though the script included elements that the Production Code banned. To navigate around this apparent difficulty, the studio attached a statement to forewarn the audience that said "No one under 18 admitted without a parent." The Production Code office subsequently agreed not to challenge the release.[23] Although it may not have been fully realized at the time, this step was a major rupture with past practice and a strong indication that Hollywood was intent on escaping the grip of the decades-old Production Code.

New Hollywood

The "New Wave" of filmmaking, a movement that first surfaced in France, had made an international impact on world cinema audiences by the mid-1960s. The fresh, modern, and morally adventurous movies from directors such as François Truffaut, Éric Rohmer, and Jean-Luc Godard had captivated upscale film audiences in many countries. In some of these films, the inspiration of American film noir from the 1940s and 1950s was very evident.

Godard's *Breathless* (1960), for example, told the story of a man inspired more by the pleasures of life and adventure than by achieving success according to society's rules. As he is joyriding in a stolen car, police take note of a traffic violation and pursue him. When they catch up to him, the relatively minor crime turns into murder when the man finds a gun in the glove compartment of the car and thoughtlessly shoots the police officer. The remainder of the film follows the man's almost pedestrian efforts to avoid detection in Paris as he becomes romantically involved with a young American woman, with whom he has a casual sexual relationship. Despite what appears to be somber subject matter, the film has an airy feel and exhibits an attitude that perhaps owes much to the existentialist philosophy that was then current in Europe.

Regardless, the film's seeming refusal to draw easy moral conclusions from the behavior of the its characters lies in striking contrast to the type of filmmaking to which American audiences had grown accustomed in the years leading up to the 1960s. Indeed, the film does not repeat the darkness that characterized the moral world of most film noir movies and instead presents its story and leaves conclusions up to the viewer. The influence of film noir directors had quickly traveled across the Atlantic, and their works soon inspired some people in Hollywood. In some cases, the connection was very direct.

Two American writers, Robert Benson and David Newman, developed a script in the mid-1960s that reflected their admiration for French New Wave cinema. In fact, they contacted François Truffaut, famous for having directed such films as *The 400 Blows*, with the thought that he would take interest in the project.[24] Although Truffaut decided against working on the project himself, he subsequently passed the script along to fellow director Jean-Luc Godard, with whom he had worked on many occasions. Not long after, Godard attended a social evening at which the American actor Warren Beatty was also present. Hearing of Beatty's interest in finding a new film project, Godard suggested the script that Benson and Newman had written.[25]

The script in question was for the film *Bonnie and Clyde*, a movie that played a pivotal role in reshaping filmmaking in the United States. Indeed, in the view of many writers, the film was instrumental in launching a movement sometimes called the "New Hollywood."

After securing the rights to the script, Beatty was successful in convincing Arthur Penn to direct. Penn was an established figure in Hollywood. In 1958, he had directed *The Left Handed Gun*, which starred Paul Newman in the role of Western legend Billy the Kid. Penn was also at the helm of *The*

Miracle Worker, in which Anne Bancroft played Helen's tutor, Annie Sullivan, and Patty Duke played Helen, the deaf and blind activist and inspirational lecturer. And Penn had directed a formidable cast, including Marlon Brando, Robert Redford, Jane Fonda, Angie Dickinson, and Robert Duvall, in *The Chase* (1966).

Perhaps most important, however, Penn and Beatty had previously worked together in the 1965 film, *Mickey One*, a film with an obvious debt to film noir and the French New Wave style. That movie met with mixed reaction. A review in the *New York Times* assessed this earlier film as "a clutter of grimly realistic and grotesquely nightmarish scenes" that "shows us the fear-ridden flight of a cheap nightclub entertainer who is trying to escape from himself."[26] *Mickey One* quickly faded from memory, but it had established the connection between Beatty and Penn.

Bonnie and Clyde is based on the true story of the Depression-era outlaws Clyde Darrow and Bonnie Parker, who embarked on a crime spree of bank robberies, holdups, and murder. Their exploits were widely recounted in the press, and their rise to notoriety came at a time that coincided with similar public attention directed to infamous gangsters such as Al Capone, John Dillinger, George "Baby Face" Nelson, Charles "Pretty Boy" Floyd, all of whom—like Darrow and Parker—were pursued by law enforcement in the early 1930s. In real life, the crimes committed by Darrow and Parker became increasingly violent. As fugitives from justice, they died as the result of law enforcement gunfire in May 1934.

Hollywood has often told crime stories and featured criminals as the main character in movies. *Little Caesar* and *Scarface* had done so in the early 1930s, during the very era that the real Clyde Darrow and Bonnie Parker were establishing themselves as the stuff of folklore. Yet the script for the movie Beatty and Penn were to make was revolutionary when compared to most previous crime films.

Although crime films had often been violent, *Bonnie and Clyde* portrayed violence much more graphically that had been permissible in the days when social norms and the Production Code played a stronger role in shaping what appeared in a film. Gun wounds, for example, had often been portrayed in movies, but usually there was scarce visual evidence of the wounds. Instead, gun-inflicted injury occurred off camera or was depicted more as style than reality. A small tear from a bullet hole on an article of clothing and perhaps a slight hint of blood, for example, might be shown as the result of a direct bullet wound. In *Bonnie and Clyde*, however, the carnage of gunfights is portrayed more explicitly and to substantially more shocking effect. Special effects—including profuse use of stage blood—were used to depict the violence in a direct way that audiences of that era were not used to seeing. For some later writers, this aspect of the film is crucial. Lester D. Friedman, for example, concludes that "the whole point of *Bonnie and Clyde* is to rub our noses in it. . . . Bonnie and Clyde needs violence; violence is its meaning."[27] But the violence was disturbing to many people with traditional sensibilities and suggested to some of them a loosening of American morality.

The sexuality infused in *Bonnie and Clyde* also challenged norms that had prevailed in the U.S. movie industry for decades. While not as explicit in terms of nudity and depicted sexual activity as would be the case in many subsequent Hollywood productions, the film was provocatively suggestive. It left little doubt in the viewer's mind of the sexual subtext that was an instrumental part of the characters' appeal to a more youthful and liberal audience than Hollywood had made movies for earlier.

Despite widespread acclaim that would later develop, at first *Bonnie and Clyde* was greeted with some skepticism. Many early reviews were brutal. *Newsweek* called it "reprehensible" and "gross and demeaning," and *Time* magazine summarized it as "tasteless and grisly."[28] *New York Times* critic Bosley Crowther wrote that the film was "a cheap piece of bald-faced slapstick comedy." He continued, "This blending of farce with brutal killings is as pointless as it is lacking in taste, since it makes no valid commentary upon the already travestied truth."[29]

Bonnie and Clyde soon attracted a substantial audience, however, and critical opinion from some sources became more favorable. *Time* magazine, which had previously published a negative review of the film, seems to have changed its perspective by later that year. Its December 8, 1967, issue featured a colorful adaptation of a still photograph from the film on its cover. An essay in that issue stated:

> Bonnie and Clyde is not only the sleeper of the decade but also, to a growing consensus of audiences and critics, the best movie of the year. . . . Blending humor and horror, it draws the audience in sympathy toward its antiheroes. It is, at the same time, a commentary on the mindless daily violence of the American '60s and an esthetic evocation of the past.[30]

Somewhat surprisingly, the movie was subsequently named "best film for mature audiences" by the National Catholic Office for Motion Pictures. A news report on this development stated that while "*Bonnie and Clyde*, a film castigated by some religious leaders and sociologists for glamorizing violence," had won the award, "the Catholic office praised the film as 'a genuine folk epic challenging the individual viewer to recognize within himself the seeds of meaningless violence which are just below the surface of an easy conscience.'"[31]

The importance of *Bonnie and Clyde* in the broader theme of American decline and ruin does not lie in its storytelling, per se. Rather, its significance is largely in the way it heralds new attitudes, reflecting a divide between forces that continued to embrace traditional views of social norms and clear-cut morality, as opposed to perspectives—at the time largely attributed to rebellious young people—that challenged or dispensed with the status quo and in some ways welcomed a weakening of tradition's hold on social behavior.

Whatever else *Bonnie and Clyde* revealed, by this time it was clear that the continued viability of the Production Code was in serious doubt. The Code was, after all, almost four decades old and reflected the social perspective of a time that had long since passed. In November of 1968, under the guidance of Jack Valenti, the new president of the MPAA, the old system was scrapped altogether. Valenti introduced the MPAA's new ratings system in its place.

The new system classified movies according to the following scheme: the rating of G was given to general-audience films (this was essentially the category of film that would have previously been approved by the Production Code); the rating of M was given to films with mature but otherwise not explicit subject matter or content (this designation was changed to GP in 1970 and then to PG—parental guidance—in 1972); the rating of R indicated a film for which persons under the age of 16 (later changed to 17) were admitted only when accompanied by a parent or adult guardian; and the label of X (changed to NC-17 in 1990) was given to the films with the most restrictions.

In addition to major changes in the American cultural landscape that had occurred by the late 1960s, the legal environment in terms of motion picture censorship had also changed dramatically. Earlier in the decade, the Supreme Court had addressed the issue of film censorship by way of prior restraint questions. A narrow 5–4 decision in the *Times Film* case of 1961 did not overturn laws that required licensing and "prior screening" of films as had been established in many areas around the country. But to the Court the matter was contentious, and Chief Justice Earl Warren wrote a harsh dissent that argued against government censorship of films.[32]

In subsequent cases, the Court began to chip away at the censorship laws of the type that had elicited Warren's objections. In *Freedman v. Maryland* (1965), the Supreme Court found that a film censorship "process which requires the prior submission of a film to a censor avoids constitutional infirmity only if it takes place under procedural safeguards designed to obviate the dangers of a censorship system" and that "the burden of proving that the film is unprotected [as constitutionally protected free speech] expression must rest on the censor."[33]

Although in *Ginsburg v. New York* (1968) the Court permitted restrictions on access of minors to material with adult content, another decision that year substantially weakened government censorship laws. *The Interstate Circuit v. Dallas* (1968) found that standards for judging films to be censored were "unconstitutionally vague." The following passage in the decision lays out the Court's reasoning:

> It is not our province to draft legislation. Suffice it to say that we have recognized that some believe "motion pictures possess a greater capacity for evil, particularly among the youth of a community, than other modes of expression," *Joseph Burstyn, Inc. v. Wilson*, supra, at 502, and we have indicated more generally that because of its strong and abiding interest in youth, a State may regulate the dissemination to juveniles of, and their access to, material objectionable as to them, but which a State clearly could not regulate as to adults. . . . Here we conclude only that "the absence of narrowly drawn, reasonable and definite standards for the officials to follow," . . . is fatal.[34]

As Kenneth S. Devol has noted, other than in cases involving hard-core pornography, "the Warren Court for all practical purposes eliminated film censorship for adult viewers."[35]

The Planet of the Apes

A film that can be interpreted as a deeply critical reading of then contemporary American society was ostensibly a science fiction film. Like films in that genre of the 1960s, the cloak of science fiction and fantasy allowed sharp commentary to be delivered to mainstream audiences indirectly. Director Franklin J. Schaffner's *The Planet of the Apes* (1968) is on many levels a socially aware allegory that deeply reflects issues of its era. Its postapocalyptic story is based on a French novel by Pierre Boulle and tells of a future American astronaut whose space craft crash-lands on a distant world.

Rod Serling, an intelligent Hollywood screenwriter and a man known for creating the famed television series *The Twilight Zone* several years earlier, prepared an early draft of the script. Serling had often used science fiction and fantasy story lines to deliver astute and often satirical social commentary, and his script for this project was no exception.[36] When the script Serling delivered was judged to have parts that would be too expensive for the film's projected budget, it was given to Michael Wilson for revision. Wilson, who at one time was blacklisted in Hollywood, had previously developed the script for the 1957 movie adaptation of Boulle's story *The Bridge on the River Kwai*.[37] (Due to his blacklisting, Wilson received credit for his work on *The Bridge on the River Kwai* some years after its release.)

The Planet of the Apes was well crafted and included special effects that were dazzling for the era. It also featured a notable cast of Hollywood regulars. The leading role of astronaut George Taylor was played by Charlton Heston, who was famous for his appearance in many films, especially Hollywood epics such as *The Ten Commandments* (1956) and *Ben-Hur* (1959). Under heavy but highly effective makeup, Roddy McDowell played Cornelius, an intelligent ape with keen knowledge of archaeology and history. Kim Hunter, known for many television roles, played Zira, an ape specializing in the study of humans. Maurice Evans, who had started his career on the British stage several decades earlier, played Zaius, a politically powerful ape who fiercely defends his society's status quo. The appearance of these and the many other familiar Hollywood actors and actresses in the film undoubtedly helped make the potentially provocative story of *The Planet of the Apes* seem less threatening to the American audience.

In the film's narrative, astronaut George Taylor crashes on an earth-like world after a very long space flight. To Taylor's surprise, these sophisticated apes are masters of that world. The apes have developed both language and a complex, human-like society. As it turns out, however, this world is also inhabited by beings with a primitive human appearance, who do not possess language and appear dull compared to the sophisticated apes.

Soon after his arrival, Taylor is captured by the apes. They mistake him for one of the planet's native humanoids. To Taylor's dismay, the humans of this world are relegated to a status little above that of other animals. They are treated as pets or trained to be docile servants for ape masters. The film largely focuses on the astronaut's struggle to free himself from this condition of slavery and to awaken in the native humans a will to rise against the apes.

The film was popular not only with viewers but also with critics. Writing in *Life* magazine, Richard Schickel praised the film and noted the effect that it seemed to have had on his four-year-old daughter's moral awakening. Schickel wrote that the movie "taught her something—that animals, and by implication all creatures different from her, are capable of feeling. It taught her, she tells me in her own way, that they can be scared of the unfamiliar and therefore as foolish and as prejudiced as more familiar beings can be."[38] *The Planet of the Apes* appears to have conveyed its indirect message and commentary about inequities in American society in a way that was understood by many people.

Although it is possible to view the story simply as a science fiction tale about another world, it is nonetheless difficult to avoid noticing the similarities of these elements of the narrative to the troubled history of race relations in the United States. And indeed, the parallels between the apparently fictional story and the real-life racial strife that had erupted in the 1960s have been widely noted. Writing several decades after the movie's debut, Eric Greene observed, "As the *Apes* series implied that blacks and whites were so alienated from each other that they required symbolic representation as entirely different species. Many saw the domestic conflicts between blacks and whites as analogous to a war between two nations."[39]

Greene concludes that the film demonstrates how "in the racist imagination, the 'lower' orders masquerading as the 'higher' threatens to compromise racial or even species purity."[40] He further notes the turbulent social and political context of the 1960s and 1970s—and particularly the controversies of the war in Vietnam, the struggle against poverty, and racial strife—"provided a stinging sense of despair that pervades" *The Planet of the Apes* and the sequels that soon followed it.[41]

Changing Hollywood

In the final year of the 1960s, Hollywood offered several popular films that directly challenged the norms and mores of traditional American society. No longer constrained by local licensing issues or the Production Code, the American film business reflected more directly the interests and tastes of a youthful audience that in many respects did not feel bound to attitudes of the past. Three such productions—*Midnight Cowboy*, *The Wild Bunch*, and *Easy Rider*—were released with weeks of each other. Movies that otherwise appear quite unrelated, they collectively reflect significant shifts in American attitudes.

Midnight Cowboy, directed by John Schlesinger and featuring the actors Dustin Hoffman, Jon Voight, and Sylvia Miles, attracted considerable public attention. In the story, Voight plays Joe Buck, a young man who drifts from Texas to New York with a plan to sell his sexual services to upscale city women. But things do not work out as he plans, and Buck becomes associated with a low-life con artist named Ratso Rizzo (Hoffman). The film is set largely in the Times Square area of New York City, which in that era had fallen into disrepute. It depicted what has been described as "a bleak descent into New York City's netherworld of drifters and losers at the margins of society and living in the midst of a crass and self-obsessed metropolis."[42] As described in one review, it was a world in which "everybody is too busy smoking pot [and] popping pills."[43]

The film was originally released with an X rating.[44] Ostensibly, the "X" was assigned due to what Stephen Farber has characterized as its many "oblique hints at homosexuality."[45] Indeed, the film directly treated sexual topics. But the main effect was mostly to demonstrate how alienating some aspects of modern urban life had become. As Farber also notes, "The film treats all sexual encounters—heterosexual or homosexual—with abhorrence."[46] Regardless of the dismal world it depicted, *Midnight Cowboy* had little trouble attracting an audience. And for its unflattering view of an aspect of contemporary urban life that was far from idyllic, it won three Academy Awards (Best Picture, Best Director, Best Adapted Screenplay).

Although Hollywood did continue to make the occasional Western film, the genre received less attention from American feature film producers as the 1960s wore on. One notable exception to this trend was director Sam Peckinpah's 1969 movie *The Wild Bunch*, which probably attracted more attention for its gore and explicitly portrayed violence than for its Western theme.

The film's narrative focuses on an aging gang of outlaws, which is led by Pike Bishop (played by William Holden). During a robbery the gang is ambushed. Leading the ambush is one of Bishop's former associates, Deke Thornton (Robert Ryan), who is cooperating with authorities in order to avoid prison. Violence erupts and many town residents are caught in the crossfire. Some are wounded and many die. Bishop and his gang are able to slip away, and they flee across the border into Mexico.

In Mexico, the gang encounters a corrupt Mexican army officer, General Mapache (Emilio Fernández), whose lawless troops appear to rule a small town. Bishop schemes to steal weapons for the general, but things go wrong. At the end of the story, the gang and the general's troops engage in a bloody fight, in which most of the characters meet an agonizing end.

In some respects, *The Wild Bunch* deals with traditional themes that are familiar in the Western genre, such as trust and betrayal, bravery and cowardice. But the film is set near the end of that historical period, at a time of transition. And the aging protagonists are fitting symbols for a story about the untidy end of an era. The movie throws into question many of the mythologized memories of the Old West period, which Hollywood's Western genre had often repeated. In this way, *The Wild Bunch* builds upon themes that Sergio Leone had introduced in his trilogy about the man with no name.

When *The Wild Bunch* was screened for members of the international press, reaction was intense. Many in attendance were shocked and outraged. Although some of the viewers did seem to appreciate the movie, others expressed their strong disapproval.[47] One critic, for example, wrote, "There is little justification for this ugly, pointless, disgusting film."[48] The director was aware of the provocative nature of his explicit portrayals of violence. He once explained, "You can't make violence real to audiences today without rubbing their noses in it. We watch our wars and see men die, really die, every day on television, but it doesn't seem real . . . I want them to see what it looks like."[49]

In his review of *The Wild Bunch*, Vincent Canby interpreted the graphic violence in the film this way: "Borrowing a device from *Bonnie and Clyde*, Peckinpah suddenly reduces the camera speed to slow motion, which at first heightens the horror and mindless slaughter, and then—and this is what really carries horror—makes it beautiful, almost abstract, and finally into a terrible parody."[50]

Overall, the film strongly reflects the social and political context of the era in which it was made. The nation had witnessed assassinations, racial and anti-war riots, and a perceived sense of increasing crime. And the United States was still in the midst of the bloody war in Vietnam, graphic images of which were regularly televised on the evening news. In this context, one writer noted that Peckinpah emphasized "the casualness of everyday violence." Perhaps the nation had long been accustomed to this. But Americans had often envisioned violence in a sanitized, almost heroic way, both on film and in American culture more broadly. Peckinpah's violence was simply violence, painful and pointless—the antithesis of anything noble.

In addition, like some other films in this period, *The Wild Bunch* was a comment on perceptions that traditional ways of understanding American life were in question and, perhaps, coming to an end in the contemporary world, just as they were for the characters in this fictionalized portrait of the Old West. As Canby astutely noted at the time, "*The Wild Bunch* takes the basic elements of the Western movie myth, which once defined a simple, morally comprehensible word, and by bending them turns them into symbols of futility and aimless corruption."[51] And because the Western was so much a part of the national myth overall, and epitomized much that was inherent in the idea of the American Dream, such an assault on this traditional understanding of the American experience was significant.

Another film from 1969, *Easy Rider*, depicted an alternative picture of the contemporary United States, in which in many ways had broken with its past. With a youthful perspective and reflecting an approving attitude of drug use and other behavior that was considered counterculture at the time, it was a film in which the American Dream narrative held little meaning. There was little doubt about the movie's nontraditional attitude. Advertisements for the film featured the tagline: "A man went looking for America. And couldn't find it anywhere."

The story of *Easy Rider* is about the journey of two young men, Wyatt (played by Peter Fonda), whose nickname is Captain America, and Billy (Dennis Hopper). Fully immersed in the counterculture of the era—"hippies" in the parlance of that time—they smuggle cocaine across the Mexican border to California, where they sell it to a Los Angeles dealer (played by Phil Spector). But they are not really interested in the drug business, per se. Their goal is to take their ill-gotten money and take a cross-country motorcycle road trip to New Orleans, where they plan to experience Mardi Gras.

The film makes extensive use of 1960s-era rock music (including work of Jimi Hendrix, Steppenwolf, and the Byrds) and is explicit in showing the fondness that Wyatt and Billy both have for recreational drug use. Some of the most memorable scenes revolve around discussions where the characters are under the influence of various drugs. This type of scene, presented matter-of-factly and with an air of implicit approval, would have been unimaginable in a major feature film just a few years earlier. Such scenes represented a significant departure from the usually implied moral underpinning that had characterized most Hollywood films since the industry's earliest days.

As the journey progresses, Billy and Wyatt are briefly jailed for a minor infraction. There they meet a young lawyer, George Hanson (Jack Nicholson), who has been detained after an alcoholic binge. Although Hanson belongs to a prominent southern family, he works with civil rights cases and is interested in countercultural ideas—ideas about an expansive view of personal freedom that extend beyond the boundaries that traditional society had long observed. Hanson is eager to explore life beyond his small-town horizon, and he decides to accompany Billy and Wyatt on their trip to New Orleans.

Soon, however, the three men run into trouble in a small Louisiana town where the locals do not take kindly to "hippies" and their presumed deviant ways. The night after a tense encounter with them, the three travelers are attacked as they sleep. Hanson is savagely beaten and dies.

Wyatt and Billy do eventually continue to see Mardi Gras, but in some ways it seems empty and is a disappointment. Later, as they are traveling along a desolate road, a random encounter with two men in a pickup truck turns violent, bringing the story to a somber end. As one writer later concluded, "Given how thoroughly audiences embraced *Easy Rider*, its unremittingly tragic ending is striking. . . . their journey, based as it was on ill-gotten gains, has been a waste."[52]

Bernard Drew, a syndicated film critic in the era, wrote that the film was "a dirge, a lament and a requiem for America, a valedictory to the spirit of freedom and justice which moulded [*sic*] us, and one of the most beautiful, devastating and important films ever made by Americans in America. It kills you, that's what it does. It kills you."[53] Writing in the *New York Times*, Vincent Canby was less impressed, though he admired Nicholson, then mostly an unknown actor, for his performance as George Hanson. As for the film overall, he appeared to be skeptical of its "decidedly superior airs." He nonetheless understood "the film's statement" as something "to do with the threat that people like the nonconforming Wyatt and Billy represent to the ordinary, self-righteous, inhibited folk that are the Real America."[54]

Films such as these presented a strikingly different vision of the United States, past and present, which was unlike anything Hollywood had issued in previous years. Though an old, venerable industry that was in many ways intimately American, the new generation of filmmakers, like their audiences, no longer automatically believed that the American way always led to success, or even that it could be reliably counted on to be good. Such feelings would give way to more nagging cynicism and alienation in many works that would be produced in the future.

END OF A TURBULENT DECADE

The month after *Easy Rider* was released, an event in rural New York provided one of the watershed moments of the 1960s-era counterculture. The festival at Woodstock, which was promoted as "3 days of peace & music," attracted a huge number of attendees—estimates range from 300,000 to 500,000 people. (Director Michael Wadleigh's concert film of the festival, simply titled *Woodstock*, was released the following year.) Over the three days, the crowd listened to rock music and, as described by writer James Perone, "lived for three days in a manner that showed a complete rejection of suburban, military-industrial-complex-based concepts of what American should be."[55] It was also, as observed in a special edition of *Life* magazine devoted to the event, "a display of the authority of drugs over a whole generation."[56]

A similar event was held in California that December. Billed as the Altamont Speedway Free Festival and attracting several hundred thousand people, this festival too featured rock music and widespread drug use by the audience. (The event, which was recorded by documentary filmmakers Albert and David Maysles, was the subject of the 1970 movie *Gimme Shelter*.) Unlike the event in Woodstock, however, the concert in Altamont was marred by violence. As a contemporary news account reported, four people died—one from a stabbing that occurred as the Rolling Stones performed—in the one-day event, in which "a handful of incidents, most involving Hell's Angels motorcycle toughs, marred an otherwise peaceful exercise in togetherness by young students, hippies, teeny-boppers and other rock fans."[57] Although it may have been "a handful of incidents," it was enough to mar the public perception of the event, especially among traditionally minded Americans who were appalled at the lifestyle and politics of those in the younger generation who embraced the counterculture. Coming in the last month of the last year of the 1960s, in some ways the downbeat aura of the Altamont Festival seemed to sum up the disturbing, disruptive decade.

The crises of the 1960s had a divisive effect on American society, significantly tarnishing the ideals and optimism that the American Dream idea had represented just two decades earlier. Assassinations, riots, and war had been a big part of this development. More than that was the social upheaval that swept across the cultural landscape. Established ways of thinking and behaving had been thrown into question. The future was unclear, since many of the things that had caused these changes in society were not yet resolved. The war in Vietnam dragged on and continued to spark dissent. A nationwide moratorium to end the war in Vietnam was held in October 1969 in communities and college campuses across the nation. An estimated quarter million demonstrators gathered to protest the war in Washington, DC.

Beyond the war, issues of race and gender—the unfinished work of the civil rights and women's movements—were still contested. Traditional social order was in doubt, as evidenced by fears of rising crime and widespread drug use. Such anxieties and doubts had chipped away at the United States' trust in its institutions, generating skepticism and disaffection. In other words, the United States' confidence in itself and its way of life was no longer unquestioned.

Evidence of this gnawing feeling of unease was easy to find. Syndicated columnist Jack Anderson reported that letters were "flooding" into his office "from middle-class Americans who are deeply troubled over the deadly drift away from the old-fashioned values." Anderson noted troublesome issues, such as rising crime, racial strife, and the ongoing war in Vietnam. With the United States facing these difficulties, he said the letters he had received "ask anxiously whether the United States is going the way of the great powers of the past whose strength was sapped by moral decay."[58]

In another example, Attorney General Nicholas Katzenbach appeared before the Senate Government Operations Subcommittee, where he discussed the urban riots that had plagued the nation. These disturbances, he said, were the result of "an American failure" and that "disease and despair, joblessness and hopelessness, rat-infested housing and long-impacted cynicism.... They are the product of generations of indifference by all the American people to the rot and rust and mold which we have allowed to eat into the core of our cities."[59]

In some ways, the enormous changes in Hollywood mirrored some of the strains that had ruptured American life more generally. Reflecting the society at large, as well as industry pressures to continue attracting audiences in an era when television was the ascendant medium, Hollywood had liberalized its attitude about what could appear on-screen. Nudity had become increasingly common as part of an overall trend toward more direct treatment of sexual behavior overall. In addition, drug use, profane language, explicit violence, and a general disrespect for American ideals and institutions could easily be found in movies that were distributed to mainstream theaters. To traditionalists in American society, such changes were profound. These developments were evidence that pointed to a breakdown in order and the system of values that to them characterized what America had been and should be. They feared that the American Dream was on a precipice and that corrective action needed to be taken to avoid the United States' fall.

CHAPTER 7

Disillusion

As the 1970s began, American society continued to grapple with the crises and social upheaval that had erupted in the previous decade. Many issues remained unresolved, and by this time American confidence was clearly rattled. A study conducted by the Gilbert Youth Research Corporation in 1971, for example, concluded that more than half of the United States' youth had lost confidence in the nation's future; fewer than 40 percent of respondents in the study agreed with the statement, "Everyone has a chance to get ahead in this country."[1] The bright world of hope, promise, and prosperity envisioned in the idea of American Dream in previous years seemed increasingly uncertain.

Indeed, the United States that emerged from the turbulent decade of the 1960s was in some ways a different nation than it had been. People expressed varied reactions to this transformation. For some, developments in the areas of civil rights, women's issues, and other causes indicated progress. For other people, however, such changes, along with the upheaval of the 1960s more generally, had altered the United States for the worse. Thus, while behaviors and attitudes with regard to many aspects of society were evolving, albeit sometimes slowly and inconsistently, a sizeable number of Americans were looking for a way to recapture the familiarity of the past.

But troubles from the 1960s lingered. Controversy about the Vietnam War continued to plague the nation, for instance. Although U.S. involvement in the war had crested, it proved to be difficult to bring the conflict to an end. In an effort to hasten an outcome acceptable to the United States, American troops were ordered to cross the border from South Vietnam into Cambodia.

Their mission was to disrupt supply-and-command capabilities of the North Vietnamese enemy that had set up bases in that neighboring country. When Richard Nixon announced the incursion into Cambodia in a televised address in late April 1970, however, opponents of the war were outraged at what appeared to them as a widening of the conflict. Not long after, an antiwar protest at Kent State University in Ohio turned violent. Four students were shot and killed by nervous National Guard troops, who had been called in to maintain order. This development horrified much of the nation, and it prompted widespread student strikes on many campuses across the United States. The polarizing effects of the war in Vietnam remained very evident.

Still, by 1972 the Vietnam War involved fewer and fewer American troops. And Nixon's national security advisor, Henry Kissinger, was close to a nego-tiated settlement that would end U.S. participation in the war. With some slight bumps in the road still to come, conditions were mostly set in the fall of 1972 for the United States to exit Vietnam. With the conflict in Southeast Asia taking a lessening role in domestic American politics, Nixon easily won reelection that November.

In the meantime, domestic problems had become a major concern. Crime, for example, was on the minds of Americans and their leaders. But it was not merely the fear of crime itself that propelled this issue to the forefront of poli-tics. Crime was an issue that stood as an example of a phenomenon broader than lawbreaking by individuals. More than that, rising crime was a symbol of American moral decline—of society on the brink of disorder and chaos. So, during the months in which the war in Vietnam dragged on, much politi-cal attention turned inward, toward the widely perceived collapse of civil soci-ety that, depending on a person's point of view, seemed imminent or already under way.

The perception of increasing crime was an accurate one, and crime had already come to be seen as a pressing issue. As one newspaper columnist wrote in 1969, "Crime is now an ever-present threat . . . people are talking approvingly about anticrime measures so harsh they would have horrified everyone only a few years ago."[2] Indeed, violent crime had doubled over the course of the 1960s, and property crime had increased also.

The upturn in criminal activity continued throughout the 1970s, causing a sense of unease among many Americans. The rate of violent crime, which hovered around 160 reports per 100,000 persons in 1960, 1961, and 1962, doubled to a rate of 328 per 100,000 by 1969. Ten years later, in 1979, it rose to nearly 549 reports of violent crime per 100,000 of the nation's popu-lation, a rate than was more than triple that of only 20 years earlier.[3]

HOLLYWOOD'S REACTION

Crime was an issue that Hollywood did not shy away from portraying. The crime film already had a long history in American cinema. The genre followed a winding path through the 1960s, when films with crime themes sometimes had taken on new attitudes. These included movies such as *Murder, Inc.* (1960), *Ocean's Eleven* (1960), *Robin and the Seven Hoods* (1964), and *Point Blank* (1967). Though influenced by the times, however, for the most part such movies were somewhat conventional and fit within audience expectations. *Bonnie and Clyde*, on the other hand, had stylishly, albeit violently, portrayed midwestern bank robbers as romanticized antiheroes.

In addition, films such as Sam Peckinpah's 1969 Western movie *The Wild Bunch* had broken new ground in the depiction of violence, which crime films of the 1970s would exploit. With the combination of the social-political context of the early 1970s—that is, Americans' growing fear of crime and the widespread feeling there was little to stop it—and the new acceptance of extremely explicit language and graphic depiction of violence on screen, Hollywood was poised to produce jarring new works.

Movies that addressed and responded to the perceived collapse of urban society gained much popularity. The actor Clint Eastwood, whose fame was cemented in Sergio Leone's popular Westerns of the 1960s, appeared in *Dirty Harry* (1971). It was a movie with populist appeal that tapped into deep-seated anxieties about moral decay and the ineffectiveness of American social institutions. Indeed, director Don Siegel's *Dirty Harry* is one of the most iconic films of the 1970s. In this film and its sequels, Eastwood plays Harry Callahan, a San Francisco police detective. These movies often focus on Callahan's sardonic attitude and tendency toward violence, along with his "shoot first and ask questions later" approach to law enforcement, which is the behavior that had earned him the reputation of being "dirty." Callahan is clearly not a man willing to be confined by official rules. Instead, the character combines the role of law enforcement officer with that of judge, jury, and sometimes executioner. He often appears as likely to shoot as to arrest a suspect.

Although a menacing and angry character, Harry Callahan nonetheless goes about his business in an efficient, almost matter-of-fact manner. He frequently makes ironic, off-handed comments to the criminals with whom he interacts. His goal is to clean up what he perceives as the scum of society. In so doing, he displays nearly total contempt for his superiors and makes clear that he thinks the rules and regulations of the criminal justice system are not only of negligible usefulness in fighting crime but also frequently work to actively make life easy for criminals.

The audiences who flocked to see *Dirty Harry*, as well as its sequels—especially *Magnum Force* (1973) and *The Enforcer* (1976)[4]—delighted in the Old West style of justice that Eastwood portrayed on screen. Indeed, the character's imposing handgun functions almost like a second leading character in the films. In one scene, for example, Callahan confronts a wounded suspect lying on the ground and reaching for a gun. Callahan looks down at the suspect and points his weapon, saying:

> But being this is a .44 Magnum, the most powerful handgun in the world, and would blow your head clean off, you've got to ask yourself one question: "Do I feel lucky?" Well, do ya, punk?[5]

Many viewers responded quite favorably to Harry Callahan's approach to justice. The movie was a popular as well as a financial success. Yet some people criticized the film and accused it of blatantly appealing to vigilantism, which, given the story portrayed in the film, is an understandable charge.

The Dirty Harry character did not only appeal to angry fringes of American society. Indeed, the film's widespread popularity suggests that the movie also had successfully tapped into growing frustration with the direction in which society appeared to be heading. Perhaps some audience members did wish to see the lawless form of justice practiced by Dirty Harry put into real-world use. But for many people, the appeal of the character may have been simply that Callahan represented a longing, or even nostalgia, for an envisioned past world in which common values and standards of behavior were respected and in which American institutions functioned in the way that people imagined they should.

The 1974 film *Death Wish*, directed by Michael Winner, was another vigilante film. Through the avenging actions of its lead character, it exhibits an attitude about crime and society similar to that which viewers had seen in the *Dirty Harry* films. *Death Wish* stars Charles Bronson, who was well suited for the very unsubtle story. Bronson was an actor with an already established tough-guy image. He had played rugged characters with an air of bravado in movies such as *The Magnificent Seven* (1960), which was an American adaptation of Akira Kurosawa's *Seven Samurai*, *The Dirty Dozen* (1967), about convicts offered freedom in return for dangerous military service in World War II, and *The Mechanic* (1972), the story of a ruthless hit man.

In *Death Wish*, Bronson plays an architect named Paul Kersey. According to the story, three young criminals break into Kersey's apartment while he is out. His daughter is sexually assaulted and his wife is beaten so badly that she subsequently dies. Over the next weeks, the shock of these crimes slowly causes Kersey to transform from a politically liberal, mild-mannered citizen into a gun-wielding vigilante seeking revenge. In one scene after another, as Kersey encounters hoodlums in the process of victimizing the innocent, he dispenses his own lethal justice. Throughout, he takes precautions to shield his identity and disappear before authorities arrive at the scenes of his vengeful episodes. Although the police launch an investigation, by then the public has made a hero of the mysterious man cleaning up violent crime. Somewhat halfheartedly investigating, a detective suspects Kersey but is told by superiors not to interfere too much. Essentially, even the police come to believe that the vengeful gunman is helping them do the job that they could not.

The brutal violence in the initial scenes of *Death Wish* was considered to be tasteless and exploitative by many viewers at the time. Some critics detested the film, believing that it pandered to the lowest common denominator of audiences. Reviewer Vincent Canby, for example, wrote that *Death Wish* "seems to have been made for no reason except to exploit its audience's urban paranoia and vestigial fascination with violence for its own sake" and that it "raises complex questions in order to offer bigoted, frivolous, oversimplified answers."[6]

Indeed, the violence is vicious. The depiction of the attack on Kersey's daughter was filmed in a way to be particularly repulsive. Yet true to the formula that the movie follows, the savagery of the assaults on innocent victims seems designed to establish a basis for the violent retribution that Kersey inflicts in later scenes. The horrible atrocities committed against innocents in the film may be intended to allow Kersey's subsequent vigilantism to have a cathartic effect on audiences. In any case, *Death Wish* appeals to viewers on a gut level, at first shocking them with horrific violence and then showing scenes in which the perpetrators get, on the film's terms, what they presumably deserve.

Overall, the vigilante movies of this era provide a glimpse into the increased social unease and nagging fears that everyday life in the United States was eroding. Although these stories show isolated cases in which anti-heroes buck the system and bring about justice on their own, the films really do not suggest that anything is about to halt the overall decay of society, which is depicted as increasingly chaotic and lawless.

These movies show slightly milder versions of the futuristic and hyperviolent world depicted in director Stanley Kubrick's *A Clockwork Orange* (1971), a British movie that initially received an X rating when it was distributed in the

United States. Indeed, the society depicted in American vigilante movies offers little to inspire confidence that things can be put right. Said differently, characters such as "Dirty" Harry Callahan do nothing to restore the American Dream in any meaningful way; they simply exact revenge in a few cases that have come to their attention. The vigilante justice is as random as the criminal violence it is intended to fight. The overall effect appears to be limited.

WATERGATE AND NIXON'S FALL

In the final months of Nixon's reelection campaign in 1972, negotiations between the United States and North Vietnam came close to an agreement, which stipulated there would be a cease-fire and eventual political resolution to the bitter war in Southeast Asia. South Vietnam, which had been largely cut out of the peace talks, balked when told of the plan. Although this stalled things for a short while, it soon became clear that the United States intended to move ahead with a settlement with or without South Vietnam's approval. The United States' South Vietnamese allies had little choice but to go along with the plan.

In January of 1973, the same month in which Richard Nixon was sworn into office for a second term, the cease-fire was announced. An uneasy truce held for a while. North Vietnam released Americans being held as prisoners of war. The hugely unpopular military draft, which had been a divisive issue in the United States at the height of the war, was also halted, removing a social irritant that had fueled much protest for nearly a decade. Within a few months, the American public started to disengage psychologically from the Vietnam experience.[7]

The bitter war in Vietnam ended with what seemed to be an American defeat. The Cold War continued, but now American perceptions were different. The Soviet Union, though still regarded warily, seemed less threatening, despite playing a continuing role as an international provocateur. Nixon had already reestablished relations with Communist China, partially to complicate things for the Soviet Union, which had an uneasy relationship with this other Communist giant. There had also been as series of treaties and agreements, significantly defusing the international political atmosphere.

Thus, although Americans may have still been apprehensive about the USSR, for the most part they no longer regarded the Soviet Union as an existential threat. The Cold War was not over, but it had surely changed over the course of the previous decades. The Soviet Union remained a concern, but it seemed less dangerous and menacing than it had at the height of the Cold War. Instead, the new spirit in American-Soviet relations was that of détente, the apparent willingness of each nation to work toward peaceful coexistence.

Yet by the mid-1970s, the United States was mired in a general malaise. The nation's confidence was deeply rattled not only by its apparent defeat in Vietnam but also by a decade of social unrest. Many Americans had lost confidence in their society's major institutions, which had been a cornerstone component of American Dream ideals for more than a quarter century. Instead, their nation appeared to be on a downward slide.

The mid-decade Watergate scandal helped fuel this sense of frustration, which was harbored by much of the American public. The major events of the Watergate affair reveal some of the reasons for the public's continuing disaffection with their own government.

In the summer of 1972, a few months before the presidential election, police arrested five men for breaking into the Democratic National Committee office at the Watergate building in Washington, DC, and attempting to plant eavesdropping devices. At first, the break-in was treated as a minor crime, of little more than nuisance value. Soon thereafter, however, troubling details began to emerge about the men who had been arrested. It seemed that they were connected to the White House in some way, although at first this connection was difficult to confirm. The connection soon became clearer. Within a few weeks, the *Washington Post* reported that a check for $25,000, which had been intended for Richard Nixon's reelection campaign, had instead been deposited into the account of one of the men accused in the break-in.[8]

In the months that followed, investigations by journalists and the FBI uncovered more information linking the Watergate break-in to the White House. An October 10, 1972, story in the *Washington Post* reported, "A massive campaign of political spying and sabotage [had been] conducted on behalf of President Nixon's re-election and directed by officials in the White House and the Committee for the Re-election of the President."[9] The report further noted that the Nixon campaign had redirected "hundreds of thousands of dollars" for the purpose of "discrediting individual Democratic presidential candidates and disrupting their campaigns."[10]

But even with these revelations, it still seemed that the crimes had been the work of low-level people and not top officials. At the time, therefore, it had not been fully established that President Nixon was directly involved in the incident. For this reason, concerns about the Watergate incident were not sufficient to derail Nixon's reelection efforts, and he handily won a second term in November 1972.

By early 1973, however, the tide turned. Slowly but steadily, suspicion about the president's personal involvement in criminal events began to mount. Two aides were convicted of conspiracy and other charges related to the Watergate break-in, and the growing scandal then led two top Nixon aides and the attorney general to tender their resignations. By May 1973, the Senate opened televised hearings about the matter. Then in June, there was more damaging evidence. A former White House counsel, John Dean, testified that he had "discussed aspects of the Watergate cover-up with President Nixon or in Mr. Nixon's presence on at least 35 occasions between January and April" of that year.[11]

Slowly the Watergate affair began to unravel the Nixon presidency. New revelations and allegations cast an ever more troubling light on the president's alleged involvement in criminal activity. Nixon came under increasing pressure as the months wore on. In summer 1974, the House Judiciary Committee passed articles of impeachment, in which the president was accused of obstructing justice. With his presidency in shambles and his future prospects looking dim, Richard Nixon took the unprecedented step of resigning from office on August 8, 1974. The nation's vice president, Gerald R. Ford, was sworn into office as Nixon's successor.

The Watergate investigations fueled additional skepticism and doubt among the American people. The disastrous end to Richard Nixon's presidency led Americans to new heights of distrust and disaffection. People from many political backgrounds became jaded about Washington and politics in general.

TURNING AWAY

By the mid-1970s, then, the United States had been rocked by a series of crises: the social turmoil of the previous decade, the unceremonious conclusion of the war in Vietnam, and the fall of Richard Nixon. All of these, in various ways, contributed to a shattering of public confidence. For many people, there was a troubling perception that American institutions were not capable of dealing with the nation's most pressing problems. Such were the circumstances that generated a widespread feeling of malaise across much of American culture at that time.

In some respects, the culture turned inward, and to a degree became self-indulgent. Novelist Tom Wolfe noticed this change and in 1976 described this time as the "me decade."[12] Wolfe attributed the development of a narcissistic streak in American culture to the post–World War II economic boom, which had elevated the standard of living, particularly for the middle classes, to an unprecedented height. These people had escaped from the cities, which were now regarded by suburbanites as largely dysfunctional, irrelevant wastelands. To many of them, urban centers increasingly seemed to be breeding grounds for social problems of many sorts, such as crime, drug addiction, and poverty. Meanwhile, from their remade lives in suburbia, the mostly white middle classes created a new version of what constituted normalcy. It was a world where people were in many ways socially disconnected from one another and where the emphasis was instead placed on building worlds of self.

In this era, popular culture often focused on nostalgia for a past that was, in fact, not much like the actual past. Productions such as George Lucas's film *American Graffiti* (1973) and the television series *Happy Days*, which premiered in 1974, envisioned small-town life in the 1950s in ways that caricatured the historical experience of that not-too-distant past. Nostalgia for the 1950s tended to gloss over the apparent fact that many of the causes for the 1970s cultural malaise had roots in that previous time.

In some ways, nostalgia served to deaden awareness of the cultural downturn by providing an escape from it. Looking back before the 1960s, the nostalgic version of Americana was a world in which people cheerfully got along with each other, were very homogenous—meaning almost exclusively white and middle class—and basically accepted the traditional premises of society. Unlike the case in the real world of the 1970s, in which many people were skeptical of society's ability to solve its problems, in the nostalgic re-creation of the 1950s, American society seemed to work seamlessly.

The excessive focus on self in the 1970s had many manifestations. One was the increasingly widespread recreational use of illicit drugs, which by the 1970s was a mainstream fact of life. Though drug laws remained strict, these were widely ignored, not only by rebels of society but increasingly by ordinary people, across social classes and locales. The drug problem often appeared in films and television as a largely urban problem—hence, safely removed from suburban experience. This was despite the fact that drug abuse had deeply penetrated suburban and rural communities, as well. The Nixon administration had declared a war on drugs some years earlier, but by the mid- to late 1970s the federal antidrug program was widely perceived as a failure. In 1973, the National Commission on Marijuana and Drug Abuse issued a report stating that the drug problem was persistent and showed no signs of abating, though it dismissed the idea this would lead to a "collapse of our society."[13] But anxiety about the continuing failure to curb drug use did not decrease, and the inability of government policies aiming to solve the problem was a concern to many people.

During this same era, the American economy was under attack from many sides. In the autumn of 1973, the Organization of Arab Petroleum Exporting States instituted an oil embargo against the United States. The stated reason for this step was to protest American military aid that had been given to Israel in the wake of an Egyptian and Syrian military attack on that nation. By this era, the United States was highly dependent on imported oil to feed its ever-growing energy needs. The result of the embargo was a gasoline and heating oil shortage, which in the following months led to long lines at the gas pumps and to rising oil prices.

More broadly, throughout this era the economy, which had been the engine for growth and prosperity, stumbled badly. Inflation, which had mostly been kept at a modest rate since mid-century, became a worrisome issue. Based on a consumer price index of 100 in 1967, the change from 1950, when the consumer price index was 72.1, to 1970, when it was 116.3, was noticeable, but represented only a slight increase, on average, from year to year. In the 1970s, the pace of inflation quickened, rising from 116.3 in 1970 to 217.4 in 1979.[14]

The slowing economy also meant that unemployment surfaced as a problem. Even college graduates felt the pinch of the tightening labor market.[15] Given that a college education had for a generation been regarded as a safe route to secure employment, this was a shock to many people.

For such reasons, it increasingly appeared as though faith in the American Dream was weakening. As journalist John Cunniff wrote in 1974, "What seems to be missing from the lives of many Americans is the dream—the vision that tomorrow could be better, the soul deep conviction that they would participate in the future."[16] Indeed, the sagging economy continued to take a toll on American confidence. In 1974, the Federal Home Loan Bank Board reported that the mortgage rate for new homes averaged 8.72 percent.[17]

Seeking to restore American confidence, Gerald Ford asked Americans to "bite the bullet" to defeat the inflation problem. In addition to other austerity measures, the Republican president proposed that families with incomes of over $15,000 per year pay a 5 percent surcharge in what one newspaper called "his most sweeping equity proposal."[18]

But confidence had eroded and the economy resisted any quick resuscitation. During a 1975 speech delivered in Boston in April 1975, the president called for renewed faith in the United States. "We must become masters of our own destiny," he declared. "The American Dream is not dead. It simply has yet to be fulfilled."[19]

The context of Ford's speech revealed some of the strains facing the nation. In fact, when the president delivered this speech in Boston, the city was in the throes of tension and violence, which had resulted from court-ordered school busing there. Thus even as the president called for unity, protesters had gathered nearby. According to a news report, "At least one fist-fight broke out on the school busing issue and police had to arrest several of about 30 persons involved."[20]

The cultural and economic malaise of the era continued to defy easy resolution. In some ways, the nation's bicentennial in 1976 was a cause for rejoicing. But despite national celebrations, the mood was restrained. A downbeat feeling continued to haunt the nation in some ways.

When Americans returned to the polls in November 1976, they wanted change. Voters passed over Gerald Ford, who had campaigned for reelection, and instead voted Jimmy Carter into office. Carter was an apparent Washington outsider who was a peanut farmer, former naval officer, and the recent governor of Georgia. The nation, it seemed, was searching for a new direction.

HOLLYWOOD AND THE UNEASE OF THE EARLY 1970s

The seeming breakdown of many previously durable aspects of American society was reflected across multiple film genres at this time. Several science fiction films, for example, envisioned the crumbling of society in ways that picked up themes that were in the news in that era. Concerns about ecology and the environment, overpopulation, economic demise, and deviant corporate plutocracy were among the ideas that can be found in these works.

One such movie was *Omega Man*, director Boris Sagal's 1971 reworking of a novel by Richard Matheson that had been the basis of the movie *The Last Man on Earth* (1964) several years earlier. *Omega Man* follows the story of a man named Neville (played by Charlton Heston), who by day appears to be the final human survivor after a war between the USSR and China that had unleashed deadly biological weapons that destroyed life across the earth. After nightfall, Neville battles hordes of creatures—reanimated dead people who had now been transformed into monstrous, mindless killers, reminiscent of vampires or zombies.

For a time, Neville believes he is the sole remaining human, but he eventually discovers a small group of other human survivors. Although he tries valiantly to protect them, by the end of the film the prospects for their survival do not appear promising. The movie's overall outlook, therefore, is decidedly pessimistic.

Another science fiction movie, with a similarly dim view of humanity's future, was director Richard Fleischer's 1973 science fiction film *Soylent Green*. It envisions a dystopian future of social breakdown, overpopulation, environmental erosion, and economic distress. Poverty and food shortages are major problems in this world. Many people survive on a food called Soylent Green, a product that its manufacturer says is made from plankton.

At first, the story appears to revolve around a futuristic murder mystery. The film's protagonist, a detective named Robert Thorn (also played by

Charlton Heston), has been assigned to investigate the murder of a prominent board member of the corporation that makes Soylent Green. But things are not as they seem, and eventually Thorn discovers the terrible secret that had led to the executive's murder. Due to the eroding environment, the oceans no longer produce enough plankton to keep up with the demand for Soylent Green production. As a result, the company has resorted to processing the corpses of recently deceased humans, using them as the main component in the Soylent Green product. Thorn is understandably horrified by the discovery and in the closing moments of the movie frantically warns his superior, "Soylent Green is people!"

Some writers have seen in this movie thematic connections to real life that transcend the shock value of the script. Noreena Hertz, for example, has written of the "apocalyptic world of *Soylent Green*," in which "the corporate interests—literally or metaphorically—feed off our carcasses."[21] And although some critics were not impressed—one reviewer said the film was "occasionally frightening but it is rarely convincingly real"[22]—*Soylent Green* does reflect serious concerns of that era, albeit in a somewhat overwrought form.

In one telling scene, for example, a character longs for the days before the United States and the world had descended into its dire state. He laments, "You know, when I was a kid food was food—before our scientific magicians poisoned the water, polluted the soil, decimated plant and animal life."

But as Thorn replies, this was before "a heat wave all year long. Greenhouse effect. Everything is burning up." In such exchanges, the film reveals concerns about ecology and the environment, which were ideas that had picked up considerable social traction, especially in the decade since the birth of the ecological revolution. The general outlook in the film thus has some similarity to ideas expressed by Rachel Carson in her groundbreaking book *Silent Spring* a decade earlier. In that work Carson had written, "Can anyone believe it is possible to lay down such a barrage of poisons on the surface of the earth without making it unfit for all life?"[23]

Importantly, the dangers faced by the United States as depicted in *Soylent Green* are not like those of the 1950s science fiction and Cold War films that it superficially resembles. In movies such as *Invasion of the Body Snatchers* and *Invaders from Mars*, to name two examples, the destruction of the United States and human life more generally requires vigilance to threats emanating from outer space. In other movies, such as *Invasion U.S.A.*, the dangers were of earthly origin, but still from a source (presumed to be the Soviet Union) from outside the United States. *Soylent Green*, however, is an early instance in which the threat of catastrophic American ruin is portrayed not as the result of an external enemy but rather as a consequence of assaults undertaken by internal dynamics—corporate, cultural, and social—that had developed within American life. It was similar to themes that had been embedded within the earlier *Omega Man*, which, as Robin L. Murray and Joseph K. Heumann observed, addressed "both the dangers of technology and biological weapons, clearly illustrating apocalyptic repercussions of exploitative human actions."[24]

More than that, many of the great dangers depicted in the film are exaggerated forms of traits that otherwise would fit innocuously into standard accounts of everyday American life and values. It is the excesses of people's own behavior that are the sources of the problem—the failure to responsibly protect the environment, or to promote presumably sensible limits on population growth (often perceived as a looming disaster in that era), or to control corporate excesses. Said differently, the failure to maintain balance in human affairs and environmental affairs means, in the context of *Soylent Green*, that things that had previously led to the "good life" had ended up veering out of control, thus contributing, ironically, to that good life's destruction.

Beyond the science fiction genre, other types of films also reflected Americans' concerns about the decline of society. One variation on the theme portrayed imminent danger and the destruction of American life from within. *The Parallax View* (1974), for example, is for the most part a contemporary thriller, with a hero who uncovers an evil secret and seeks to expose injustice. But the secret he aims to uncover is not one of simple moral corruption or evildoing on the part of an individual. Such a story would not be an indictment of the American system, but rather a story of an immoral individual choice. By contrast, *The Parallax View* suggests that a more thorough corruption has penetrated the American system, which is here represented by the fictional Parallax Corporation. For as the hero seeks to unravel the story of what appears to be a simple if spectacularly staged murder high atop the Seattle Space Needle, he discovers that not one person or even a few people are to blame. Instead, he learns that an entire corporation—one that is well known and otherwise respectable—is literally in the assassination business. And this is not assassination as a means to achieve some other ends. Assassination is this company's main product. Murder, in other words, has been transformed into a banal commodity.

In another film portraying the idea that corruption had become entwined deep within the institutional structure of American life, director Sydney Pollack's *Three Days of the Condor* (1975) tells the story of a bookish intelligence analyst (played by Robert Redford) who works as a translator in an nondescript CIA office in New York City. One day, the analyst leaves the office for lunch. When he returns, he finds that everyone there has been murdered. Shocked and panicked by this grisly discovery, he calls his CIA superiors to report the news and seek instructions. Soon, however, he comes to realize that someone, or some group, wishes to kill him, also. He then comes to distrust everyone, including the CIA contacts with whom he communicates only by telephone. In the end, the story reveals that the murders are not the result of the United States' external enemies, but rather have been perpetrated by traitorous elements within the CIA itself. In the context of the skeptical and cynical 1970s, this is perhaps not a very surprising plot twist. But when considered in light of the usually reverential treatment of the nation's espionage efforts only 20 years earlier, the story of *Three Days of the Condor* is revealing in how matter-of-factly it offers a scenario about moral collapse from within a major American institution.

In a very different filmmaking vein, Robert Altman's 1975 film *Nashville* presents a picture of more ordinary existence that is also unsettling. The film, which contains long sequences of country music, follows the stories of two dozen characters. Some are people in the country music business, and others are involved political campaigns. The movie thus combines observations about the intersection of politics and the entertainment business in the United States. At times the movie is a wry musical, but at other times it is a dark satire of the United States' view of itself. Altman's overall picture of life in the United States in the era of the nation's bicentennial is not flattering.

Nashville is structured as a series of interlocking narratives. The musical portion of the production features songs with lyrics that both reveal and conceal aspects of life that are not necessarily visible on the surface. Like the glittery entertainment business overall, the songs, as well as other aspects of the film, show that there is a difference between how people appear and how they really are. The elements of the story dealing with the political world are equally revealing and often jaded. Indeed, the film ends on a decidedly downbeat note with the assassination not of a political figure, but of a musical entertainer.

A sense of sadness and mistrust permeates much of the narrative, which is unusual for a musical film. Some writers have since commented on the film's dark portrayal of American life. Lester D. Friedman interprets one scene as depicting the "exposure of the empty American Dream" that can "no longer gaze at this mythless landscape,"[25] for example. In a similar vein, Chris L. Durham noted that Altman's vision of the United States in the movie has a "dystopic narrative structure" that is "defined in terms of polarized communities, a bankrupt political culture, and the threat of random violence."[26] Indeed, it is difficult to imagine this story finding resonance with audiences in an era before the calamities of war, assassination, social protest, and mistrust had severely damaged Americans' confidence in their society and its institutions.

Some observers have taken *Nashville* to represent an even stronger indictment of the traditional United States, which by the mid-1970s appeared to be an idea that, if not broken, was at least one in need of restoration. Along these lines, the film has also been interpreted as an explicit condemnation of then-recent developments in American politics and society. Michael Klein, for example, writes that it depicts "a sympathetic view of people as victims of commercial capitalist-induced cultural dislocation.... [These people are] oppressed by inversions of humane personal values and idealized familial relations of the past."[27] In some ways, *Nashville* suggested that the surface of American life looked prettier than it really was.

A film released the following year, Martin Scorsese's much-admired *Taxi Driver*, dispensed with this positive veneer altogether. Instead, Scorsese's film looks straight on at city life in which decay and moral ruin are very much out in the open. The film arrived in American theaters early in 1976, providing an image of the modern United States that, in its darkness and cynicism, contrasted markedly with the more upbeat portrayal of the nation that was heavily promoted during the year in which the U.S. bicentennial was celebrated. *Taxi Driver* brings together several themes, including some recognition of the Vietnam War, as well as crime themes that had been treated in the vigilante films earlier that decade. Overall, then, *Taxi Driver* explores ideas such as alienation, reactionary responses to urban problems, moral decay, and sexual exploitation, among others.

The main character in the film, Travis Bickle (played by Robert De Niro), is a psychologically scarred Vietnam veteran who drives a New York City taxi all night as a way to cope with life. During his encounters with people of varying races and ages, he becomes fixated on the darker side of city life at the time. Imagining himself as a hero, he acquires a number of guns and then prepares to avenge people he thinks have been victimized by New York thugs and criminals. He is particularly troubled by the plight of a young prostitute, a 12-year-old runaway girl (played by Jodie Foster) who is exploited by a pimp named Sport (played by Harvey Keitel). In the latter part of the film, Travis sets out to right this situation, and over the course of a series of violent scenes he kills the pimp as well as other men who had been exploiting the girl. In the process of carrying out this revenge, Bickle is seriously injured by gunfire. Although at first it seems that Bickle will die, it is then revealed that he has survived. But more than that, he has been dubbed a "hero" by the New York news media and resumed his life as a cab driver.

Scorsese channeled multiple social and film themes in this film. The later sequence of revenge and redemption takes ideas from the revenge films and has some affinity with movies such as *Dirty Harry* and *Death Wish*. Yet, while the earlier films portrayed revenge as cleansing and righteous actions that in some ways restore moral order, the revenge portrayed in *Taxi Driver* is unsettling and cynical. Though Bickle is regarded as a hero by the public, viewers know he is a deeply disturbed and alienated man whose actions are rooted in a disconnect with reality.

Escapism in the Cinema

Despite the many serious films in this era, Hollywood continued to release escapist films, as it had done since the industry's beginnings. And as had been the case in previous eras, some of the most popular movies—and some of those making the biggest impact in popular culture—were of this latter sort. Of these, probably no work from American popular culture in the late 1970s received more attention than the iconic movie *Star Wars* (1977) from director George Lucas. Cloaked in the guise of science fiction, it is a film that reflects many movie-making traditions and is strongly connected to the historical-cultural era in which it was released.

Many commentators have noted the mythic qualities of the story, but in many respects the movie hearkens back to genres that had a powerful past in Hollywood—the Western and the World War II film. Similarities to both kinds of films are evident on many levels, but in terms of placing *Star Wars* in the cultural narrative of the time, the most striking feature that it offered its 1970s audience was moral clarity. Regardless of the futuristic setting, this is a story of a long and difficult war. But it is a war more like World War II than the more recent war in Vietnam. The enemy in *Star Wars* is clearly villainous and evil. The heroes exhibit innate goodness and virtue. The conflict in *Star Wars*, especially in the first movie in what became a protracted series, is therefore clear-cut. There are no questions about who is in the right or about whether the fight is worth the cost. Like Westerns and World War II movies produced prior to the 1960s (and in some cases later), the narrative in *Star Wars* presents an unambiguously moral struggle that does not require the audience to reflect about deeper questions. Thus, as Stephen P. Miller has concluded, *Star Wars* can be interpreted as "a fantastic ideological alternative to Vietnam."[28]

The memories of the recent war in Southeast Asia evoked feelings that were altogether different. Though the bitter years of the Vietnam War had ended several years earlier, downbeat effects of the conflict lingered in the United States. The end of the war had been unceremonious, to say the least.

There had been no celebrations and, indeed, many people seemed eager to avoid thinking or talking about it.

The peace accords that the United States negotiated with North Vietnam did allow for the withdrawal of troops in early 1973, effectively concluding the war for the United States. But in Vietnam the fight was not over. It continued two more years without American troops. Then, in 1975, the government of South Vietnam fell. In the end, therefore, the battle that the United States had invested in so deeply was lost. And so Americans came to see the war in Vietnam as an American failure, even though the country had exited before that outcome had arrived. This feeling of loss—the disturbing thought that perhaps the whole involvement in Vietnam had been in vain— was very troubling to Americans. This stood in marked contrast to the feeling of jubilation only 30 years earlier that emerged with victory at the end of World War II. The perceived loss in Vietnam had an impact on American morale. It was not an easy idea for Americans to accept. The outcome was thus a major blow to American self-confidence. Indeed, by 1978 many Americans regretted American involvement in the war that had ended so badly from their perspective. A poll conducted by the Chicago Council of Foreign Relations, for example, found that 72 percent of respondents believe that the war had been both a mistake and a moral error.[29]

Hollywood and the Vietnam War

Hollywood had not directly confronted the Vietnam War to any significant degree when it was ongoing. Indeed, the war received very little attention from Hollywood during the years of fighting. Aside from the 1968 movie *The Green Berets*, which portrayed the war in a positive light and which starred and was codirected by the staunchly anti-Communist John Wayne, few other films touched directly on the subject.

However, the war was in the background of many film narratives of the era. One example of that was the 1971 film *Billy Jack*, which was directed and cowritten by its star, Tom Laughlin. It tells the story of an unconventional hero, a man of Native American and European ancestry, who is a Vietnam veteran and skilled in combat. Billy Jack, the main character, uses his abilities to fight for vaguely counterculture causes. The movie thus treats the Vietnam War as backstory rather than addressing it as a main subject. Even the 1975 *Taxi Driver* treated the war as something in the past without touching on the subject very directly.

Overall, Hollywood's avoidance of the Vietnam conflict in the 1960s and early 1970s was in marked contrast to its active treatment of wartime themes during World War II. Of course, a critical difference between the two conflicts was that the earlier war had the overwhelmingly support of the American people, whereas the war in Vietnam had come to be seen as a symbol of division and dubious wisdom.

Finally, in the mid- to late 1970s, more Hollywood films about the war in Vietnam started to appear. But the vision of the war experience that was initially portrayed reflected this doubtful, sometimes bitter mood. Michael Cimino's movie *The Deer Hunter* (1978), for example, tells the story of three men (played by Christopher Walken, Robert De Niro, and John Savage). They were friends with a strong bond. They had been prisoners of war together in Vietnam. After they return home, their lives are haunted by their war experiences. Violent scenes in the film reveal the psychological and physical brutality and terror that they had endured. Probably the most famous scene in the film shows the men as prisoner-of-war captives, living like caged animals in primitive swampy surroundings. The men have been dehumanized and are at times playthings for their captors. At one point, an unnerving scene shows how they were forced to play a deadly game of Russian roulette simply for their captors' amusement.

Back home in rural Pennsylvania sometime later, they try to return to some sense of normalcy in the small mill town where they live and work. But it is difficult. The three men have each been changed by their wartime experiences, both mentally and physically. One man, for example, is fixated on taking death-defying risks, and another has lost his legs.

Although the Vietnam War plays a major role in the film, the politics and morality of the conflict—elements of the war that had caused so much dissent and controversy in the previous decade—are not much evident. A review in *New York* magazine noted that the movie was not about the American experience of the Vietnam War as a whole, but rather simply about the lives of the three main characters. But in making this point, the writer asked a question that was on the minds of many Americans at the time: "How could there be a central story on that bewildering catastrophe?"[30]

Some people were upset that a film dealing with the war did not address, in ways they found satisfactory, the overarching moral issues that the war had raised. Some writers interpret the film in a broader way. Stephen P. Miller's conclusion is a common one. In his view, *The Deer Hunter* portrays "America's terrible psychological vulnerability in the wake of the Vietnam War."[31] In its era, the film was critically praised. It won the award for Best Picture at the Academy Awards. But outside the Academy Awards ceremony in April 1979, a group of demonstrators from Vietnam Veterans Against the War protested outside the event.[32]

Other films from the era touched upon the Vietnam War in various ways. For example, director Hal Ashby's *Coming Home*, also released in 1978, deals with a disabled Vietnam War veteran's troubled life after the war. Like *The Deer Hunter*, it was well received and seemed to indicate a new willingness to talk about the conflict that had divided families and generations 10 years earlier.

In the following year, Francis Ford Coppola's film *Apocalypse Now* was released to much advance notice. Coppola based his film's story on the Joseph Conrad novella *Heart of Darkness*, which had been published 70 years earlier, and on Michael Herr's popular book *Dispatches*, which was directly based on his Vietnam War experiences. Working with a script that combined these elements, Coppola produced a film that was an expansive, abstract epic that presented the war as a confusing event and that lacked clear-cut heroes and villains.

The film's narrative focuses on the secret mission of Capt. Benjamin Willard (played by Martin Sheen). The young American officer has been ordered to make his way up river, deep into the jungle, where he is to find and kill—"terminate with extreme prejudice," as one character says—an American officer, Kurtz (played by Marlon Brando), who has apparently gone mad and is carrying out violent, unauthorized missions. As Willard makes his way deeper into the jungle, hitching a ride on a PT boat and enlisting the aid of the air cavalry to help him along the way in his clandestine mission, events become increasingly bizarre and surreal. The violence seems random and extreme, even in the context of war.

Willard encounters some scenarios that are so dreamlike—or perhaps more accurately, nightmare-like—that they seem hallucinogenic. One of the many such examples is a scene depicting an impromptu entertainment extravaganza staged in a remote region in enemy territory. In another instance, a surfing display is arranged in a hostile area that has just been the scene of a fierce battle. Through it all, Willard seems to become increasingly disconnected from the bizarre circumstances around him.

As he makes his way closer and closer to the remote area where Kurtz has established a base, Willard becomes increasingly troubled. Kurtz has persuaded the local population that he is a near godlike figure and has convinced them to follow his violent and seemingly irrational orders. These frequently involve brutal displays of violence with no clear purpose. By the time the film ends, the story seems primitive and elemental. The narrative no longer appears to be connected to anything resembling the actual war in Vietnam in which it is set. Willard has seemingly followed Kurtz into madness.

Initial reaction to *Apocalypse Now* was decidedly mixed. The film, coming from the director who had delivered the acclaimed *The Godfather* only a few years earlier, had been eagerly anticipated. This prompted many people to have elevated expectations about what the film would be. At first, it appeared that Coppola had not presented a film that matched these expectations, probably because his vision had veered so far from the traditional war narrative that many viewers presumed they would see. A Harris poll conducted for the Veterans Administration, for example, found very divided opinion about how American soldiers were depicted in the film, with 40 percent finding the portrayal to be favorable, but 44 percent finding it to be unfavorable.[33]

Uncertainty about the film persisted with some people well after its release. One writer, Frank P. Tomasulo, claimed that Coppola had tried to "have it both ways."[34] He further suggested, "The narrative goes out of its way to justify the actions of Colonel Kurtz."[35] Such responses to the film—and especially to the manner in which the story slowly evolves from a narrative about a specific historical situation into a perhaps more universal commentary on the madness of war—do not need to be accepted or rejected in order to appreciate the film's importance as a milestone of American culture in the late 1970s. The fact that the story may be saying that the Vietnam War was not something a person could make sense of is perhaps closer to what many Americans actually felt about it at the time than has sometimes been acknowledged.

Indeed, many people had come to see the war as a major American failure. They were unaccustomed to such an outcome. Losing the war was a psychologically difficult result. And if World War II had "the good war"—a war perceived with moral clarity and that ended with a decisive U.S. victory—then the war in Vietnam was the opposite of those things to many people. In Vietnam, American power had not been able to defeat a tiny enemy, albeit one that had been supplied by the Soviet Union. And the troubles of the 1960s revealed very clearly that if the conflict had moral clarity, it was not the sort of moral clarity about which people widely agreed. Thus, if *Apocalypse Now* was a story that seemed to make sense at the beginning and increasingly seemed bizarre and ambiguous by the end, this was actually quite close, metaphorically, to how many people already saw the conflict.

Apocalypse Now reveals the dampened, dimmed view that many Americans, in varying degrees, had come to have about their nation's recent experience. Perhaps some people had expected Coppola to produce a post–Vietnam War film that would have been the contemporary equivalent of the many World War II films that had been produced (and were still being produced) after that conflict. Those films had been largely reassuring, showing the United States as a moral leader whose triumph was achieved at the cost of heroic sacrifice. Most of the World War II films confirmed the same ideals upon which the American Dream had been realized in the decades following the war. But Coppola's work does not affirm anything of the sort. Indeed, it blurs heroes and villains and calls into question whether the conflict in Southeast Asia, which had claimed over 58,000 American lives, had been worth the trouble.

Cinematic Doubts about the United States in Other Genres

In a more general sense, throughout the later 1970s many American films portrayed negative aspects of society and the decline of American Dream ideals. In *The Stepford Wives* (1975), for example, director Bryan Forbes tells the story of life in an idyllic, suburban Connecticut town, steeped in the appearance of American Dream ideals. In fact, time seems to have passed over this community in many ways. The men go to work, while the women are housewives who cheerfully conform to stereotypical and sexist expectations that resemble assumptions from a generation earlier. They cook and clean, and their lives are generally organized around the goal of pleasing their husbands. The twist to the story, of course, is that the "wives" are robots.

A seemingly unrelated 1975 film is director Paul Bartel's *Death Race 2000*, the cast of which included Sylvester Stallone and David Carradine. It depicts the United States in the future, in which financial collapse has resulted in the United States' transformation into a fascist state. To pacify the population, the nation's totalitarian government stages something akin to a modern-day gladiatorial contest, here in the form of a transcontinental automobile race. But this is no ordinary race. To win the hugely popular spectacle, the battling race car drivers not only must achieve the fastest speed, they also must hit and kill as many pedestrians as they can in the process. The event thus pacifies a mass audience by killing ordinary people at random. The film is another movie in which American society has collapsed, with whatever remains benefiting only the very few.

In 1978, the science fiction classic *Invasion of the Body Snatchers* (the original was released in 1956) was updated in a popular remake by director Philip Kaufman. The story of pod people slowly replacing humans, which was depicted in the earlier film, was retained. In the context of the late 1970s, however, the story seems not so much an allegory for potential Communist invasion, as it had in the 1950s, as a commentary on "feelings of contemporary urban mistrust."[36]

The China Syndrome (1979) is a very different kind of film, but its negative slant on some aspects of American society is similar. Director James Bridges's film tells of a potentially disastrous accident at a nuclear power plant and about the great lengths that the company running that facility will go to in order to keep the truth from coming out about it. The narrative therefore focuses on the intent of corporate and elite elements of society to deceive and possibly victimize ordinary Americans.

The deviousness of large corporate interests is a central part of the story in *Alien* (1979), which was directed by Ridley Scott. Set in the future on a spaceship, a key element of the narrative revolves around how the company financing an apparently routine expedition has withheld the real purposes of the mission and the extreme danger that the crew faces. It soon becomes apparent that the company regards the crew as expendable and that it has even planted a robotic spy on board to make sure crew members do not interfere with the company's effort to secure an alien life form, which the firm hopes to adapt to military purposes. Overall, then, the film reinforces ideas that corporations do not necessarily have the best interests of their employees in mind and, more generally, that they can be extremely untrustworthy.

These films, which are only a few examples of films with a similar impulse, all contain other thematic elements in addition to their apparent background commentary on American Dream ideals as perceived in the latter half of the 1970s. But the cynicism and apparent crisis in faith about these ideals is far from hidden. For a decade that had seen the nation's apparent failure in war, shocking corruption in government, and the faltering of the economy, this was perhaps not surprising.

AMERICAN POLITICS IN THE CARTER YEARS

As might be gleaned from Hollywood's output at the time, in the latter years of the decade the nation was searching for an answer to the doubt and uncertainty that had intruded into American life. After voters ousted Gerald Ford from the presidency in 1976, Jimmy Carter had tried to spearhead an American renewal. Indeed, as early as his inaugural address of January 1977, he announced lofty goals for his presidency. Seeking a better life for Americans at home and a more secure world abroad he said, "These are not just my goals, but our common hopes. And they will not be my accomplishments, but the affirmation of our nation's continuing moral strength and our belief in an undiminished, ever-expanding American Dream."[37]

Yet, within a few months, Carter had encountered continuing fallout from the crises that had preceded his presidency. Hedrick Smith, a *New York Times* writer, described an April 1977 speech delivered by the president as "the unmistakable message that the time has come for some elemental transformation in the American way of life."[38] In this instance, Carter had proposed that Americans begin to limit their use of automobiles and confront a long-term energy problem. This was not a new thought, of course, since the oil crisis of 1973 had exposed the potential consequences of the United States' dependency on foreign oil. Still, the automobile was a potent symbol of American success and freedom, and suggestions to place limits on or reduce its use were politically sensitive. As Hedrick Smith also wrote, Carter's suggestion appeared to challenge "what some people regard as one element of the American Dream."[39]

Meanwhile, little progress was made in the campaign against drug abuse. While public disapproval of illicit-drug use remained strong, by this time there was little doubt that drugs were regarded as a fact of life in the modern United States. Still, officials were in a quandary as to how to address the problem.

Many ideas were floated as public leaders struggled to find an approach that would work. In 1977, for example, Senator Sam Nunn (a Georgia Democrat) and Senator Charles Percy (an Illinois Republican) took the unusual step of requesting the Pentagon to become involved in the war on drugs. In the view of newspaper writers Jack Anderson and Les Whitten, "The sheer magnitude of the drug problem has led the [Senate] subcommittee to seek drastic countermeasures."[40] Thus, as drug use persisted, so too did increasingly harsh rhetoric about it. By this time, the drug problem was viewed as more than only a drug problem. Many people, especially those with traditional values, saw it as a major symptom of American moral decline.

The American economy continued to face challenges, as well. A 1978 survey conducted by David Caplovitz at the Graduate School of the City University of New York concluded that more than a third responded that they no longer had faith in the American Dream and that they expected their standard of living would be lower.[41]

A New Crisis

Yet despite these many challenges to his presidency on the domestic front, the most significant crisis that confronted Carter did not come until late in his term. On November 4, 1979, a group of Islamic revolutionaries attacked the U.S. embassy in Tehran, the capital of Iran. Earlier that year, militants had overthrown the government and deposed the dictator Mohammad Reza Pahlavi, who was widely disliked by the Iranian people, but had been a reliable U.S. ally for decades. After years of perceived oppression, however, religious revolutionaries, under the guidance of Ayatollah Khomeini, swept the Shah and his regime from power, setting the stage for a long confrontation with the West.

As a result of the siege on the American embassy, 52 American citizens were taken captive. The resulting ordeal, known as the Iranian hostage crisis, focused Americans' attention on the plight of the prisoners. The Carter administration struggled to resolve the situation. With other avenues yielding few results, a secret mission to free the hostages was approved. In late April 1980, Operation Eagle Claw was launched, with the hope that American military personnel could swoop into Tehran and remove the hostages to safety.

The mission went horribly wrong. The operation called for the use of helicopters to deliver American military personnel and transport the hostages. But Tehran was a long way away from where the mission was to originate, on an aircraft carrier. This required a refueling stop in a prearranged spot. And although all but one of the helicopters arrived safely at the refueling location, at a remote makeshift airstrip, a sandstorm contributed to the development of mechanical problems. Then, during refueling, one of the helicopters crashed into an American C-130 tanker aircraft. Eight soldiers died and others were wounded. This setback was too severe to overcome, and the operation was aborted.

When news of the failed rescue attempt was revealed, the damage to the United States' reputation was significant. In probably the highest-stakes military operation since the Vietnam War, the United States had failed. Carter's political fortunes fell dramatically. A presidential address in late April, in which Carter attempted to explain and justify the failed operation, did little to stop his political reputation from sliding further.

As the 1980 presidential election approached, the mood of malaise and diminished national confidence seemed further heightened by the lingering Iran hostage crisis. Campaigning against this mood, almost in a throwback to the swagger that had been more evident two decades earlier, came the figure of Ronald Reagan. He was not only a former governor of California but also a Hollywood actor of considerable fame. Reagan championed traditional conservative values and advocated renewed national pride. His message resonated with many voters.

In the November 1980 election, Reagan easily defeated Jimmy Carter. Although other factors played a role, Carter's failure to secure the release of the hostages in Iran surely aided Reagan's cause. As if to add insult to injury, Iran released the American hostages on the very day that Reagan assumed the presidency on January 20, 1981.

Perhaps Jimmy Carter summed up the mood of the nation best in his farewell address to the nation made during his final days in office. His words reflected, in part, a bittersweet appraisal of where the nation stood and where the path it was on might lead. These words from his address point to the choices the United States faced at that time:

We live in a time of transition, an uneasy era which is likely to endure for the rest of this century. During the period we may be tempted to abandon some of the time-honored principles and commitments which have been proven during the difficult times of past generations. We must never yield to this temptation. Our American values are not luxuries, but necessities—not the salt in our bread, but the bread itself.[42]

Once again, the United States appeared to be at a crossroads. And whether the American Dream ideals, upon which the post–World War II nation had been built, would continue or instead unravel remained an unknown.

CHAPTER 8

Shimmering Façade

Ronald Reagan was swept into office proclaiming a positive message about the United States. He promoted a view that hearkened back to the traditional American values that were often articulated a generation earlier, before the upheaval of the 1960s and 1970s. As he assumed the presidency, a new spirit was in the air. This positive, unabashedly American mood was a reawakening that would eventually be called "morning in America." Indeed, the Reagan years were an era that many people saw as a time of renewal and newfound optimism in the American story.

Yet the skepticism and cynicism that had become intertwined in the American psyche remained present. And an apprehensive strand in the American narrative, which had been a subtext in U.S. culture throughout the post–World War II era, lurked in the background, albeit it in continually transforming manifestations. In this subtext, visions of ruin and the end of the American Dream persisted in various guises, gnawing at the reemerging self-confidence that often took center stage.

As Reagan championed a new confidence in the nation, violence made occasional appearances in the political sphere. In some ways this was reminiscent of the 1960s. Reagan was in office only a few weeks when a young man named John Hinckley attempted to assassinate him outside a hotel in Washington, DC. The president suffered a serious gunshot wound, and three others were also injured. It was not a politically motivated attack. Instead, the would-be assassin appears to have modeled the attack on the character of Travis Bickle from *Taxi Driver* a few years earlier.

The incident was not the last time that assassination plots would be in the news during the 1980s. The following year, a gunman attempted to assassinate Pope John Paul II in Vatican City, causing him serious injury. The same year, a deranged gunman murdered musician John Lennon, who had risen to fame in the 1960s as a member of the Beatles, outside a New York apartment building. The public recovered from the shock of these episodes, but such incidents reveal the lingering violence that occasionally punctuated public life.

The Reagan era was sometimes plagued by violence in other incarnations, as well. In 1983, during the years of the Lebanese civil wars, a multinational peacekeeping force, including an American contingent, was stationed near Beirut. On October 23 of that year, suicide bombers detonated huge truck bombs that destroyed barracks housing American and French troops. The death toll for the U.S. soldiers was high, totaling 241. Dozens more were injured.

In 1985, another violent incident alarmed the West. Islamist extremists hijacked TWA flight 847, which was traveling from Athens to Rome. Several passengers were beaten. A 23-year-old American navy diver, who was traveling on the flight, was singled out and tortured. The hijackers killed the sailor and tossed his body onto the airport tarmac to the horror of Americans who were following the unfolding spectacle in the news media.

A few months after the TWA hijacking, armed men commandeered an Italian cruise ship that was sailing in the Mediterranean Sea. The attackers claimed ties to the Palestinian Liberation Front and took the crew and passengers hostage. Their goal was to secure the release of fellow Palestinians who were then imprisoned in Israel. During the ordeal, the hijackers killed an elderly Jewish passenger, an American tourist named Leon Klinghoffer. They then threw his body overboard. The victim was 69 years old, disabled, and confined to a wheelchair. His brutal murder disgusted and alarmed Americans. Although the hijackers were ultimately unsuccessful and settled for secure passage to Tunisia for themselves, it was yet another episode of violence precipitated by the tense politics of the Middle East.

Indeed, the Middle East was proving to be a place where projections of American power seemed unpredictable. And U.S. policies appeared unable to bring about the results that Washington leaders sought to obtain. The United States continued to have a major voice in regional conflicts, but American influence proved to be of little use in stabilizing the region, as later events would make clear.

RENEWED COLD WAR

Throughout his presidency, Reagan revived Cold War rhetoric. His attitude about the Soviet Union was clear. To him, the Soviet system was "a Godless tyranny."[1] The invocation of the atheist label, combined with his description of the USSR as morally evil, renewed much of the deeply polarizing language from the days of the Cold War three decades earlier. This view of the Soviet Union breathed new life into the otherwise fading idea that the United States was engaged in an all-out moral struggle with a despicable enemy.

As Reagan and other leading neoconservatives railed against the USSR, some of the harsh rhetoric was no doubt based in a genuine perception that the Soviets remained a dangerous threat and should not be taken lightly by an American public that seemed more interested in domestic matters than in foreign policy. But some of Reagan's zeal in promoting a new awareness of the Communist threat was probably based in his already-stated desire to move the nation beyond the "Vietnam Syndrome." This was Reagan's term for the sullen, withdrawn mood that Americans seemed to have with regard to U.S. engagement in the world in the post–Vietnam War years. To Reagan and like-minded Republicans, this Vietnam Syndrome was thwarting American policy, dampening the American spirit, and undermining the nation's authority on the world stage.

As early as 1983, Reagan enthusiastically endorsed the idea of using new technologies in a planned Strategic Defense Initiative. The goal of such a plan was to develop a system that would act as a protective umbrella for the United States by providing the U.S. with the defense capability of destroying incoming missiles in midair, before they could reach American targets. The plan was cutting edge and one version of it involved high-powered lasers. But many scientists were skeptical that it could be made to work. The popular press began to refer to the scheme as "Star Wars," a reference to George Lucas's 1977 hit film. (Lucas protested the use of the term in this way.) Regardless of whether or not it was a realistic plan, controversy about the Strategic Defense Initiative demonstrated that the president of the United States regarded the Soviet Union as much more than simply a rhetorical threat.

Reagan was a skilled speaker, even gaining the popular nickname of the "Great Communicator" during his days in the Oval Office. His plain manner of speaking projected an aura of authority and trust. Some of his communication skills were undoubtedly the result of his years as a Hollywood actor. But there can be little doubt that he firmly believed in what he was saying. People sensed a man with straightforward conviction, and when Reagan spoke, he gained attention.

Some particularly telling comments about his view of the Soviets were delivered in Orlando, Florida, where Reagan spoke to a gathering of the National Association of Evangelicals in 1983. In these remarks, he presented a dire picture of the state of relations with the Soviet Union:

> So, in your discussions of the nuclear freeze proposals, I urge you to beware the temptation of pride, the temptation of blithely declaring yourselves above it all and label both sides equally at fault, to ignore the facts of history and the aggressive impulses of an evil empire, to simply call the arms race a giant misunderstanding and thereby remove yourself from the struggle between right and wrong and good and evil.[2]

Reagan's comments were an unambiguous declaration of how Reagan viewed the USSR. It was not simply an adversary or rival. It was an "evil empire." In expressing such views, Reagan was not so much presenting new ideas as he was resurrecting and updating much of the Cold War rhetoric that had held sway in American political culture in the anxious days of the 1950s. And when viewed in light of his description of the USSR as a "godless tyranny," it is apparent that Reagan viewed the Cold War with the Soviet Union though a lens of morality.

As Reagan and other leaders in the United States were ramping up rhetorical conflict with the Soviet Union, the USSR was experiencing major internal challenges. Since 1979, the Soviets had become involved in a long and costly military campaign in Afghanistan, where the national government was under attack. Soviet leader Leonid Brezhnev, who had focused on military expansion since he assumed leadership of the USSR in the mid-1960s, was eager to shore up the besieged pro-Soviet government in Kabul. He promptly dispatched Soviet troops to Afghanistan to help quell the insurgency.

Unfortunately for Brezhnev, however, the Soviets had no better luck intervening in Afghanistan than had previous foreign forces. Although some stability was achieved in urban areas, control of the rugged countryside remained contested. The USSR quickly became bogged down in a fight that eventually grew to be unpopular among Soviet citizens.

The Soviet military incursion into Afghanistan had been strongly advocated by Yuri Andropov, who rose to power upon the death of Brezhnev in 1982. But Andropov apparently became disillusioned with the military campaign's lack of progress. Afghanistan was becoming a substantial drain on

Soviet resources and further exacerbated deteriorating domestic conditions that had been years in the making.

Throughout this time, Soviet relations with the United States remained tenuous. Reagan's "evil empire" declaration at this time demonstrated that this mistrust was not narrowing. Meanwhile, the USSR faced mounting internal problems, in addition to foreign policy setbacks. Andropov terminated plans for the weapons systems that had precipitated the "Star Wars" fears in the United States, but the overall political climate between the two superpowers mostly remained tense.

The icy situation was not yet ready to thaw. An incident in 1983 elevated concerns. In that episode, a Soviet fighter jet shot down a Korean passenger jetliner, flight KAL 007, which the USSR claimed had flown over Soviet airspace. Over 250 people were killed in the crash, including a member of the U.S. House of Representatives. The Soviets claimed that the aircraft was involved in an espionage mission, and for a time the two nations were at a diplomatic standoff over the incident.

In the following year, Andropov died while still in office. Konstantin Chernenko became the new Soviet leader, but he also died. All the while, the war in Afghanistan was becoming increasingly burdensome, and the Soviet economy was under duress. (By 1988, the Soviet position in Afghanistan was clearly unsustainable. The USSR started a gradual military withdrawal that was completed by the following year.)

Despite displaying bellicosity in many international situations, the Soviet Union was already showing signs of strains from within, and it was increasingly unable to enforce its authority over nations within its orbit. The most obvious example of the latter situation was Poland, where the Solidarity trade union developed into a potent political movement that directly challenged Communist rule and Soviet influence. With its charismatic leader, Lech Walesa, Solidarity exerted a powerful anti-Moscow influence throughout parts of the Soviet sphere.

Mikhail Gorbachev had assumed leadership of the USSR after Chernenko's death in 1985. Gorbachev was a realist, and eventually he developed a personal rapport with Ronald Reagan. The Soviet leader ushered in policies that were startlingly new for the USSR. The key reforms that he promoted were *perestroika*—restructuring the Soviet system—and *glasnost*—transparency and openness in governance. Such policies paved the way for the eventual demise of Communist rule and the dissolution of the USSR in 1991.

New Soviet policies also signaled the coming end of the Cold War. In 1987, the end of this era was foreshadowed in words spoken by Ronald

Reagan during a visit to West Berlin: "General Secretary Gorbachev, if you seek peace, if you seek prosperity for the Soviet Union and Eastern Europe, if you seek liberalization: Come here to this gate. Mr. Gorbachev, open this gate. Mr. Gorbachev, tear down this wall."[3]

The Iran-Contra Affair

The biggest controversy of the Reagan years was the Iran-Contra scandal, which was intimately related to the president's perceptions about the seriousness of the 1980s incarnation of the Cold War. In that era, a pro-Soviet government held power in the tiny Central American nation of Nicaragua. Although Cuba was the most notable irritant in the hemisphere, the United States had long looked unfavorably at any Soviet influence in the Americas. Reagan was particularly disturbed by what appeared to be a flaunting of Communist influence in what he perceived as the backyard of the United States.

Given the president's attitude about the situation, it was not surprising that the administration was eager to assist rebel forces, known as the contras, who sought to bring down the Nicaraguan government of socialist Daniel Ortega. Reagan called these rebels "freedom fighters."

But the options were limited. Congressional leaders, like many U.S. citizens, were still wary of foreign entanglements. The memory of the failed American experience in Vietnam was still too fresh, and so restrictions were placed on what would be allowed. With these legal impediments, the administration was unable to directly fund the contras. To maneuver around these restrictions, a circuitous plan was devised to secretly send aid to the contras indirectly, using a third party as an intermediary to supposedly get around the legal restrictions.

As it happened, at about the same time a small group of Americans were being held hostage by extremists with ties to Iran. The Reagan administration—anxious to secure the release of the hostages—made a decision to attempt secret negotiations with the hope the captives would be set free. The clandestine nature of the discussions was partly due to the sensitivity of such situations, but it also obscured details of the negotiations, which, if made public, would have been embarrassing for the administration since Reagan had publicly vowed never to negotiate with terrorists.

Eventually, a deal was finalized. The United States arranged for Iran to acquire missiles that would come from Israel's arsenal of American weapons. (The United States was to replace Israel's missiles, but those that were sent to Iran would technically not be property of the United States.) In the proposed transaction, cash would change hands unofficially, and the Iranians would press the terrorists to release the hostages. It was a convoluted scheme, but one that essentially was an "arms for hostages" deal of the type Reagan had publicly disavowed as an option. But the plan was put into effect and eventually the hostages were released.

As these events were unfolding, Lt. Col. Oliver North, a National Security Council staff member who was then stationed in the White House, devised a new plan. He concluded that the funds were already changing hands through a third party. He reasoned that these funds, which were not technically in the United States' possession, could be diverted and instead sent directly to the contras in Central America. According to this reasoning, the administration could secure funding for the contras while seemingly, in a technical sense, not violating the Boland Amendment, which specifically forbade the administration from funding the contras.

North subsequently put the plan into action, while apparently being quite vague about it to other people in the White House, at least according to some later testimony. In any case, the Iran-Contra affair brought together the United States' political difficulties in the Middle East and its renewed Cold War apprehensions. It does not appear to have been very successful in addressing either concern, however.

For a time, the entire set of transactions remained secret. Since it was out of view, there was no opportunity for questions about it to emerge. That changed in 1986, however, when a Lebanese publication made some details about the arms deal public. From that point forward, increasing revelations fell into public view. And as more information became known, the situation developed into a major political crisis for the White House.

The scandal that erupted culminated in dramatic congressional inquiries, which were televised in the summer of 1987. These high-profile hearings made a media star of the besieged Oliver North, whose patriotic demeanor was appealing to many Americans. The controversy, which resulted in federal trials for some of those involved, proved to be a deeply polarizing episode and a political scar on the administration's record. For his part, however, Reagan later claimed to have not been aware of the full details, and his reputation recovered as memory of the crisis faded.

HOLLYWOOD AND THE FINAL DAYS OF THE COLD WAR

As conservatism was reenergized during the Reagan years, many Hollywood films similarly extolled traditional American virtue and a triumphant spirit, albeit with a shiny 1980s veneer. This era in Hollywood was also marked, as Chris Jordan notes, by "a return to principles of bottom-line conservatism in movie-production practices and record-setting profits for the filmed entertainment industry. . . : [and to] its production of movies that resonated within the culture of conservative backlash promoted by Reagan."[4]

Much of Hollywood's output during this time reflected these trends, though not necessarily consciously on the part of filmmakers. Yet many of the most popular films were consistent with a traditionalist perspective, updated to appeal to contemporary 1980s audiences. For example, *Raiders of the Lost Ark* (1980) and its sequels, *Indiana Jones and the Temple of Doom* (1984) and *Indiana Jones and the Last Crusade* (1989), were unabashed throwbacks to adventure films of the 1930s and 1940s. Series hero Indiana Jones (played by Harrison Ford) is a swashbuckling archaeology professor (surely an unlikely combination) whose quest for ancient artifacts is presented in an adventurous, almost innocent way. The film somewhat glosses over a potentially dubious colonial ideology. And many of the indigenous peoples of non-Western cultures that Jones encounters are portrayed as primitive and superstitious.

The three Indiana Jones films from the 1980s (as well as the much later 2008 sequel, *Indiana Jones and the Kingdom of the Crystal Skull*) tell their stories from a distinctly American point of view and in ways that extoll American virtue. *Raiders of the Lost Arc* established this tone for the series by resurrecting Nazis as the primary enemy, a choice that removed any possibility that the audience would hold sympathy for the villains or see the conflict of the narrative as possessing any moral ambiguity. The film therefore comfortably fits within a way of viewing the world in terms of stark moral choice between good and evil, a perspective consistent with the dichotomous manner in which Reagan saw the then-contemporary world.

The revival of Cold War rhetoric from Washington coincided with new productions from Hollywood that brought back and updated Cold War themes very directly. And like the films in this vein from the late 1940s and 1950s, these new works envisioned the United States engaged in a bitter struggle against a thoroughly evil foe. These movies had stories in which the stakes were high. The battles depicted in these stories were not only for the survival of the American way of life but also for the very soul of the nation.

One such film was the 1984 movie *Red Dawn*, from director John Milius. The movie features a cast of 1980s box office favorites, including Patrick Swayze, Charlie Sheen, Lea Thompson, C. Thomas Howell, and Jennifer Grey. *Red Dawn* is perhaps the most blatant Hollywood film steeped in the newly reinvigorated Cold War of the Reagan era. The movie centers on American youths as they battle invading Communist forces in the heartland of the United States. As World War III appears under way, these young students engage in a counterinsurgency against seasoned troops from the USSR and its allies. Many Americans have already fallen victim to the invaders. In one scene, an enemy soldier takes the weapon of a dead American civilian, who is lying on the ground near a vehicle with a bumper sticker that reads: "They can have my gun when they pry it from my cold dead fingers."[5]

Most of the film follows the story of the group of young Americans, who quickly become a formidable threat to invading Soviet troops. But they are vastly outnumbered, and much of the United States has already succumbed to Communist control. Those who resist the Communists are variously sentenced to "reeducation" camps, subjected to torture, or killed. The Soviet invasion is therefore apocalyptic in tone and quickly threatens to cause the United States' total collapse and ruin.

The young American students at the center of the story heroically resist, but their valor can achieve only limited results against the onslaught of the brutal Communist invaders who have destroyed their world. Although a scene at the very end of the film implies that after a period of time, the United States would eventually repel the invasion, it is nonetheless clear that this was not to happen until destruction and sacrifice had first pushed the nation to the brink of oblivion. An inscription from a future time, which is read aloud by a surviving character in the closing moments of the movie, tells the story: "In the early days of World War III, guerillas, mostly children, placed the names of their lost upon this rock. They fought here alone and gave up their lives, so that this nation shall not perish form the earth."

Red Dawn is not a subtle film, and much of the story and action that it portrays stretches credulity. Yet it does reflect the renewed perception, strongly held by some Americans at the time, that the Soviet Union remained a powerful and truly evil enemy, despite widespread thinking among other Americans that the Communist threat had significantly lessened.

Details in the film's narrative reveal ways in which the threat to the United States had evolved by the 1980s. In the movie, Cuban and Nicaraguan troops assist the USSR. They have crossed the border from Mexico (which Communists had already toppled) "like ordinary illegal aliens," as critic David Denby wrote in a *New York* magazine review.[6] Moreover, as Denby also notes, the film "stretches right-wing paranoia into masochistic wish fulfillment. Battered but still proud, America stands alone, surrounded by hostile forces, ... betrayed by most of its allies."[7]

In a related way, during the 1980s Hollywood issued new films in which the Vietnam War figured prominently. These tended to be very different responses to that conflict from the works produced in the previous decade.

Some of the most well known of such productions reflect the reemergence of Cold War attitudes and patriotic renewal that coincided with the Reagan era. The most prominent films of the 1970s with a Vietnam War theme had emphasized a perspective in which the war was confusing and ambiguous and had been a damaging experience for the American troops who had served there. That way of thinking about the war, however, contrasted sharply with the way in which Reagan and other neoconservatives envisioned it. Reagan, after all, had proclaimed that the war in Vietnam was not a mistake at all but rather a "noble cause."

Actor-director Sylvester Stallone tapped into Reagan-era patriotism and the seemingly renewed Cold War with the Soviets in several films from 1980s. The two movies involving Stallone that most clearly exhibit a Hollywood version of this political spirit, both from mid-decade, are *Rocky IV* (1985) and *Rambo: First Blood, Part II* (1985). Although the characters and plots of the two films are different, each has a story that emphasizes the bold, unapologetically American worldview that was popular in the era.

Stallone's greatest popular successes have been in largely formulaic films that reduce, even more than most Hollywood films, the world into clear-cut morality. Such was the case in *Rocky IV*, an entry into the already popular series of films that focused on the uphill struggles of a boxer named Rocky Balboa. The typical Rocky story portrays the character as a simple, but hard-working and good man, who seems to face overwhelming odds as he strives for success in his sport.

In *Rocky IV*, which Stallone directed, the boxer finds himself doing battle with a fearsome Soviet boxer named Ivan Drago (played by Dolph Lundgren). Drago has defeated Rocky's friend Apollo Creed (Carl Weathers) in a match so vicious that Creed subsequently dies of injuries. This motivates Rocky to accept a match against Drago to avenge Creed's death. The bout between Rocky and Drago is scheduled in the Soviet Union, and the entire affair is portrayed in a way to emphasize the rivalry between not only the boxers but also the nations they represent. There is little subtlety in the nationalistic flavor that is woven into the movie. For example, Rocky blatantly wears the colors and stripes of the American flag in the pivotal scene.

Unsurprisingly, given the structure of the narrative, it appears that the Soviet boxer is, if not cheating, then at least stretching the limits of fairness as he trains. By the story's climax, the odds have been stacked against Rocky. But in the end, he is victorious, of course. His valor and skill even seem to win over the very partisan Soviet onlookers. In a way the film mirrors conservative foreign policy inclinations of the 1980s, which argued for standing up to the Soviets, with the view that presenting a strong front would surely cause the USSR to back down, yielding results in international affairs that were aligned with American interests.

Rambo: First Blood, Part II (often called simply *Rambo II*), directed by George P. Cosmatos from a script by Stallone and James Cameron, places Stallone in a more directly patriotic role. Here he is cast as an avenging military hero, John Rambo, which was a role he had played earlier in *First Blood* (1982). In the previous film, it was shown that Rambo was an innocent Vietnam veteran who was unfairly treated by local officials. This led to a battle between Rambo and police and military pursuers in the dense forests of the Pacific Northwest. Despite his apparent innocence, Rambo is eventually captured and turned over to the criminal justice system for prosecution. The whole story portrays Rambo as the victim of a heartless government that had consistently neglected and mistreated military veterans, such as Rambo, who had served in Vietnam War.

In *Rambo II*, audiences see that the heroic veteran has suffered yet more indignities at the hands of the government. He has been imprisoned for fighting back, literally and violently, in the events portrayed in the earlier film. Yet despite continuing mistreatment, the government wants more from Rambo. They seek his services on a dangerous, clandestine mission. He is to return to a remote region of Vietnam and secretly search for surviving American prisoners of war, who are reportedly being held in the wilderness under brutal conditions, despite the fact that the war had ended a decade earlier.

Rambo undertakes the mission and eventually discovers that Communist Vietnamese forces, inexplicably assisted by a Soviet advisor, are holding American troops. (Why either the Vietnamese or Soviet military are still devoting any attention to keeping prisoners of a war that is long over is never adequately explained, but it does not matter to the story.) Rambo frees the American prisoners, and then they make their way to a rendezvous point, where an American helicopter is supposed to pick them up.

But it turns out that devious American bureaucrats have double-crossed Rambo. The entire mission is a sham and meant only for show. The people who planned it have predetermined that it should not succeed in order to cover up their previous failures. They now intend to abandon Rambo and the rescued hostages, leaving them to die in the Vietnamese wilderness, rather than return to the United States and reveal embarrassing details about how American soldiers had been abandoned in the first place. In the end, an honorable American officer discovers the injustice, and Rambo and the freed prisoners are rescued.

Overall, the plot of *Rambo II* replicates in exaggerated and metaphorical fashion many of Reagan's themes regarding the way in which the United

States had dealt with the memory of the Vietnam War and with the American soldiers who had served in it. The film portrays elements within the government as treacherous and decidedly unpatriotic. Only by standing up to them, which Rambo does at great personal sacrifice, can the United States' moral virtue be restored.

Although critics generally gave *Rambo II* negative reviews, the film was a huge commercial hit. Audiences responded very positively to the patriotic message. It was not uncommon for viewers to burst into applause at Rambo's triumph at the film's end. At one theater, news accounts report that those in attendance spontaneously started cheering and chanting, "Rambo, Rambo, USA!"[8]

Other films of the era addressed similar themes and presented similar views of a United States that had lost its toughness and was in need of a heroic comeback. *Missing in Action*, a 1984 film directed by Joe Zito and that starred the actor and martial arts expert Chuck Norris, was perhaps the most notable of examples. That movie and its two sequels—*Missing in Action 2: The Beginning* (1985) and *Braddock: Missing in Action III* (1988)—espoused a worldview that clearly reflected the conservative ideology of the time.

Still other films, while did not directly addressing the Vietnam War, reflected a flattering view of U.S. power and the military in the renewed Cold War. For example, *An Officer and a Gentleman* (1982), directed by Taylor Hackford and starring Richard Gere, revolved around the struggles and triumph of a dashing young hero in the U.S. Navy flight school. A few years later, the action drama *Top Gun* (1986), directed by Tony Scott and starring Tom Cruise, tells the story of swaggering young American pilots who were clearly undaunted by the military's Vietnam-era past and were ready to confront any danger.

"MORNING IN AMERICA"

Much of Ronald Reagan's vision for the United States involved reestablishing its role in the international sphere and, importantly, in reinforcing the confidence that Americans had about their country. But a large part of Reagan's vision was focused on life within the United States since in addition to seeing a need for a resurgent United States in international politics, he also saw a nation in need of renewal—along economic, moral, and spiritual dimensions.

As part of this inward look at the United States, the Reagan presidency was marked by a shift in official attitude about the nation's economy. Eager to put the malaise of the 1970s firmly in the past, Reagan touted the benefits of "supply-side" economics. The way to assure future economic stability and growth, in this view, was for government to reduce taxes and regulations, both of which supply-side economists regarded as burdens on the private sector. They reasoned that with less to pay in taxes, there would be more available funds to invest in businesses. What was not collected in taxes could therefore be directed to adding employees, improving services, expansion, and innovation. Similarly, freed from what were seen as the onerous burdens of regulation, businesses would be better able to focus on their core activities and be better situated to compete in the marketplace.

Perhaps not unexpectedly, under Reagan initiatives the wealthy were among the most obvious beneficiaries. This, however, was a desired effect in supply-side thinking, which predicted a "trickle-down" effect. The theory was that as wealthier classes retained more of their money due to less taxation, their spending and investment activities would have the net result of raising living standards broadly across the middle and working classes. Whether such policies actually had such effect was widely debated for decades after Reagan's tenure. But regardless of whatever the judgment of the future would be, in the 1980s the president was able to make the case for this way of addressing the nation's economic concerns in an effective way.

Inherent in this economic approach—which was sometimes called "Reaganomics"—was a core belief that the president brought to the White House. His unyielding view was that government had grown too large and was now more contributing to the nation's problems than helping to solve them. As Reagan had said in his 1981 inaugural address, "Government is not the solution to our problem; government is the problem."[9]

A number of Hollywood films reflected these major concerns in various ways. One film that directly commented on some of these issues was Oliver Stone's *Wall Street*, a 1987 film that captured, in somewhat exaggerated manner, some of the excesses that were part of the seeming reinvigoration of the economy and society during the Reagan years.

Despite a recession in the early 1980s and occasional bumps along the road, the Reagan era coincided with a revitalization of the United States' financial sector. And in keeping with the supply-side view of economics heralded by the administration, those people with wealth and access to it had many opportunities to generate money. Investment, however, took on increasingly stylized forms, as entrepreneurs devised creative ways to increase their profits within the existing rules of the time. In this era, so-called corporate raiders made huge sums by acquiring companies and then selling off or otherwise restructuring what were seen as underperforming parts.

But this tactic was sometimes viewed as extreme and predatory. This was especially the case with those who had become accustomed to traditional ways of understanding the business world and had a vested interest in older ways of doing things. Moreover, corporate takeovers at times left many people unemployed or with diminished benefits. Many people thought that the quality of goods and services declined in these situations, as well. In a way, the business world was reassessing the assumptions of the past. New questions were raised about the proper relationship between employers and employees, between workers and owners, and so forth.

Some financial-success stories from the era were spectacular. But in some cases, excess seemed to be the operative word, in terms of both the sheer wealth that had been generated and the ostentatious ways in which it was sometimes used. The wealthy class fascinated the general public. By mid-decade, a syndicated television series called *Lifestyles of the Rich and Famous* was a staple of American broadcasting. The popular program, which ran for a decade, focused on extravagance and plenty. It showcased a world of rarified individuals. They were unlike ordinary people, but they presented a new model of what American success might be. And many people seemed to readily subscribe to the vision of success that it showcased.

This picture of the super-wealthy was quite different from the earlier, more humble picture of success that the American Dream idea had traditionally referenced, however. Personal financial security had been one of the foundational components of this concept, of course, but the usual way of understanding the idea did not envision a life of opulence. Moreover, the perhaps caricaturized picture of the newly rich, as conceived in popular culture (such as was portrayed in the *Lifestyles* program), was seemingly at odds with other core values that had been accepted in both conservative and liberal visions of the American Dream of the past. That idea, which had focused largely on middle-class life and ethics, stressed widely accepted values such as work, personal integrity, and responsibility. While people upholding those values may have generated new wealth, this part of the equation was missing from the picture of success promoted in popular media. Instead, the media reflected only the end results and the luxuries of success. And it remained uncertain, in the minds of many people, whether some of these successes had been achieved with adherence to traditional principles.

It was in this milieu that director Oliver Stone's film *Wall Street* was released. The story ostensibly focuses on a young Wall Street trader named Bud Fox (played by Charlie Sheen), who is impatient at the seemingly slow pace at which he is achieving success. He longs to be a major player, a Wall

Street star, in the vein of his apparent idol, a corporate raider named Gordon Gekko (played by Michael Douglas).

The Gekko character is among the most memorable in 1980s American film and one deeply connected to specific attitudes of the day. Gekko is fantastically wealthy and successful in terms of how Wall Street defined success. And he has the lifestyle and bravura of someone who sees himself as more than an ordinary person. Gekko has a gift for seeing the world for what it is, and he is adept at exploiting situations to his advantage. He makes no apologies for what he is or what he does, and at one point in the film he says, "Greed, for lack of a better word, is good." As Vincent Canby wrote in his *New York Times* review, "Gordon Gekko is a good character. He's ruthless, ironic and, under the circumstances, completely practical."[10]

But Stone does more than simply observe the financial world of that era. Indeed, this is a film in which the director has a point of view that is specifically and unsubtly developed. As Canby also noted at the time, "Mr. Stone takes a dim view of the moral climate in which insider trading can flourish and corporate raiders are role models for the young."[11]

Stone, whose widely admired Vietnam War movie *Platoon* (1986) had recently been released, was accustomed to attracting media attention from beyond the entertainment press. And even before he started filming *Wall Street*, he reported encountering "enormous paranoia" from real Wall Street firms as he searched for locations at which to film part of the movie. As Stone also said, "There's sensitivity in the air because of what's going on in the news. They're scared of this film." Yet Stone's perspective seemed to be that he was merely seeking to capture in a fictional story part of the real world. In his view, he said, "We're presenting a very balanced look. We're not emphasizing greed and corruption."[12]

Wall Street was a commercial success and was in many respects well received, though not universally without reservation. A review in the *Washington Post*, for example, seemed to express mixed feelings about the film. In the paper's review, Desson Howe wrote, "In *Wall Street . . .* you will see the evil, capitalistic impulses of man. Towards the end, you will see the self-righteous impulses of liberal finger-pointers. It's hard to tell which is worse."[13] The *New York Times* described the film with faint praise, saying it was "an upscale morality tale to entertain achievers who don't want to lose touch with their moral centers, but still have it all."[14]

Beyond reaction from film critics, the subject of the film and its largely unflattering portrait of Wall Street traders and financiers brought attention from people with a stake in financial industry. For example, Kenneth

Leibler, then president of the American Stock Exchange, was quoted in newspaper reports saying, "I thought it [*Wall Street*] was stereotypical and somewhat clichéd in terms of the sharp depiction of some of the characters."[15] But the perception that Wall Street was riddled with bad behavior and excess was not necessarily a widely held view, especially among conservatives. Indeed, to many people Wall Street's problems were mostly isolated and not reflective of the business world as a whole.

PERCEPTIONS OF CULTURAL DECAY AND MORAL DECLINE

Reagan and his allies were interested in more than simply restoring vigor to the American economy. In a broad sense, Reagan's agenda was aimed at remaking American society—or, said differently, restoring the American moral condition—in a way that would undo many of the policies that liberalism had installed over time. It was very much an agenda that focused on returning the United States to the years of hope and promise, which were typified in the underlying American Dream ideals that had been championed at mid-century. Key to achieving this end was the necessity of not only placing the United States on sound financial footing but also moving the nation beyond addictions, crime, and moral breakdown—all of which were, in the eyes of the new conservatives, largely the result of misguided liberal policies of the past.

Drug abuse, for example, was a major concern. Richard Nixon had declared a war on drugs a decade earlier, but in the assessment of many observers that "war" was not going well. Marijuana remained widely used, and many Americans, particularly conservatives, were alarmed at how deeply it had penetrated middle-class life in suburbia. Meanwhile, cocaine had become a drug of choice, and its use was increasingly common among a wide swath of the United States from all walks of life. In fact, U.S. demand for cocaine had fueled the development of powerful drug cartels in Colombia, where it was produced. It was American demand, for example, that enabled the growth of the infamous Medellín cartel, an alliance of cocaine kingpins that included Pablo Escobar, the Ochoa brothers, and several others. By 1981, this group had organized a massive and violent illegal drug-trafficking business that flooded the United States with cocaine. With strong American demand for the drug, by the end of the decade Pablo Escobar, the most powerful member of the Medellín group, had amassed a fortune. *Forbes* magazine ranked him as the seventh-richest person in the world in 1989.

Despite a high-profile antidrug public relations campaign featuring First Lady Nancy Reagan and her "Just say no" to drugs message, alarm about the drug situation worsened. By mid-decade, a powerful new and highly addictive variant of cocaine, called "crack," had made a frightening appearance in major urban areas. The so-called crack epidemic panicked many antidrug crusaders and lawmakers, and the negative publicity surrounding its chilling effects helped spur passage of sweeping new legislation. The Anti-Drug Abuse Act of 1986 directed about $1.7 billion to the antidrug effort and established mandatory sentences for many drug law violations. The effectiveness of the former aspect of the law is questionable, but the results of the sentencing requirements were soon quite visible. American prisons quickly filled with drug-law violators. The percentage of drug offenders in federal prisons in 1980 was roughly a quarter of the total prison population; by 1990 it was over half.[16]

Drug use was taken to be a potent symbol of continued American moral decay, though concern for the United States' drift from traditional values of God and country—a concern that was especially strong among the new conservatives—involved much more than only drug use. This general idea found widespread expression in American culture and politics of the time.

The criticism that liberalism was the source of what ailed U.S. culture was implicit in views voiced by Reagan and like-minded people throughout his presidency. This idea received a lofty airing in the widely discussed book, *The Closing of the American Mind*,[17] written by University of Chicago philosophy professor Allan Bloom. This 1987 work skewered the U.S. higher education system for succumbing to moral relativism and for falling victim to what Bloom viewed as the questionable ideas of leftist, 1960s-era radicals. Bloom saw the nation sliding into an abyss.

Bloom's criticisms were but one part of what is sometimes called the "culture war" of the 1980s. In fact, there were many critics of what the United States had become over the past several decades. Some people, such as Bloom, criticized the culture for having become intellectually shallow. Others, including leaders of the rising Christian evangelical movement, railed against immorality and called for a return to religiosity. Overall, the very public national debate about the United States' presumed cultural decline, which was often laden with hyperbole, took on an increasingly partisan and polarizing tone as the 1980s progressed, and it would remain a major theme in subsequent years.

Also in 1987, a major controversy erupted when Reagan nominated Robert Bork to fill a vacancy on the Supreme Court. Bork's interpretation of the Constitution was very conservative and emphasized the original intent of that document's authors. This "originalist" position led him to reject many less literal interpretations of the Constitution. The more liberal way of interpreting the Constitution had been the basis for Supreme Court decisions favored by liberal lawmakers and by women's and civil rights groups. Ultimately, Bork's nomination was defeated in the Senate, but the episode was another indication of how polarized opinion was becoming on major social issues and about increasingly strong disagreement as to whether policies of the past decades had been leading the United States in a positive or negative direction.

Throughout the 1980s, a group called the Moral Majority had exercised much influence in conservative American politics. The group espoused a return to Christianity in both public and private life. Tim LaHaye, one of the people involved in the Moral Majority from the beginning, wrote a book entitled *The Battle for the Mind*, which was a favorite among conservative Christian readers. LaHaye argued that a conspiracy existed among "humanists," who in his words were people who sought "to solve . . . problems independently of God." LaHaye believed such efforts had been failures, but that these humanists had "treacherously" failed to acknowledge this and had instead blamed "traditional religion or ignorance or capitalism or religious superstitions."[18] According to this way of thinking, Hollywood producers, the National Association for the Advancement of Colored People, the National Organization for Women, and other liberal groups were among the conspirators.[19]

Some people, especially those who held more liberal values, strongly criticized the Moral Majority and feared that it exerted too much power. Indeed, it was a major player in 1980s politics and was regarded as wielding much influence. Yet exactly how much of a real, as opposed to a perceived, effect the group actually had, especially on Hollywood, is difficult to determine. Author Stephen L. Carter, for example, saw little effect, especially in terms of changing the course of American movies. As he wrote, "It turns out Moral Majority could not deter Hollywood from creating films it did not like . . . Moral Majority's membership was a tiny fraction of Falwell's public claims, or the media's public fears."[20]

What the viewpoints of many critics of American culture had in common was a basic affinity for the critique that had been offered by Reagan. They therefore shared the view that the United States had drifted far from its traditional roots and was in grave danger of falling off the precipice into national ruin. This incarnation of the theme of American demise resonated strongly with some segments of U.S. society, and it became a powerful narrative strand in the increasingly polarized political realm of national life over ensuing decades.

HOLLYWOOD AND MORALITY IN THE 1980s

Although many, if not most, Hollywood films did not set out to challenge widely accepted American morality, Hollywood occasionally issued films that ignited controversy. These were often highly polarizing films, with vocal supporters as well as vocal detractors.

For example, director David Lynch explored the dark and troubled underside to life in an ordinary American community in *Blue Velvet* (1986). The story includes many iconic elements of American life and cinema, but the director uses them in to expose hidden corrosion and dysfunction. As Lynch has said, "It's a strange world. This is the way America is to me. There's a very innocent, naive quality to life, and there's a horror and sickness as well. It's everything. *Blue Velvet* is a very American movie."[21]

The story opens with a grim discovery. College student Jeffrey Beaumont (played by Kyle MacLachlan) is visiting his hometown when he finds a severed human ear in a nearby field. With this in the background, the narrative follows Beaumont's efforts to solve the mystery as to whose ear it was or how it had come to be there. He is aided by Sandy Williams (Laura Dern), a local high school student and love interest, whose father is conveniently a police officer.

From the beginning, then, Lynch plays with conventions of American myth and film traditions. As one writer later observed, "The opening sequence in *Blue Velvet* seems to parody the American fantasy—that is, what's advertised as the all-but-trademarked American dream—but what's happening on the screen may be without any satiric meaning at all, and impossible to immediately understand."[22]

As Beaumont seeks to unravel the mystery, he slowly becomes aware of the town's seedy underworld. Believing that a local nightclub singer (played by Isabella Rossellini) may somehow be involved, he sneaks into her apartment to investigate. The singer discovers him, but instead of turning Beaumont in to authorities, she unexpectedly initiates a sexual encounter with him. This episode is abruptly interrupted, however, when another man arrives at the singer's apartment. Beaumont then hides in a closet, from which he secretly witnesses the man (Dennis Hopper) engage in bizarre and violent sexual activities with the singer. It is then revealed that the man has kidnapped the singer's husband and son in order to force the singer to comply with his wishes.

As the story progresses, Beaumont encounters more mysterious people who seem to be involved. Eventually, one shadowy figure is revealed to be a member of the local police department. Beaumont continues to unravel clues, but he becomes more entwined in the dark and hidden world camouflaged beneath the community's innocent surface as the story progresses. When the mystery is finally solved—a result that is accompanied by more violence—the film then seems to reach a conclusion. What viewers are left with, however, is a sense that the world of normalcy apparent on the surface is something of an illusion. For they have seen that just beneath, hidden from view, is a far darker and more lurid world than can be seen at first glance.

Stylish and provocative, especially in its linking of sex and violence hiding almost, but not quite, out in the open in an ordinary community, *Blue Velvet* received positive reviews from many critics and solidified Lynch's reputation as a director with a unique vision. In many respects, however, the film plays on long-standing impulses in American cinema, which had frequently been expressed (though usually without as much flair). *Blue Velvet* draws quite heavily on film noir conventions and sensibilities and in some ways is reminiscent of Roman Polanski's late-noir classic, *Chinatown* (1974). Yet Lynch's treatment of the story challenges the conventions upon which it draws. And it startled audiences at the time. "The shock comes from the material itself, which is genuinely cruel and sometimes obscene, and from Lynch's artistic control over it," as critic David Denby concluded.[23]

The film seemed compelling to many viewers, though some people had reservations. Stephen Hunter later wrote, "The most appalling aspect of the entire 'Blue Velvet' phenomenon isn't the document itself, wretched and seamy thought it may be, but the uproar raised by certain critics who've professed to see consistent humor, coherent vision and even genius in this twisted work."[24] Leaving aside questions of artistic merit or originality, however, the public's fascination with the film in the midst of the culture war of the 1980s is noteworthy. For the movie surely skewers the traditional view of the United States, portraying a seemingly idyllic small town and its people as deeply flawed and hiding inner moral weaknesses.

Another film that spurred controversy was Martin Scorsese's *The Last Temptation of Christ* (1988). Condemned by some groups as an affront to religion, it provoked protest and indignation from many people in the conservative Christian community. The scenes in which Jesus of Nazareth is tempted by lust particularly offended many faithful Christians. The Moral Majority, for example, called the film "an utter blasphemy." Jerry C. Nims, president of that group, wrote a letter to the chairman of MCA in which he condemned the people associated with the film of "privately and personally profiting from the blaspheming of our Saviour." News accounts in August reported that a mob of demonstrators "lugged crosses and picket signs to the gates of Universal Studios ... to protest" the film the day before its opening.[25] The protest, which was coordinated by conservative Christian groups such as the American Family Association and the Trinity Broadcasting Network, snarled traffic in the area and drew much attention.

Throughout the decade, themes of moral decay and society's descent into lawlessness and pervasive violence appeared in a number of films. Some of these combined the motifs of revenge and vigilantism, which had been prevalent in such movies as *Dirty Harry* and *Death Wish* in the 1970s. The new films often addressed similar themes in narratives that were set in future dystopias, which are vaguely or overtly postapocalyptic.

A movie that foreshadowed themes that would appear in the 1980s was *Mad Max* (1979), which had been imported from Australia. It became a substantial hit with American audiences. In the film's narrative, outlaws savagely attack and abuse the innocent in a postapocalyptic world, and society's remaining system of law and order is incapable of protecting anyone. The film's hero (played by Mel Gibson) is a police officer who experiences the inadequacies of the system firsthand. Marauding criminals murder his wife and child. Eventually, he adopts the methods of the outlaws and takes matters of justice into his own hands. As with the revenge films earlier in the 1970s, government is ineffective and irrelevant. Only strong heroes who step outside the constraints of society can save the timid population that has been weakened by the pampering and pacifying influence of modern civilization.

Escape from New York (1981), from American director John Carpenter, similarly involves a future world plagued by savage chaos and brutality. In the society depicted in this film, the urban problems plaguing New York City have descended into such hopeless violence and criminality that the entire borough of Manhattan has been sealed off from the rest of society and made into a penal colony. The city is now a place where society's worst criminals are dropped off and left to their own devices and violence and to rot and victimize each other for their remaining days. True to form in such films, the main antihero and protagonist, Snake Plissken (played by Kurt Russell), is sent on a rescue mission to New York. The president of the United States has become stranded there after the crash of Air Force One. Although the president is ultimately rescued, as the story unfolds viewers see not the noble leader of a strong nation, but a flawed and selfish man scarcely deserving of his nation's respect.

Director Ridley Scott's *Blade Runner* (1982) is a striking depiction of crime and gloom in a future world. The film, an adaptation of Philip K.

Dicks's science fiction novel *Do Androids Dream of Electric Sheep?*, starred actor Harrison Ford, who by then was famous for his work in *Star Wars* and *Raiders of the Lost Ark*. The film was another big-budget production, with stylish direction and visual design.

The story in *Blade Runner* envisions a future, dystopian world of dark and dreary megalopolis. Buildings tower into cloudy and rain-filled skies, creating an environment in which the lower classes of society seem to literally be stuck at the bottom, near the ground level, while the upper classes reside high above. The dank and nightmarish urban setting makes one of the film's most powerful impressions, and even viewers unfamiliar with Scott's vision of a dark, depressing future as portrayed in this film may recognize its look from the many films that have been influenced by it. The bleak setting is a fitting backdrop against which the narrative of the film unfolds.

In the movie's version of the future, advanced androids—called replicants—have been mass-produced to perform work on other worlds. They so strongly resemble humans in appearance and intelligence that only experts can recognize them as not being human. They are also so advanced that some of them have internalized the desire to continue their existence well beyond what amounts to their expiration date—the predetermined time that the manufacturer has established for the replicant's termination.

The replicants who defy their scheduled termination are regarded as a danger to society in this future world. Authorities therefore send specialists to find such rebels and enforce the termination orders. The plot of *Blade Runner* centers on Rick Deckard (Ford's character), who serves in this capacity and functions more or less as a bounty hunter. Deckard is called to deal with difficult cases, and as the story unfolds, it is clear that the case to which he has newly been assigned is complex and challenging indeed.

Blade Runner touches on many themes of social and environmental ruin that had emerged in both films and popular discourse in the preceding years. Its vision of a quasi-totalitarian corporate state, for example, is reminiscent of films such as *RoboCop* (1981), which had been released the previous year. Its depiction of an environmentally bleak future is not unlike themes from films of several genres that cast doubt on the ability of humans to act responsibly in ways that do not inflict ecological disaster. And its depiction of androids suggests that inherent in humankind's technological innovation and ingenuity lie hidden ramifications with troubling consequences. In this respect, *Blade Runner* has similarities to some science fiction films of the 1950s, which also focused on human achievement leading to dire unintended consequences. (Among earlier movies with such themes were *Them!*, *Godzilla*, and

The Fly.) More generally, the film's way of portraying future society appears to show how American goals and aims could turn out terribly wrong.

Blade Runner opened to mixed reviews and lackluster audience enthusiasm, but over time it has become a viewer favorite thanks to cable broadcast and several recut versions that have been released in home video formats. It has also attracted the attention of scholars, who have examined its many thematic strands in detail. Guiliana Bruno, for example, interpreted the film as "a metaphor of the postmodern condition."[26] The world it envisions, she writes, "creates an aesthetic of decay, exposing the dark side of technology, the process of disintegration."[27] Sean Redmond has analyzed the film as a "powerful story of social class.... [that] offers up a particularly depressing and pathological vision of the working class, both through the representation of the film's central protagonists [the replicants], and through the teeming hordes who populate the lower levels of *Blade Runner*'s city."[28] Mike Davis commented that the film had inadvertently assumed another role in the cultural landscape: that of Los Angeles's "dystopic alter ego" and "official nightmare," which he observed had influenced some people's thinking about the future of Los Angeles in the real world.[29]

Scott's film offers a picture of the future that contrasts markedly with the positive vision for the United States that had swept into the political landscape with the rise of Ronald Reagan and the new conservative philosophy that he championed. *Blade Runner* presents a future that is uniformly unappealing and resembles a totalitarian environment that has some commonality with the future as envisioned in Fritz Lang's *Metropolis* (1927), in which workers lead a deadening existence to support the elites of society. It has nothing in common with Reagan's vision. Indeed, as the president said in a 1984 speech, his was "a dream of an America that would be a shining 'city on a hill.' "[30] (The "city on the hill" language connects Reagan's vision to the ideas that had been among the foundational concepts in the formulation of the American Dream idea, in this case to a sermon delivered by John Winthrop in 1930.)

A less sophisticated film that was nonetheless a commercial hit was *The Terminator*, director James Cameron's 1984 science fiction story. It similarly includes elements of a future world gone awry. The narrative involves time travel and attempts to thwart an imminent apocalypse that would render humanity obsolete. Similarly bleak portrayals of future society continued in two 1987 films, *RoboCop* and *The Running Man*. Both depict futuristic worlds in which cities have decayed and morality has collapsed. As with many other films with similar themes, huge, faceless corporations have taken control over society, but care little for the welfare of citizens, who appear to be regarded as largely disposable.

In a slightly different but related vein, director Tim Burton's hugely successful *Batman* (1989) presents the famous superhero fighting crime in dark and downtrodden Gotham City. As a review in the *New York Times* indicated, the city in this film, which is a fictionalized version of New York, is "a nightmare version of megalopolis, an urban landscape without sun, seen through pollutants and despair. Everything seems foreshortened, squeezed, angry, rotten."[31]

The Batman character had first appeared in comic books in 1939, at a time when the United States had not yet recovered from the Great Depression. In intervening years, Batman had continued to be a popular comic book character while occasionally appearing on-screen in various incarnations, most famously in a popular mid-1960s television series that spoofed the character. Burton's 1989 update, however, reflected major changes in how the world the character inhabited was portrayed.

In most eras, Batman is shown fighting powerful enemies who present traditional society with challenges that only a superhero could meet. But the society itself is usually shown as very traditional. Batman's heroics in such stories, therefore, are aimed at protecting the status quo, at ensuring that the good life of the United States would continue. In the 1989 movie, however, Batman lives in a world that is already decaying. Indeed, in some ways, as James Berger notes, "Gotham City was already dead."[32] The hero does not so much save the city as attempt to prevent it from descending even further into chaos. Indeed, Gotham City seems dystopian in the movie, and the world depicted is quite similar to that portrayed in the other films with this theme.

Movies such as these, which were issued across the decade and are in some ways quite varied, nonetheless share common features. They depict a United States (or a society very much like the United States) that has fallen into ruin and in which many people lead bleak lives. Some major challenge (usually in the form of a villain) arrives on the scene and makes matters worse. But the people in these societies are ill-equipped to address these challenges. They exist simply as victims until the arrival of some hero, possessing strength and virtues that had traditionally been associated with American heroes. The day is therefore saved by the strength of an individual (not by a government) and by heroes that either had never lost their American moral strength or at least somehow come to acquire it.

Do the Right Thing

Hollywood had changed in many ways since previous eras and even from just a decade earlier. But some things had not changed much. The stories

Hollywood told, and the people telling those stories, still reflected the perspectives of the nation's racial and ethnic majorities. A quarter century had elapsed since the height of the civil rights movement, but the film and television businesses still tended to tell the same sorts of stories from the same, basically white points of view.

In 1989, however, a relatively small film captured the attention of American audiences and critics with a story about an African American community dealing with racism and other problems during a sweltering heat wave. *Do the Right Thing* made its director, Spike Lee, instantly famous. His movie was startlingly direct and did not gloss over the realities and emotions of a struggling neighborhood. Nor did it shy away from depicting scenes in which anger and frustration boil over and lead to alarming violence and dire consequences. Indeed, the film possesses an almost take-it-or-leave-it attitude, as Lee refuses to sugarcoat the inner life of a community that seems to exist apart from the white society on the outside.

In many ways, the film is relatively tame in its implied criticism of persisting racism and unfairness that shape the community's everyday experience. "Still," as William Grant has written, "theater owners and film critics feared that the film would ignite the flames of racial violence."[33]

Indeed, a white pizza shop owner (played by Danny Aiello), who in the narrative functions as a representative for the white world more generally, does not even regard himself as racist. He maintains what he believes is an honorable relationship with his African American employee Mookie (Lee played this part himself) and is later shocked to discover that Mookie feels otherwise.

One of the most important films of the era, *Do the Right Thing* shares with some other movies of the 1980s a view that surface appearance is deceiving. The riot that erupts near the end of the film seems shocking to the white community, which has failed to notice—perhaps because it did not wish to notice—that conditions in the neighborhood had been fueling discontent and frustration for some time. The resurgent American Dream ideals in which many people were immersed in the Reagan years had not, after all, solved the escalating crises in American cities. But by the late 1980s, many middle-class white Americans did not think much about such things. By then, problems of the so-called inner city seemed separate and remote to much of the white United States, which the language itself revealed. After all, phrases such as "inner city" were words that were often used to say African American or other "minority" communities without saying so. The term "inner city" was laden with hidden meanings that were nonetheless understood on some level, even as the communities so labeled were marginalized by the greater society.

FROM RONALD REAGAN TO GEORGE H. W. BUSH

The Reagan era continued beyond his term somewhat, with the election of George H. W. Bush in 1988. Bush had been vice president and his election seemed, to many people, to be a way for the Reagan conservative revival to continue. By this time, a sea change in American politics had occurred, with a firmly ensconced and revitalized new conservative presence that would persist well into the future.

At the same time, the United States' old rivalry with the Soviet Union seemed destined to end. Perhaps nowhere was the foreshadowing of this development more evident that in the demolition of the Berlin Wall in 1989. A potent symbol of the Cold War, it had physically divided the city into Communist and democratic zones since its construction in 1961. When it fell, there was a palpable feeling throughout much of the East as well as the West that the era it represented was coming to a close.

Americans were quick to take credit for the end of the Soviet Union when it came somewhat later. For the conservative onlookers, the impending collapse of the "evil empire" appeared largely due to Reagan's hard line against the Soviets. Other observers were less sure that this was the cause, however. Surely it is true that the end of the Communist authoritarianism in the USSR had a long genesis and was hastened by the leadership of that nation making questionable decisions, alienating their own citizens and the people they ruled, and ineffectively overseeing the nation's economy. But there were probably many reasons for the end. And whatever differences of interpretation may exist, the end result was the same.

The era of two unquestionable superpowers was ending, at least for the moment. Yet the demise of that potent foe did not mean the end of fears of American demise and moral decline, as would slowly become apparent in the following years.

CHAPTER 9

Hollow World

National pride and the promise of prosperity from a renewal of American Dream ideals had been prominent developments in the 1980s. But that decade had also been wracked by a bitter culture war and haunted by occasional controversy. The reinvigorated national spirit had been achieved at the cost of rising cultural and political polarization. The increasing logjams in Washington were only one incarnation of this latter trend, which was to grow only more pronounced in the 1990s. Underlying many of these controversies were markedly different ideas about the state of the nation and about the direction in which it was heading. American power and might were still not securely reasserted, in this view. And within the U.S. homeland, continuing moral decline was a constant worry. If left unchecked, it was feared, the American Dream would be seriously threatened.

The 1990s were also the end of a millennium, according to the Western, Christian calendar. Though in everyday life, this was merely to be a change of the calendar, the coming of the year 2000 caused many people to take stock of where they and their nation had been and where it was going. As the twenty-first century approached, then, undercurrents of apocalyptic, end-of-millennium anxieties, frequently repeated in popular-culture contexts, sometimes added fuel to the concerns about the United States' ultimate fate.

Yet in the 1990s, many of the old worries and threats from earlier decades faded away. The Cold War, which had largely defined the United States' outlook on the world for nearly a half century, disintegrated. This apparently left the United States as the victor and sole remaining superpower. But it would soon become evident that a changed world was not necessarily a safer world.

Meanwhile, many of the divisive questions that had come to public prominence in the so-called culture war in the previous decade were far from settled. In fact, American political culture seemed to be becoming more, rather than less, divided. From a conservative perspective, unfinished business from the Reagan years remained undone, and the conservative revolution had yet to be completed. Liberals, meanwhile, were disturbed at what they perceived as backpedaling on social and political issues that, to their way of thinking, had been settled in the era before the rise of neoconservatism. Hot-button issues such as abortion, affirmative action, and the very role of government in American life remained highly contested. And the willingness of the two major political parties to work together seemed increasingly in doubt.

Hollywood and the entertainment business had consolidated during the 1980s. The industry remained a major economic powerhouse, and it was a major force in American culture. And as the polarization of American political culture became more apparent in the new decade, Hollywood would take on an increasingly evident role as a major player in the continuing culture wars. The industry had long been implicated in the struggle for the United States' moral condition, but now it would be taken to task for what was perceived as heightened partisanship.

A NEW WORLD ORDER

The final collapse of the USSR in 1991 and the resulting end of the Cold War was partially overshadowed by events of a different sort, which were also a herald of more profound refocusing of American fears and anxieties. The Middle East had been problematic since the end of World War II and especially since the establishment of the State of Israel in 1948. Although there had been a series of conflicts and crises in that region since that time, the United States had mostly managed to refrain from major military involvement.

In the new decade, however, that changed. At the direction of dictator Saddam Hussein, in July of 1990 the armed forces of Iraq poured over the border of the tiny neighboring nation of Kuwait, with which Iraq had long had disputes. At stake were oil fields and access to marine shipping. The invasion immediately drew the attention of Washington. American officials not only were concerned that Hussein had violated international borders; they also feared that he planned to attack Saudi Arabia, a staunch U.S. ally in the region as well as a major supplier of oil to the United States.

When Hussein refused international demands to vacate Kuwait and to respect the previous borders, preparations began for a military campaign to compel him to do so. With the backing of a UN mandate, the United States coordinated and led a counterattack to free Kuwait. In January 1991, Operation Desert Storm commenced to achieve these ends.

Under the charismatic field leadership of General Norman Schwarzkopf, the American-led action made speedy progress. A series of airstrikes pummeled strategic locations, which included Iraq's capital city, Baghdad. The cable news network CNN reported live as American missiles exploded in the city.

By February, a land-based assault began in earnest, as American and coalition troops moved into Kuwait and the southern part of Iraq. The operation moved more quickly and more successfully than had been anticipated. With Kuwait quickly freed and Iraq apparently in no position to continue resistance, President Bush declared a cease-fire on February 28. The crisis was seemingly brought to an end, with relatively few American casualties suffered in what had, at the time, been the largest American military conflict since the unceremonious end of the Vietnam War over 15 years earlier.

The spirit of American pride and patriotism during these events rose to heights that had not been seen in recent memory. In this fight, Iraq had clearly seemed the aggressor, and so there was not the moral ambiguity that many people had perceived during the Vietnam conflict. The short war appeared to reassert the United States' superpower role in the emergent post–Cold War world.

Yet the seeds of discontent had been planted even amid the United States' victory in Iraq. Once the objectives of securing Kuwait's freedom and limiting Iraq's future military capability had been secured, the operation was mostly terminated. Peace was enforced by patrols of coalition aircraft. The Iraqi regime remained in place, however. This meant that Saddam Hussein, Iraq's dictatorial ruler with a reputation for brutality, remained in power. And so, while most Americans rejoiced over the swift victory in the region, some worried whether ceasing the operation before removing Hussein from power was the right decision. As things would turn out, the decision would have serious implications a decade later.

But in 1991, these complications were both unclear and very much in the future. What seemed clearer was that the huge surge in popularity enjoyed by President Bush would surely bolster his upcoming campaign for reelection in 1992. Yet after the brief war, the American economy came under stress. And despite having pledged not to raise taxes, Bush reluctantly oversaw tax increases in response to the growing national debt. These developments were damaging to Bush's reelection bid. Subsequently, in November 1992 he was defeated.

Voters instead sent William Jefferson Clinton, a Washington outsider, to the White House. The presidential tenure of Bill Clinton, as he preferred to call himself, was marked by an increasingly polarized era of American politics. Yet threats from the outside were never far from the surface. In many instances, these challenges were a long way from American shores.

In February 1993, however, an assault reached into the heart of New York City, presaging the more horrific attack on the same target eight years later. In the 1993 incident, terrorists exploded a large bomb in the basement of the iconic World Trade Center. Crudely executed, the plan resulted in six deaths and many injuries. The attack was not immediately recognized as a warning sign of much bigger trouble to come. Yet it was one of a series of events that seemed to show an unsettling vulnerability that Americans were unaccustomed to considering. Indeed, throughout major conflicts of the twentieth century, few had touched the American homeland directly. In the 1990s, however, questions emerged about how long the United States could hope to keep violence on the outside.

Later in 1993, a traumatizing incident in Africa inflicted deep psychological pain on the United States. The nation of Somalia had descended into anarchy. In the assessment of the United Nations, Somali citizens were suffering at the hands of battling warlords. Operating in support of UN efforts to stabilize the country and reduce violence, the U.S. military intervened. The operation achieved some of its aims, but in what later became known as the Battle of Mogadishu, the American intervention went horribly wrong.

During the mission, American troops attempted to mount an airborne daylight assault on a target in the lawless capital city.[1] But what was planned as a quick operation soon turned into a deadly 17-hour ordeal. American soldiers, hampered by inexperience and communications difficulties, were pinned down in a fierce firefight. The U.S. forces were outnumbered and suffered many casualties as the struggle continued.

As the battle raged, an American Black Hawk helicopter was shot down. Survivors of the crash were captured and beaten by hostile forces. To the horror of Americans, the body of one fallen soldier was dragged through the streets. This image, shown on television throughout the world, deeply shocked the nation. In the end, the Battle of Mogadishu cost 18 American soldiers their lives, with another 73 wounded. This turn of events was traumatic for the Clinton administration and the American people. Many observers openly question American policy. They wondered if whatever was being achieved was worth the price.

The Battle of Mogadishu was quickly absorbed into the United States' evolving narrative about itself. It was remembered as an episode in which American soldiers had heroically tried to bring security to a lawless region at great personal sacrifice. The soldiers were remembered as valiant warriors. However, American political leaders, at whose direction the intervention had been initiated, were widely perceived in a lesser, and less noble, role. (The incident was later memorialized in director Ridley Scott's 2001 film *Black Hawk Down*, which was released only a few months after the seismic terrorist attacks of September 11 that year.)

The administration was sent reeling by the Battle of Mogadishu. And in the polarized world of 1990s American politics, the Clinton administration was harshly criticized for its handling of the situation. In coming months, the president was more cautious about when and under what circumstances to commit American troops. The administration's policy was not to intervene unless there was a clear American interest in a given situation. When other events in Africa veered out of control—and especially in the violent situation that led to genocide in Rwanda in 1994—the United States was reluctant to intervene. For the moment, at least, the horror of Mogadishu sidelined American interest or willingness to use its military power in areas where it did not perceive a direct threat. The Cold War victor thus seemed in danger of becoming, in the eyes of some critics, a toothless tiger.

In 1995, the United States became involved, by way of its membership in NATO, in a bloody civil war in Eastern Europe. Bosnia had declared independence from Yugoslavia several years earlier, which led to a long siege of Sarajevo, the Bosnian capital. Over a four-year period, residents lived in a state of fear, as Serbian forces surrounded and bombed the city. Thousands were killed and many more thousands injured. Concern for the plight of Sarajevo eventually led NATO to intervene in 1995, with a cease-fire declared the following year. Although officially a NATO action, given the pivotal role of the United States in NATO's command and military structure, it was obviously also an important foreign policy matter for the Clinton administration.

As these international events were unfolding, the situation in Washington was rapidly eroding. Republicans and Democrats had always been opponents, but the level of distrust between them appeared to be rising. The discord between the two major political parties threatened the ability of the federal government to function at all.

In the 1994 elections, Republicans seized control of the House of Representatives. Promoting a document called "Contract with America," a new breed of conservatives promised to downsize government and restore guiding traditional values to Washington. Within months, the new Republican majority in the House of Representatives made its presence felt. Emboldened by their electoral success, they soon challenged their Democratic colleagues and the president on the pace of progress being made toward balancing the federal budget. The deficit had been substantially reduced in the time since Clinton had assumed office. But these had not made a big enough impact on the budget to please the Republican House majority. Conservative House members demanded more cuts from Medicare, Medicaid, education, and environmental programs. Most Democrats, including the president, thought that the requested additional cuts would be too damaging to the citizens using these programs.

In an address to the nation, Clinton announced he would not yield to Republican pressure if it meant agreeing to budget cuts he believed would inflict harm on the citizens who relied on the programs in question. The president knew what was at stake, and said:

> Remember, the Republicans are following a very explicit strategy announced last April by Speaker Gingrich, to use the threat of a government shutdown to force America to accept their cuts. . . . But it is my solemn responsibility to stand up against a budget plan that is bad for America and to stand up for a balanced budget that is good for America. And that is exactly what I intend to do.[2]

The situation evolved into a legislative standoff. With no new budget agreement, the result was a brief government shutdown. To those who may not have been following the disintegrating relationship between the two political parties, the incident was surprising as well as troubling.

Meanwhile, threats from within the United States had also become a cause for concern. Fringe groups with reactionary political views were a growing concern. Sometimes, these factions fought against their own government. For example, a 1993 standoff between members of the Branch Davidian religious sect and federal authorities in Waco, Texas, resulted in the deaths of more than 70 men, women, and children. Two years later, an American citizen named Timothy McVeigh detonated a massive truck bomb outside a federal building in Oklahoma City. More than 160 were killed, including 19 children. Indeed, the polarization in American political culture that was obvious in Washington at times extended far beyond that city. As society continued to change, some Americans were willing to resort to violence with the hope of forestalling more changes.

CULTURE WARS AND POLARIZATION IN WASHINGTON

Thus, as the bipolar world of the Cold War slipped away, apparently leaving the United States as the world's sole superpower in the international arena, American politics and culture were becoming increasingly polarized. As the 1990s progressed, there appeared to be fewer and fewer circumstances in which politicians on the left and the right were willing to work together in Washington. And beyond the confines of government, cultural leaders and observers similarly showed that there were vast differences in their assessments of the nation's current state or its likely prospects for the future. As the 1990s wore on, these diverging worldviews would become ever more obvious.

Although in some respects it seemed new, the "culture war" of the 1980s really had been a manifestation of cleavages that had been developing for decades. During the Reagan years, a constellation of worldviews—political, cultural, and religious—had come together with a force that had not been seen in a long time. That impulse continued into the 1990s and became more pronounced after Bill Clinton's arrival in Washington.

The Hollywood Connection

Clinton's brand of politics was attractive to many progressives and liberals in the entertainment industry. There soon developed a widespread perception that the Hollywood establishment was actively supporting the Democratic president and his causes. Hollywood's money was one source of concern among the president's critics. There was also worry about perceived attempts to influence public opinion. The tendency of some celebrities and Hollywood insiders to make pronouncements about political matters was irksome to many of those critical of the industry's seeming tendency toward liberal political activism.

More than that, conservative observers believed that Hollywood productions on-screen were intentionally skewed to present liberal ideals in a favorable light, while slighting conservative and traditional ideas and values. As polarization of American politics accelerated in the 1990s, then, many conservatives came to view Hollywood with increasing distain and suspicion. This was not a wholly new development, of course, since political distrust of the entertainment industries dated back decades. But in an era when the connections between the White House and high-profile Hollywood figures were well publicized, this mistrust became prominent.

Indeed, Hollywood soon became a near code word for political liberalism and a powerful symbol, for many people, of the United States' perceived moral decline. Writer James Hirsen, who has sharply criticized the entertainment industry on moral and political grounds, represented this view when he referred to Hollywood as "a liberal bastion."[3] In a scathing critique of

Hollywood, Hirsen criticized what he perceives as Hollywood's blatant liberalism, but he raises concerns that are broader than that. Hirsen particularly objects to the infusion of implicit political and cultural messages into screen productions that may persuade viewers to accept these messages, even in the context of fictional stories, as a type of truth saying about the world, perhaps at a subconscious level. As he writes: "Movies, TV shows, and other entertainment products don't merely amuse us or divert us from reality: often they convey messages about political, social, and cultural issues."[4] And in Hirsen's analysis, such messages "usually come with a distinct lefty twist."[5]

The claim that films of recent decades have actually projected a "lefty twist" was a familiar argument. In fact, it had long been believed that implicit messages and worldviews had the power to influence the behavior and beliefs of people encountering such works. Washington hearings in the 1940s and 1950s were based in large part on the premise that what Hollywood projected on screen could influence how viewers, or at least some viewers, subsequently behaved or thought about things.

Yet, while recognition of Hollywood's potential to influence everyday beliefs and behaviors was not new—at least not to people who paid attention to such matters—the overtness of the Clinton administration's perceived Hollywood connection was a new wrinkle. Even Ronald Reagan, whose early fame and career was entirely based on his role as a famous Hollywood actor, had not seemed to play up his close association with the industry as much as did the Clinton White House.

Hollywood vs. America

By the 1990s, the suggestion that there was a connection between Hollywood and perceptions of the United States' moral decay was a source of controversy and consternation among some leading conservative commentators. In a 1992 book entitled *Hollywood vs. America*, for example, Michael Medved sharply criticized immorality and anti-Americanism in movies and in the U.S. entertainment industry more generally. At the time, Medved was cohost of the popular syndicated television show *Sneak Previews*, on which he reviewed current movies. Yet he felt strongly that a corrosive liberalism had taken hold in Hollywood, and that its effects were deeply damaging to American society.

Medved argued that Hollywood had lost whatever moral compass it had once had and that it was now issuing works that were violent and vulgar. It was his view that as the movie business had increasingly focused on making films that displayed disregard for decency and morality, the resulting works appealed to fewer and fewer viewers. He was especially disturbed by what he saw as the entertainment industry's active "assault on religion."[6] He wrote, "Hollywood's persistent hostility to religious values is not just peculiar, it is positively pathological."[7] In a related vein, Medved also criticized what appeared to him as the industry's tendency to promote immoral behavior with respect to sex and violence.

Medved's critique of Hollywood was multifaceted and multilayered. Looking beyond questions of personal religious faith and moral behavior, he also condemned the movie business for what he perceived as hostility toward the institutions that had made the United States a powerful nation and a moral beacon to the world. On this matter he wrote, "Unfortunately, when it comes to deep-seated disgust with America and its institutions, the personal biases of the entertainment establishment show up with increasing regularity in the movies, television, and popular music."[8] The industry's "antipathy"[9] in its portrayal of the U.S. military was deeply troublesome to Medved, who was apparently surprised about Hollywood's "failure to capitalize on the public's enthusiastic support for Operation Desert Storm [in the Persian Gulf War of 1991]," which he said showed that the industry's "deeply held biases can interfere with its commercial self-interest."[10]

Though it was perhaps mildly unexpected for a movie reviewer—presumably an industry insider—to express such negative feeling about the entertainment industry, these and other criticisms in Medved's book were also not new charges. Moral leaders and conservative pundits had been making similar charges since the end of World War II, as even a cursory review of congressional hearings involving the entertainment industry makes clear. In some ways, whatever his personal beliefs Medved's commentary at this time can be seen as evidence of a nagging perception among conservative voices of that era to the effect that the new conservative movement had stalled.

The American renewal that Reagan had championed had prompted many changes in the United States. In the process, however, the political realm had become deeply divided and increasingly at an impasse. And Hollywood had come to symbolize, for some people, everything that was wrong about the United States' moral situation.

The Industry in Flux

Hollywood had become a major part of the decade's political world, but it remained a business in search of success in a fast-changing society. The film industry constantly searched for ways to regain the luster of its glory days some decades earlier. Films continued to be produced at a brisk rate, but increasingly many of these were not released in theaters, but instead on video-tape for home viewing. Indeed, videotape sales and rentals became an important part of industry revenues during this time.

Meanwhile, Hollywood's search for new ideas proved to be difficult. With stiff competition for viewer attention from broadcast and cable television, there was increased emphasis on producing movies that immediately would command attention and generate robust ticket sales. The sales a film could gross over its opening weekend took on a new significance, and thus movies that offered spectacle or an attention-getting gimmick, or that could generate massive publicity, became more common.

As average production costs rose, the financial backers of movies were eager to ensure their investments. For many productions, a significant part of this increase was in the salaries demanded by major stars, which had sky-rocketed. But producers were willing to pay for a top star. The idea was that such actors and actresses were worth the money since their participation in a film alone could help assure that a movie would attract a substantial audience.

It was also an era of many remakes. Producers scoured old television shows and films for source material, reasoning not only that such stories had been tried before and thus were somewhat audience tested but also that nostalgia and familiarity with such past productions would yield a good return on their investments.

Additionally, innovations in sound technology and special effects, especially digital special effects, could add great expense to production costs. But their use provided viewers with a visceral experience that was difficult to match by watching the era's cathode ray tube televisions.

Despite the frequently bold and splashy aspects of many 1990s Hollywood productions, however, much of the industry's output in the era displayed a sense of hollowness. The movie industry had always appealed to the senses and to fleeting sensations and experiences. Indeed, it largely evolved from arcade-style attractions such as Kinetoscopes, which appeared in the late nineteenth century and which were popular largely because they offered the novelty and surprise of simple moving images. By the 1990s, the contrast between the impressive spectacle offered by some films and the shallowness of their content was at times pronounced, even for an industry that had often displayed that tendency.

Money remained the most powerful motivation in Hollywood filmmaking. Indeed, it was an era in which the financial returns on investment could be staggering. The decade's biggest hit, director James Cameron's 1997 film *Titanic*, ran far over budget during production and there were serious concerns about whether it would make back its ballooning initial investment, which was rumored to be around $200 million. By the end of the 1990s, however, it had become the first film to gross over $1 billion, eclipsing even the amount generated over 20 years by the formidable *Star Wars* (1977).[11] One of Cameron's earlier films, *Terminator 2: Judgment Day* (1991), produced at a cost of approximately $100 million, went on to gross over $200 million in the United States; when international box office sales are added to that figure, the total gross was over $517 million.[12] The lure of such outcomes often overrode other factors, but the financial risks remained substantial. Sometimes things did not work out, as was the case with the financially disastrous film *Waterworld* (1995), which was said to have cost $175 million to produce but generated only about $88 million in U.S. ticket sales.[13]

SOCIAL DYSFUNCTION

In March 1991, a young African American man named Rodney King led Los Angeles police on a high-speed chase. Police finally stopped King, who had a criminal record, but he was uncooperative. When they judged that King was failing to comply with their directives, four police officers—three white and one Hispanic—resorted to force. They beat King on the head and body 56 times.

As it happened, an onlooker recorded the incident, preserving on videotape the image of the police officers brutally beating a man who seemed to already be subdued. The videotape was eventually offered to a local television station. When it became public, it sparked widespread interest and outrage. The tape was subsequently repeated on newscasts around the nation. This brought an incident that may otherwise never have become widely known to international attention.

The outcry over the incident eventually led to criminal charges against the officers who had been involved in it. The subsequent trial also garnered much attention. But on April 29, 1992, a jury acquitted the four police officers involved in the beating.

Many people almost immediately perceived the not-guilty verdict as a racist outcome to the trial. When it was announced, the South Central part of Los Angeles erupted into violence. When the riots ended three days later, dozens people had died. Rioters destroyed thousands of businesses and caused damage that was estimated at more than $1 billion. That section of the city was devastated and had the appearance, according to a report in the *Christian Science Monitor*, of "a bombed-out war zone."[14]

The riots shocked much of the United States. They were a reminder that while the nation had changed greatly since the days of widespread racial strife a quarter century earlier, many things had not changed. Economic hardship, racial inequities, and other issues still haunted the United States' "inner cities." For a generation, such circumstances had largely been neglected by the society on the outside, but now it was out in the open. After the riots, there was much soul-searching on the part of national leaders, but many of the underlying problems remained unresolved.

Both the beating of an African American suspect and the riots that resulted from the acquittal of the police officers involved in the incident revealed that even in the 1990s, there was much volatility beneath the surface of American life. Indeed, despite the relative calm of everyday life in much of the United States, lurking in the shadows was the prospect of a breakdown of civil society—a threat similar to the concept of *anomie*, the term the sociologist Émile Durkheim used to refer to the breakdown in social norms and common values, particularly in fast-growing societies. The riots stood as stark reminders that not everyone accepted the United States as it was. This jolted much of mainstream American society. After all, many Americans had come to believe that the racial and economic strife, which the riots seemed to expose, was something in the past. Instead, however, the massive violence of those three days in Los Angeles was a potent reminder that the glue holding the multifaceted nation together was not necessarily impervious to all eventualities.

More generally, American society continued to grapple with complex social circumstances that had evolved over time. And at various times throughout the decade, Hollywood issued films with stories in which society was at or near ruin and collapse. Some are far-fetched dystopian science fiction sagas, while others portraits of everyday characters mired in moral bankruptcy. But whatever their form or genre, the appearance of such works in the context of the United States' culture wars and disagreements about the nation's future role in the world appears to mirror the uncertainty that had become part of the national psyche.

SCIENCE FICTION NIGHTMARES

Future dystopias, in which society has come to ruin, were a major thematic strand running through 1990s science fiction films. The genre already had a long history of dealing with nightmarish scenarios and plots, but the tone and content of science fiction films were now updated in a way that reflected the anxieties of the new decade.

Along these lines was a film from early in the decade, James Cameron's *Terminator 2: Judgment Day* (1991). It was the first of several sequels to the original and more modest film from 1984. And it was perhaps representative of the darkening picture of the future that this genre typically depicted.

In the narrative of the film, the future American civilization is on the verge of being destroyed by robots. Eager to secure victory, robots in the future world send a powerful, nearly indestructible cyborg (Robert Patrick) with shape-shifting abilities back in time to kill a teenage boy named John Connor (Edward Furlong). The future cyborgs have undertaken this mission to prevent the boy from reaching adulthood, when he would threaten the robots' quest to dominate the earth at humanity's expense. But the battle between humans and cyborgs has not been settled in the future. So, human resistance fighters in the future, having learned of the plan to kill the boy, respond by sending a robot of their own back in time to thwart the intended assassination. Ironically, however, the cyborg (Arnold Schwarzenegger) now protecting Connor—and by extension, humanity—is an older model with a human shape and is an exact replica of the machine that, in the first film, had tried to kill Connor's mother (Linda Hamilton) so that the boy would never be born.

Terminator 2, which was a huge commercial success, played to the film industry's 1990s penchant for spectacle and special effects. The battle scenes between the two warring cyborgs are loud and visually overwhelming. Computerized special effects feature prominently in scenes with the new-model cyborg. In some scenes, for example, the new cyborg (played by Robert Patrick) melts into pools of liquid metal. In others, it shape-shifts around and through solid objects. This visual technology was both advanced and expensive to produce at the time. Audiences marveled at these effects, and the technological aspects of the movie were undoubtedly a large part of the film's appeal.

The combination of live photography and the computer effects was well executed for the time, which may have drawn attention away from some underlying plot elements that were ambiguous. On the one hand, the story is that of independent heroes fighting to save the day. But on the other, it is a commentary on human folly and, in the words of a *New York Times* review, a "pistol-packing plea for peace."[15]

Indeed, the film is partially in the vein of action movies, which had become popular in the 1980s. These usually had stories in which solitary heroes rescue the day or solve some crisis by refusing to be bound by society's normal rules and conventions. This type of film, which includes such earlier movies as *Rambo: First Blood, Part II* (1985) and *Die Hard* (1988), presents a dire situation that American society's traditional institutions are unable to successfully address. Instead, some hero emerges—usually unappreciated or actively resisted by the traditional authorities—who is unbound to society's "rules" and official protocols. Instead, the hero takes a stand and independently solves the problem, almost despite society's official efforts.

Richard Brown and Kevin S. Decker have astutely observed the flip side of the narrative in *Terminator 2*, which appears to deal with humankind's frequent inability to see how it is planting the seeds of its own destruction. As they have written, "Part of the drama in the Terminator story is that most of society functions normally, oblivious to the future threat of the machines. Not only is humanity mostly oblivious but some humans are actually hurrying the 'moment of singularity,' the moment when artificial intelligence exceeds human capability."[16] Although this is perhaps one of the most telling aspects of the story, the film's overwhelming spectacle and bombast may have hidden this message, almost in plain sight, from many viewers at the time.

12 Monkeys

In the future world of director Terry Gilliam's *12 Monkeys* (1995), humanity has been devastated by a plague, and the prospects for the species' survival look grim. In a desperate effort to get information about the deadly and mysterious virus that has wiped out much of the population, scientists from the future send a man back in time on an information-gathering mission. The man is a convict named James Cole (played by Bruce Willis), and his motivation is clear: if he succeeds he will earn his freedom.

The scientists plan to send Cole back to the mid-1990s, at the time when they believe terrorists have released the deadly virus that would kill nearly all of humanity. But their plans go awry, and Cole inadvertently arrives from the future not in 1996, but six years earlier. He will therefore not be able to accomplish his mission for several years. Complicating matters, Cole is soon arrested. Believing he suffers from mental illness, authorities send him to a psychiatric institution. The scientists from the future eventually retrieve Cole and question him about a person named Jeffrey Goines (Brad Pitt), whom he met while institutionalized. The scientists believe Goines may have some involvement with the deadly plague, but are uncertain of what that involvement may be.

Cole is sent back in time again, and on this occasion he arrives in 1996 as originally had been planned. But in this trip, things begin to become murkier.

Cole develops a bond with a psychiatrist named Kathryn Railly (Madeleine Stowe), who eventually comes to believe that Cole may, indeed, be from the future. Yet Cole becomes increasingly uncertain whether his experiences in the future world are real or the result of hallucination. He also begins to doubt whether Goines, who has founded an animal rights organization called the Army of the Twelve Monkeys, is the true source of the virus.

The future scientists again bring Cole back to their time, but he convinces them to send him back once again. On this final trip back to 1996, he discovers that Goines was not the central figure in the plague, after all. Cole tries to stop the scientist who is actually responsible but is killed in the process. In a twist of fate, a small boy is watching as Cole is shot. The small boy is Cole himself, when he was young. The film ends with the implication that the plague is unlikely to be prevented.

This film has some similarities in plot to the popular Terminator films, which also are stories in which beings from the future are sent back to the late twentieth-century United States as the result of some future apocalyptic event. More generally, *12 Monkeys* fits within Hollywood's attention to doomsday themes. In some ways, it has an affinity for postapocalyptic cinematic visions as varied as *Waterworld* (1995), *The Matrix* (1999), and numerous others. The film suggests, as Frederick Buell has observed, that while nature remains a powerful force in shaping the word, "human interventions in it are enormously risky and potentially disastrous."[17] It also demonstrates that in "hunting monsters of its own making, society fails to see what a monster it has made of itself,"[18] as Joshua D. Bellin has astutely noted.

Like bleak visions in some other films, the general tone and attitude of *12 Monkeys* differs markedly from many movies with a similarly dire outlook from decades earlier. As Peter Rainer has pointed out, *12 Monkeys* is not really an apocalyptic film that is warning humankind to change its behavior to stave off disaster. Indeed, it seems to have a gloomier message than that. It appears to be a movie suggesting "that existence *pre*-apocalypse wasn't so hot, either—maybe we deserve to be wiped out after all."[19] This is a far more fatalistic attitude than was found in films with similar themes from the mid-twentieth century. But it was an attitude that had been building over time and appears to run parallel to the rising cynicism that had become so apparent in American thinking, especially since the unsettling crises of faith in the United States that had shaken national confidence in the 1960s and 1970s. It is also consistent with the widespread apathy and feeling of disengagement among much of the population, which was a feeling that also had been building in recent decades.[20]

Gattaca

The 1997 production *Gattaca*, which was written and directed by Andrew Niccol, is a science fiction film concerned more with ideas and moral questions than monstrous aliens and special effects. Set in the near future, the story involves the struggle of a man named Vincent (Ethan Hawke) to free himself from the limitations that society and science have placed upon him. Vincent is a normal human, though he has health problems including a heart defect. There would be nothing extraordinary about this were it not for the fact that in the world Vincent inhabits, most people are the products of sophisticated genetic engineering, which has increased their longevity, beauty, intelligence, and health. The genetic engineering aims to eliminate random defect, essentially making people perfect.

To his misfortune, however, Vincent has been born as the result of natural reproduction, without genetic enhancements. In this world, such natural people are looked down upon and relegated to society's lower ranks. As such, it is a foregone conclusion in his world that he will die by the age of 30 and never amount to much.

Despite the social handicap of his "natural" genetic makeup, however, Vincent has exhibited an indomitable spirit since a young age. He has even managed to defeat his genetically enhanced brother in swimming competitions, which according to prevailing views in this society should not be possible. Indeed, Vincent has great plans and even wants to participate in a space mission that is reserved for society's best and brightest. But the debilitating social effects of his genetic status are nearly omnipresent. His natural state places him in the category of an "in-valid," ineligible for any important role in society. Such is the presumption about, and the prejudices against, those who lack technologically enhanced genetic perfection.

Determined to overcome these barriers, Vincent devises a plan. He secretly makes a deal to acquire samples from a genetically enhanced man, with the idea of passing himself off as similarly engineered. He will have to work hard, but he is convinced that if he can outwit authorities by faking the identity of a genetically enhanced person, he will be able to earn a spot on the space mission's crew. But the danger of being detected is high. Genetic samples are collected routinely, and the office in which he works is regularly swept for genetic material that could indicate infiltration by an "in-valid." Should even a single eyelash fall and be collected, his true genetic identity could be revealed.

The movie has other plot elements, such as a murder mystery and a romantic subplot. But overall it is a film that focuses on ideas that have much in common with Aldous Huxley's *Brave New World*, a 1932 novel that depicts a futuristic dystopia in which people are similarly engineered in a factory-like setting. As with *Gattaca*, this search for perfection has a deadening effect on society. Indeed, the societies in such works (George Orwell's 1949 novel *Nineteen Eighty-Four* has similar themes) are excessively conformist and have totalitarian and fascist tendencies.

DARK PORTRAITS OF AMERICAN LIFE

Although science fiction movies contain some of the most obvious and occasionally flamboyant portrayals of society descending into ruin, more straightforward dramas of the era also explored that theme. The declining, troubled aspects of life in the United States are not necessarily the main narrative elements of such movies, but this bleak interpretation on life—or at least on some parts of it—is often an important part of the overall story.

The Bonfire of the Vanities

Director Brian De Palma's *The Bonfire of the Vanities* (1990) was an adaptation of a novel by Tom Wolfe that was, in the words of the film's marketing slogan "an outrageous story of greed, lust and vanity in America." At the center of the narrative is a hit-and-run accident that places an African American youth in a coma. In the car are a wealthy and hedonistic investor (played by Tom Hanks) and a woman (played by Melanie Griffith), who is interested in his money and lifestyle.

As the story moves forward, a journalist (Bruce Willis) begins to investigate. Before long, the car is identified. But the story takes place in New York City, where underlying tensions and mistrust are very much in the air. Given the racial aspects of the incident and already existing tensions between the affluent and underprivileged classes of the city, the story soon becomes a sensation. Different factions opportunistically seize upon the events for their own purposes. The resulting story is a portrait of cynicism, in which genuine caring and concern are seldom seen. Instead, the incident is used as a means to various ends by a variety of shallow and self-centered people with dubious motives. As critic Vincent Canby wrote, rather than a cause for soul-searching or motivation to bring about justice, the case "becomes everybody's ticket to fame, fortune, community influence or political office."[21]

Natural Born Killers

Oliver Stone's 1994 film *Natural Born Killers*, which is based on a story by Quentin Tarantino, was instantly controversial. Its apparently cavalier treatment of violence was troublesome for many viewers. Some critics saw it as a work that almost extolled the vile behavior it depicted. The film was even accused of prompting real-life murder.[22] In his research on controversies in American cinema, Kendall R. Phillips suggests that "it was the film's anarchic tone that seemed to produce the strongest reactions, and the film's chaos seemed to spill out of the movie theaters and into the real streets of America."[23] Writer Daniel Green concluded that the film was a picture of "American decline" and the nation's "shattered idealism."[24]

The narrative follows Mickey Knox (played by Woody Harrelson) and his wife, Mallory Knox (Juliette Lewis). The young couple has a troubled and abusive background and is essentially on an extended road trip that revolves around serial murder, rape, and other acts of violence. They leave a trail of corpses from their travels around the American Southwest, where they indiscriminately murder good and bad people they encounter. They have few second thoughts about their actions and show no remorse. They seemingly take delight and satisfaction in their crimes.

The large number of murders soon attracts the attention of law enforcement officials. One of these is a detective, Jack Scagnetti (played by Tom Sizemore), who hides dark, violent secrets of his own. The couple's exploits, which in some ways seem a dark, sadistic parody of *Bonnie and Clyde*, also attract interest from the tabloid press, and particularly from the opportunistic Wayne Gale (Robert Downey Jr.)

After the first part of the story, which involves a killing spree, the narrative focuses on Mickey and Mallory Knox after they have been captured, tried, and imprisoned. It appears that Mickey Knox, in particular, is delusional and immersed in a psychological world of self-centered grandiosity. Meanwhile, both Scagnetti and Gale have their own agendas and actively seek to exploit the situation. Scagnetti concocts a scheme to kill the murderous couple in a staged escape attempt. Gale, meanwhile, has alighted upon an idea to interview the convicted couple as an opportunity to achieve media stardom. Both plans go horribly awry, however, resulting in a prison riot and more mass murder. In the end, the couple escapes and, as shown at the end of the film, they again take to the road.

In a book that analyzes violence in postmodern media, Christopher Sharrett later discussed that aspect of the film. In his view, "*Natural Born Killers* makes evil and violence, in a word, attractive. It does not simply reflect those realities but ceremonially feeds that 'demon.' "[25] Director Stone, however, has argued against this interpretation of the film, which he believes is a misreading of the narrative. According to Stone, suggestions that the film "glorified violence and was part of the [society's] problem" are misguided.

Instead, he said, "By saying that, you are trying to kill the messenger because it's not the filmmaker's fault that society is where it is. The filmmaker does his best to reflect society the way he sees it. And our society is culturally in a very violent and bankrupt mode."[26]

Pulp Fiction

A film by Quentin Tarantino, who had written the original story for *Natural Born Killers*, was released in the same year. It also contained much violence and exhibited a cynical attitude about society. Indeed, *Pulp Fiction* (1994) pictures disturbing aspects of American life. In some respects it is an updated, somewhat postmodern gangster film. Two of the principal characters are Vincent Vega (played by John Travolta) and Jules Winnfield (Samuel L. Jackson), both of whom are ruthless hit men for a mobster named Marsellus Wallace (Ving Rhames). In the course of retrieving a mysterious case and conducting other criminal business, they savagely undertake murder, while engaging in quasi-philosophical small talk in between such episodes. The parts of the film following these characters reveal the matter-of-fact manner in which they act violently and the minimal effect this seems to have on their daily lives.

Another major character is Butch Coolidge (Bruce Willis), an aging boxer. Coolidge has been bribed to intentionally lose an upcoming match so that Marsellus Wallace can profit from gambling on that otherwise unlikely outcome. However, the deal does not proceed as planned. Coolidge double-crosses Marsellus and wins the fight. The boxer bet a large amount of money on himself and stood to reap a substantial profit. But having won, he must now flee before Marsellus Wallace can seek revenge.

The complex, nonchronological narrative of *Pulp Fiction* has many other elements, but most deal with the underside of American life. Violence, drugs, abuse, and callousness appear throughout the story. And while Tarantino decidedly does not focus on everyday life or ordinary Americans, per se, his film functions somewhat like David Lynch's *Blue Velvet* several years earlier by showing a vulgar world of random cruelty and victimization not far from the more peaceful existence on the surface of American life.

Although many critics were impressed with Tarantino's film, others had reservations. The movie's explicit and frequent violence concerned some. In this respect, the major worry was that such violence, especially portrayed in the almost offhand manner that Tarantino presented it, could have a negative influence on viewers. This was similar to a complaint about violence and other antisocial behaviors in movies that had been made for decades. For

Tarantino, however, the violence was less commentary than an aesthetic part of film that exerts little influence in inducing imitative behavior. According to a report in the *Boston Phoenix*, the director defended that aspect of the film by observing, "I don't think anyone in Rwanda has seen any of my movies, and yet they've machete'd [*sic*] 500,000 people to death there."[27] (This comment was made just after the Rwandan genocide of 1994.)

Yet, if the violence in *Pulp Fiction* and similar films is simply an aesthetic element of the film and taken as such, this appears to itself be a perhaps unintended comment on how much American culture was no longer much affected by violence.

HOLLYWOOD BORROWS FROM COMIC BOOKS

The Crow

Tim Burton's film adaptation of *Batman* had introduced a comic book-inspired world that was darker and more sinister than people unfamiliar with the evolution of comic book narratives might have expected. In fact, comic books had become more sophisticated, if stylized, than they had been a generation earlier when Congress had worried about their possibly negative effects on young minds. (Congressional hearings on the matter were held in 1954.) In the 1990s, stories that originated in comic books were the sources for films that at times similarly portrayed a bleak world, in which heroes can be very flawed.

The Crow (1994) was directed by Alex Proyas. Based on a successful comic book from the late 1980s, the film version of *The Crow* received much advance publicity when star Brandon Lee (son of the legendary martial arts star Bruce Lee) died from an accidental gunshot wound during the film's production. The movie combines supernatural themes and revenge plot elements. With respect to the latter, the film has some affinity with the line of films running back to *Dirty Harry* two decades earlier.

The film is set in Detroit, which is depicted as a lawless city where random and terrible violence is common. According to the story, Eric Draven (played by Lee) and his romantic partner Shelly Webster (played by Sophia Shinas) are attacked by vicious hoodlums. Draven is stabbed and thrown out of a window to his immediate death. His fiancée, Shelly Webster, is sexually assaulted and beaten; she succumbs to her injuries sometime later. It is a horrific crime that remains unsolved.

A year later, a crow lands on Eric Draven's grave. This mysteriously causes Draven to rise from the dead. He is now consumed with the thought of avenging the crimes against Shelly Webster and himself. But Draven has not only been reanimated; he is now nearly invulnerable to injury. With the crow guiding him to those responsible for the murders, much of the film follows Draven as he tracks down the killers and their associates. When he finds his targets, he dispenses violent revenge, dispatching each of the guilty parties to grisly deaths. As with most revenge-oriented films, then, the story portrays a dark and violent world so that a hero (or, more accurately, anti-hero) can issue lethal justice that the ordinary American system has been unable to produce.

Blade

A slightly different story that was also based on a comic book character was the 1998 film *Blade*, directed by Stephen Norrington. The hero, Blade (played by Wesley Snipes), is for the most part human, but he also possesses some vampire qualities as the result of a vampire attack on his mother just before his birth. That assault claimed the his mother's life, which later motivates Blade to commit his life to hunting down and killing vampires to rid the world of their presence. And in the world of the film, there are many vampires.

Indeed, vampires apparently make up a large part of the population in Blade's United States. The vampires mostly blend in with the human population, though they sometimes appear as extravagant, rebellious upstarts. The younger, more openly hostile of them even hold wild dance parties, in which they celebrate their victimization of humans and treat human blood as something akin to a designer drug. They appear to be pseudo-sophisticates, immensely impressed with themselves and feeling entitled to a hedonistic lifestyle.

But not all of the vampires agree about the future. The old guard wants to maintain the status quo. They would prefer to harvest only what they need from the human population, mostly leaving humankind to go about its business. The younger and more rebellious vampires, however, want to rule over the human world openly.

Blade, meanwhile, is committed to thwarting such schemes and killing as many vampires as he can find. Since he possesses both vampire and human strengths, as well as an arsenal of weaponry customized for battling vampires, he appears well suited for this task. Most of the film follows his exploits in battling the vampires. The prolonged and hyperviolent fight scenes, many of which are awash in blood, are reminiscent of exaggerated sequences from earlier comic book films, such as *Batman* (1989), and also feature "acrobatics borrowed from Hong Kong action thrillers,"[28] as has been noted by film critic Stephen Holden.

Though *Blade* is cartoonish in most respects, its underlying thematic content connects it to a long line of movies across multiple genres that look with dismay and anxiety at what American life has become. While a review in the *New York Times* largely dismisses the film, it also notes that the movie can be seen, in part, as "a dark urban satire."[29]

Indeed, though visually indulgent and lacking nuance, *Blade* tells a story, albeit through the exaggerated lens of a comic book character, in which the vampire enemies are closely modeled on the metaphorically darker and more sinister elements of society that had already had a long history in American popular culture. For example, the vampires are villains who obscure their identities as they work toward domination, which is a plot element that has parallels narratives about the fear of Communist infiltrators in American life a half century earlier. From another perspective, the younger and more aggressive vampires can be interpreted as the latest incarnations of the youthful rebels who had threatened to destroy American life and civilization for decades. Such characters had appeared in cinematic guises ranging from motorcycle hoodlums to urban drug gangs. From yet another viewpoint, *Blade* metaphorically lambasts Corporate America. Scenes from film in which the vampires are plotting their takeover are reminders of corporate villains—as had appeared in many films and in much popular rhetoric—who were seen by some people as constantly scheming to take over many aspects of American life.

Blade does little more than suggest such themes, as its main purpose is not social commentary. But its story is interwoven with multiple connections to real-world anxieties about the direction in which society was heading. It therefore provides a useful illustration of how seemingly escapist movies reflected dark cultural themes of ruin and metaphorical apocalypse.

MORAL CRISIS

Throughout the decade, then, some American films looked at society gone awry. Across multiple genres, various films depicted stories in which the ideals of the American Dream were either wiped away or irrelevant. Meanwhile, in Washington, there was continued disagreement about the condition of American morals. In the second half of the decade, a scandal that was perhaps emblematic of these bitter debates overwhelmed the political sphere.

By the time he had arrived in Washington, Bill Clinton's moral character had already been the subject of speculation and criticism. Rumors of extramarital relationships had emerged before his election to the White House. At one point in 1992, he appeared on television with his wife, Hillary

Clinton, for an interview in which he denied such charges. Although Clinton was mostly able to sidestep negative effects from such claims, he did not fully escape his reputation with respect to rumored inappropriate relationships with women. Many people—even some of the president's supporters—believed that this was a weakness in his character. But despite disapproving of his personal behavior, the public remained divided about whether this was a matter of private or public concern.

Clinton was mostly able to withstand the rumors, but eventually allegations surfaced about an inappropriate relationship with a young woman who had served as a White House intern. According to reports, the relationship between the president and the young woman began in 1995. This matter did not initially become known. In 1987 Linda Tripp, who was a confidant of the intern, brought concerns about the matter to editors at *Newsweek*. But even after a briefing about Tripp's concerns, the editors decided not to publish the allegations.

Still, the story began to unravel. In December of that year, the intern was subpoenaed to testify in a trial in which a woman named Paula Jones was suing Clinton on charges of sexual harassment. At that time, the intern denied having had an intimate relationship with the president.

Then, early in 1998 Linda Tripp, the intern's confidant who had gathered some evidence against the president, met with Kenneth Starr, an independent counsel who already had been charged to investigate the Clintons for potential wrongdoing in the Whitewater real estate scandal, which was otherwise unrelated. On the basis of information provided by Tripp, Starr soon requested approval to expand his investigations into possible perjury or obstruction-of-justice charges against the president related to presumed false testimony in the Paula Jones case.

Not long after, *The Drudge Report*, a conservative Internet commentary and news site, reported that *Newsweek* already had information about "a White House intern [who had] carried on a sexual affair with the President of the United States," but that the magazine had declined to publish the story.[30] Pressured by this revelation, *Newsweek* changed course and went forward a report on the allegations.[31] By this time, the story was a full-fledged scandal.

Initial reactions from the people close to Clinton were anger and indignation. Appearing on the popular NBC television show *Today* in late January 1998, Hillary Clinton defended her husband against what she called a "vast right-wing conspiracy" that was "politically motivated."[32] (At the time, Mrs. Clinton was unaware that the charges against her husband were largely true.) The scandal soon overwhelmed most other events in

Washington. Not surprisingly, given the ideologically polarized context of that era, the controversy soon escalated to near crisis proportions. Months of protracted legal wrangling followed, in which Starr slowly gathered evidence from many sources.

Starr eventually delivered a massive amount of material to the House Judiciary Committee along with a report that was more than 400 pages long and listed 11 offenses that were grounds for impeachment. The Republican-controlled committee slowly began releasing highly embarrassing information from the Starr investigation. Calls for Clinton's resignation began to mount. The full House of Representatives voted to proceed with the matter in early October. Televised hearings soon followed. After weeks of public debate, in early December the House voted to approve articles of impeachment. Bill Clinton thus became only the second U.S. president to face an impeachment trial, which under procedures specified in the Constitution would be undertaken in the Senate.

The trial phase of the proceedings was scheduled for January 1999. At the time, Clinton was the beneficiary of strong public approval ratings, due, in large measure, to the strength of the national economy. Unsurprisingly, the trial was tense. But a month after the Senate commenced the impeachment proceedings, the president was acquitted of the charges. Still, the damage inflicted on his reputation would be slow to heal. In the eyes of conservative critics and some others, for whom Clinton's behavior was emblematic of a wider national problem, the episode was seen as confirming evidence of the United States' continuing moral decline.

The nation, or at least Washington, had been obsessed with Bill Clinton's personal behavior for months. To some people, the attention was justified since to them Clinton symbolized a weakening of American moral virtue. Other people, though disapproving of Clinton's personal conduct, felt that the amount of attention paid to the scandal trivialized government.

The Massacre at Columbine

Not long after Clinton was acquitted of the charges against him, an incident revealed that the United States faced serious problems for which it was ill-prepared. A violent episode at a seemingly typical American high school served as a reminder that just below the surface of everyday life, society faced severe and troubling problems.

On April 29, 1999, a scene of brutal murder horrified the nation. During what otherwise might have been an ordinary school day, two students walked into the public high school of Columbine, Colorado, and subsequently began a shooting spree that yielded deadly results. At the end of the frightening episode, the attackers killed themselves. But by then they had terrorized the entire school and murdered 12 students and 1 teacher. Another two dozen students were injured. The deadly event traumatized not just the Columbine community but also the entire nation. It was a senseless, cruel rampage, and it had occurred in a setting that few people associated with crimes on such a shocking scale.

The psychology behind the attacks was complex, but some aspects of it seem clear. The shooters carefully planned the attacks and appear to have been motivated partially by revenge. They held grudges against other students and authorities. But although they were deeply alienated and exhibited symptoms that might have been warning signs, their violent outburst caught the community, and the nation, by surprise. It was more evidence that surface appearances can be deceiving and that disturbing undercurrents in everyday life remained very much part of the American scene.

The Columbine massacre prompted deep reflection and soul-searching, as Americans tried to comprehend how things could have gone so wrong. Although more security precautions were instituted at many schools, the nation was rattled and continued to ask how the massacre could have happened. Unfortunately, it would not be the last time that Americans would ask themselves such questions. (Documentary filmmaker Michael Moore used the incident as the basis of his 2002 film *Bowling for Columbine*.)

AN UNEASY NATION

Despite the appearance that the United States had won the Cold War, in the years leading up to the end of the decade this perceived victory did not seem to mean very much. Threats from militant Islamists appeared to be surfacing against American interests in many parts of the world. And the danger had even been manifested in an attack in New York City.

In 1998, suicide bombers had attacked American embassies in Kenya and Tanzania. Twelve Americans were among the hundreds of victims killed in the attacks. The nearly simultaneous assaults were powerfully symbolic, and the violence provoked a swift response from the Clinton administration.

Speaking at a press conference at Andrews Air Force Base in Maryland a few days later, Clinton honored those who had died. He also explained the administration's interpretation of the events:

No matter what it takes, we must find those responsible for these evil acts and see that justice is done. There may be more hard roads ahead, for terrorists target America because we act and stand for peace and democracy; because the spirit of our country is the very spirit of freedom. It is the burden of our history and the bright hope of the world's future.[33]

The administration aimed to back up this assessment with action. Later in the month, American naval vessels launched cruise missiles in response. The targets were a terrorist training facility in Afghanistan and a factory in Sudan that was thought to be producing nerve gas.

The perpetrators of the embassy bombing appeared to be among the growing number of extremists following a man named Osama bin Laden. Although officials in Washington had long been aware of him, bin Laden was not a name that most Americans had yet come to recognize. But the embassy bombings made clear that this shadowy figure was now a major nemesis.

In the 1990s, it thus appeared that many people had come to believe that some form of national ruin or decline was perhaps unavoidable. This did not mean that the majority of the population agreed with those who expected a literal apocalypse to emerge at the millennium's end, of course. But it does suggest that a sufficient number of cracks had appeared in the façade of American life to suggest that perhaps the nation had peaked. The twentieth century, after all, had been regarded as "the American century," but many people began to doubt the United States would be able to retain its power—political, military, and moral—and its influence to such a great extent in the future.

To some people, especially conservative thinkers and politicians, any further decline of the United States was almost too terrible a thought to envision. They were deeply committed to American Dream ideals, at home and abroad, and to a traditional way of understanding the proper, perhaps God-given, role that the nation could and should play in world affairs. To forestall the erosion of U.S. power, therefore, a group of conservatives established the Project for the New American Century (PNAC), a think tank that would "promote American global leadership."[34] The organization's Statement of Principles laid out the essential questions: "Does the United States have the vision to build upon the achievements of past decades? Does the United States have the resolve to shape a new century favorable to American principles and interests?"[35]

For those holding a worldview that was so strongly connected to the primacy of American power and beliefs, then, the thought of any significant diminishment of them was tantamount to comprehensive national failure.

THE NEW MILLENNIUM

As the date approached, there was much talk and speculation about the potential significance of the year 2000. Although some people did believe that it could bring a worldwide cataclysm, for the most part such talk was focused on more mundane possibility. One topic was the potential for a worldwide computer glitch associated with the changing date and whether that would cause a global financial crisis. Yet no major disruptions occurred. January 1, 2000, was celebrated around the world, but it did not spark major catastrophes.

Prior to that date, however, end-of-millennium apocalyptic dread was a fairly widespread cultural theme. Often it was accompanied by warnings and discussions with an overtly moralistic tone. The Christian implications of this were obvious. (It is important to recall that only in the Western calendar system, which is based upon a Christian reckoning of time, was a millennium even ending. In other traditional calendar systems, this was not the case.)

Although they did not make much of an initial impression on the secular book market, a series of novels based on the End Times of Christian prophesy proved to be hugely popular among Christian readers in this era. Written by Tim LaHaye and Jerry B. Jenkins, the first and most well known of these books, *Left Behind*, was published in 1998. The novel sold well and was subsequently used as the basis of a low budget film. It was released late in 2000 on home video and then in theaters, where it had made little impact, in early 2001.

To some Christian believers, the Second Coming of Christ and the battle of Armageddon appeared close at hand. To others, the impending transition to the Third Millennium may have been more of an opportunity to take stock of the nation's moral standing, and to think about what changes should be made for ensuring the future health and prosperity of the United States. Indeed, for many Christian believers, the important point in the Bible's teachings about the Apocalypse, in the biblical sense, was to be prepared for it by bringing one's actions and beliefs in line with Christian teaching. The exact date when the End Times would occur is, theologically, less important.

Beyond those mentioned already, a number of films from the 1990s can be interpreted, in part, as visions of the impending disaster that may befall the United States, and even the world, at the close of the millennium.[36] These are typically stories of enormous disaster, sometimes on a global scale. In *Volcano* (1997), for example, an eruption in the center of Los Angeles wreaks havoc on the city. *Armageddon* (1998), a visual spectacle directed by Michael Bay, tells the story of efforts to stop a huge asteroid from colliding with the earth and destroying much of human life. A film with some superficial similarities, *Deep Impact* (1998), also has a narrative dealing with a comet that may destroy earth.

In the science fiction genre, other films continued the invasion and destruction themes that were established decades earlier. *Independence Day* (1996), for example, is an action-oriented movie about American military pilots thwarting an invasion by an otherwise seemingly unstoppable force of alien invaders. *The X-Files: Fight the Future* (1998) combines surreptitious alien invasion and government conspiracy themes. An uninspired American remake of the Japanese original, director Roland Emmerich's *Godzilla* (1998) updates the story of the story of the gigantic monster that threatens to level New York City.

Real-world events did not live up to the new millennium's hype or to the catastrophic visions that appeared in Hollywood movies. Yet in 2000, the final year of Bill Clinton's presidency, global dangers remained quite evident. Terrorism against Americans and American interests was a constant concern. And there was little to suggest that the terrorist threat to the United States was diminishing. As a global superpower with a presence across many parts of the globe, there were many possible targets both within the United States and elsewhere. But Islamic extremists remained keenly interested in those targets that symbolized American power.

In October 2000, an American naval vessel, the USS *Cole*, entered a Yemeni harbor en route to join the U.S. Navy's Sixth Fleet, which was enforcing sanctions against Iraq that had been put into place after the Gulf War. Although on alert for possible threats, a small boat managed to pull up next to the American warship. On board the unrecognized craft were suicide bombers, who detonated powerful explosives once they had maneuvered their boat next to the *Cole*. The resulting blast tore a 40-foot hole in the naval vessel, killing 17 sailors and injuring 38 others.[37]

The president soon vowed to "find those responsible." But as *Time* magazine writers noted, Clinton's words possessed a "numbing familiarity" that "betrayed a sense of dread about America's exposure to terrorist attacks and the country's apparent inability to prevent them."[38] A year later, this assessment would appear prophetic.

CHAPTER 10

Apocalypse Realized

The United States had survived a long Cold War with the Soviet Union, which came to an end in the 1990s. On the surface, this was a great American victory. A foe that once had sparked apocalyptic fears of global destruction was vanquished, leaving the United States as the world's only genuine superpower. The assessment of the conservative think tank PNAC probably summed up how many Americans viewed the situation:

> After the victories of the past century—two world wars, the Cold War and most recently the Gulf War—the United States finds itself as the uniquely powerful leader of a coalition of free and prosperous states that faces no immediate great-power challenge. The American peace has proven itself peaceful, stable and durable. It has, over the past decade, provided the geopolitical framework for widespread economic growth and the spread of American principles of liberty and democracy.[1]

Yet, while an old enemy no longer posed a threat, there were many potential dangers looming on the horizon. Some people in the political sphere were reluctant to simply accept the apparent realization of a new *Pax Americana* as a condition that would last on its own and urged proactive vigilance. Neoconservatives, for example, advocated strengthened American defense as part of an agenda for continued U.S. hegemony in the new century. Others seemed less concerned. Indeed, for the most part Americans seemed to regard existing threats as manageable and, importantly, as external.

As the year 2000 began, the American Dream seemed mostly intact. Many people had achieved the good life that their parents had wished for them a generation earlier. They shopped and traveled and lived in relative comfort in homes that were larger and filled with more consumer goods than ever before.[2] Some economic problems did arise, such as the bursting of the so-called dot-com bubble in March 2000, but many middle-class Americans enjoyed a standard of living that had grown considerably better over the years.

Hollywood entered the 2000s still engaged in its continuing search for new material that would attract modern audiences. By this time, cable television networks, such as HBO and Cinemax, were major players in screen entertainment, and the quality of their productions often equaled or surpassed that of many feature films. Cable series such as *The Sopranos* (1999–2007) and *Oz* (1997–2003) were critical as well as popular successes. In addition, the Internet was growing, and it, too, seemed poised to provide strong competition for the attention of viewers.

THE MOMENT OF APOCALYPSE

When the votes were tallied after the bitter presidential campaign of 2000, the results were inconclusive. In large measure, this was due to questions about ballots that were cast in Florida. The election was quite close. In the popular vote, Democratic candidate Al Gore, the sitting vice president, edged out Republican candidate George W. Bush by a close margin. According to the American system of choosing a president, however, it is the vote count in the Electoral College that determines the winning candidate, not simply the national vote total. And controversies about how votes were to be counted in Florida meant that the final tally in the Electoral College was in doubt.

Uncertainty about who had actually won the election dragged on for weeks. Eventually, the Supreme Court decided the matter in the case *Bush v. Gore*. The Court's intervention was a highly unusual development and the source of partisan controversy. But it was the Court's decision that determined that George W. Bush would become the 43rd president of the United States.

The early months of Bush's presidency seemed unremarkable, but all of that changed eight months after his inauguration. Despite frightening episodes of terrorist violence in the previous decade, few were prepared for the events that occurred under a bright blue sky on September 11, 2001. On that date, box cutter-wielding terrorists commandeered four jetliners. Two of the aircrafts were then flown directly into the World Trade Center's twin towers in New York City. A third smashed into the Pentagon shortly thereafter. A fourth hijacked jet crashed in rural Pennsylvania after passengers, who had learned of the fate of the other hijacked aircrafts, attempted to overpower the hijackers.

The attacks of September 11 crystallized decades of fear and anxiety. At that moment, the apocalyptic event that Americans had dreaded since the early days of the Cold War seemed to have abruptly become a reality. New York City was not destroyed by an atomic bomb or wiped out by a natural disaster. But when the commandeered jetliners flew into the twin towers of the World Trade Center, a potent symbol of everything that the American Dream embodied, the shock and horror was almost too much for Americans to bear. And when the towers crumbled, claiming thousands of lives, the sense of grief and anguish was immense. The anger and bewilderment that followed were surely heightened by the intense emotional pain of the attacks.

Though each of the 9/11 attacks resulted in tragic loss of life, the events in New York City received the most media attention. The fall of the twin towers and the deaths of thousands horrified Americans. Not since the death of John F. Kennedy had the nation experienced an event that was so thoroughly traumatic.

For decades, Americans had largely escaped from violence of such magnitude on their home turf, even during times of war. But now, on live television, Americans helplessly watched as thousands of their follow citizens perished. And there was no assurance that even more horrifying destruction was not in the offing. The eerily quiet skies—the result of a hastily declared halt to all nonofficial air traffic after the attack—seemed ominous. Americans anxiously waited. They hoped that there would not be another blow, but they feared that it was imminent.

Most of the world quickly condemned the 9/11 attacks. Messages of support were received in Washington from around the globe. Meanwhile, on the home front, a strong feeling of solidarity quickly emerged among Americans. They were in shock about the attack, but public opinion polls showed that they overwhelmingly stood in support of George W. Bush as his administration mapped out a retaliatory response.

Osama bin Laden and al-Qaeda, the radical Islamist organization he led, were soon identified as the people who orchestrated the attacks. American officials knew of bin Laden, but few ordinary U.S. citizens knew much about him. After the attacks, that quickly changed. Osama bin Laden became a household name in the United States (and around the world). He would come to symbolize the new American archenemy.

Bin Laden's hatred for the United States had been a long time in the making. At one time, he had been active in fighting the Soviets during the conflict in Afghanistan. It had a profound effect on him. He later said of his participation in the struggle: "In our religion there is a special place in the hereafter for those who participate in jihad. One day in Afghanistan was like 1000 days in an ordinary mosque."[3]

Deeply sensitive to what he perceived as affronts to Islam, bin Laden was enraged when Saudi Arabia permitted American-led coalition forces to establish military bases and stage operations there during the Persian Gulf War in the early 1990s. The memory of that perceived invasion of Islamic ground lingered with bin Laden and festered. From his perspective, the United States had directly assaulted Islam.

Some of bin Laden's subsequent thinking was apparent in a 1998 interview he granted to a Western journalist. In that context, he laid out his interpretation not only of affairs in the Islamic world, and especially the Middle East, but also of the world more generally. It was a view that pictured the United States as an enemy of God and of Islamic peoples everywhere. This view mandated, in bin Laden's view, the waging of a holy war. Bin Laden was quoted as saying that war against the United States was justified because the United States had sent "tens of thousands of troops to the land of two Holy Mosques" and was guilty of "meddling in its affairs and its politics, and its support of the oppressive, corrupt and tyrannical regime that is in control."[4]

Asked about the use of terror as a weapon, and specifically about its use against ordinary citizens, bin Laden said, "Every state and every civilization and culture has to resort to terrorism under certain circumstances for the purpose of abolishing tyranny and corruption."[5] It was clear from these and other comments that prior to September 11, 2001, bin Laden had developed a rationale for the methods of violence that he maintained were necessary to achieve what, according to him, were just ends. With the events of 9/11, these views were put into action.

REACTIONS TO TERRORISM

Beginning immediately at the time of the attacks, the tragedy of the twin towers barraged television news. Videos showing the deadly impact, the crumbling towers, and street-level pandemonium were constantly repeated. Audiences in the United States—and around the globe—were transfixed on the event. (The incidents at the Pentagon and in Pennsylvania, both of which occurred outside the media-intense environment of New York, were less emphasized.) Douglas M. Kellner has well explained the significance of this aspect of the event:

> Powerful media spectacles help shape social memory, constructing individuals' views of history and contemporary reality. Resonant images help construct how people see and interpret the world, and the oft-repeated images of airplanes hitting the WTC [World Trade Center], the buildings burning and then collapsing, and piles of rubble left in their wake were among the most compelling ever witnessed by global media culture.[6]

Americans had some experience with terrorism on their home soil. They had witnessed, for example, both the Oklahoma City bombing and a mostly unsuccessful attack against the World Trade Center in the previous decade. But as terrible as previous episodes had been, they did not compare with the scale of the September 11 attacks, the psychological impact of which was enormous. Indeed, the initial trauma was so great that the 9/11 attacks seemed to cause worry about the future survival of the nation.

In retrospect, however, it was probably never likely that the terrorists who were behind the attacks could have defeated the whole of the United States through such acts of violence. So it is difficult to envision the attack as existential in that way. Possessing the mightiest military in the world and with a population of more than 280 million people scattered over a continent 3,000 miles wide, Americans did not literally face total annihilation. But this was of little consolation and in no way seems to have reduced the intense fear that the 9/11 attacks caused in the United States.

The very word "terrorism" probably added to the level of anxiety. While the term is brimming with frightening associations, it is often used loosely and to some extent it can seem unclear. Regardless of which technical definition one might apply to the term, however, few people would dispute that the 9/11 attacks constituted acts of terrorism. But beyond a general sense of what the word means, the concept is often unexamined.

"Terrorism" is a word with shades of nuance that give it variations of meaning. In an analysis of the term that was published before the 9/11 attacks, Martha Crenshaw pointed out that "the concept of terrorism is deeply contested."[7] In attempting to clarify its meaning, she has provided a useful examination of the concept:

> The use of the term is often polemical and rhetorical. . . . In principle, terrorism is a deliberate and systematic violence performed by small numbers of people, whereas communal violence is spontaneous,

sporadic, and requires mass participation. The purpose of terrorism is to intimidate a watching popular audience by harming only a few.... Terrorism is meant to hurt, not destroy. Terrorism is preeminently political and symbolic.[8]

Terrorism thus functions on a deeply psychological level. Indeed, it is intended to inflict mental anguish and doubt as much as to maim and kill human targets. It is usually an instrumental action—a means to the end of achieving some goal apart from the resulting deaths.

From this perspective, it appears that the acts of 9/11 were as much intended as symbolic acts, which would inflict as negative emotional reaction as possible, as intended to inflict massive death and suffering. These outcomes were all but assured given the scale of the attacks. Americans felt more threatened and vulnerable after 9/11 than at any time in then-recent memory.

But the attacks had another effect: for a while they united the United States more than it had been in a long time. By providing the American public with such a clear and present enemy, and by evoking a powerful emotional response, the attacks brought together a nation that had been fractured politically for many years. As one writer observed, "9/11 has transformed the city of sin into a symbol of American unity."[9] Thus for a period of months, the emergence of an unambiguous common enemy resulted in a restored Americanism that crossed party lines. This sense of unity bridged many of the differences between liberals and conservatives. This was something that American political leaders had been unable to accomplish in recent memory.[10]

Still, although they were united against a common foe, Americans remained fearful. According to a survey cited by CNN, "a year after the attacks two-thirds of all Americans said they thought about the attacks at least once a week."[11] This new sense of anxiety was apparent in the U.S. cultural and political response to the attacks in the years that followed, in which the United States soon became a hypervigilant society. Vowing to prevent all such future attacks, government leaders enacted sweeping policy changes and legislation, all of which were explicitly aimed at doing whatever would be necessary to forestall another tragedy.

Government Response

Within weeks of the attacks, Congress passed the Patriot Act. The new legislation, which went into effect on February 1, 2002, had bipartisan support and was approved by huge margins. The vote in the House of

Representatives was 357 to 66 in favor. In the Senate, there was even stronger support, with a tally of 98 to 1 in favor.

The Patriot Act was a far-reaching piece of legislation that touched many corners of American life. It provided legal tools to fight terrorism, but it also raised questions about the balance between individual rights and needs for national security. For example, Title II of the act was entitled "Enhanced Surveillance Procedures." It included controversial measures permitting "roving wiretaps" as well as covert-entry search warrants. Another part of the act, Title IV, significantly strengthened the security measures dealing with U.S. borders. These provided the government with broad new powers to investigate suspected terrorists, but to some people such provisions appeared to be at odds with traditional understanding of constitutional safeguards for citizen rights.

Maintaining a Way of Life

If 9/11 was an apocalyptic moment in the American narrative, what did that mean for the American Dream? The ideals of the American Dream had been a powerful narrative frame throughout American culture and politics for more than a half century. One could reasonably ask whether 9/11 somehow altered its place in the American saga.

In one sense, whatever new policy changes were implemented to enhance national security, American leaders were determined to see the American Dream and its ideals persist. Despite the enormity of September 11 and the initiation of a global War on Terrorism, therefore, George Bush had urged Americans to continue with their lives. Speaking to airline employees in Chicago just a few days after the attacks, he said:

> We are too strong a nation to be carried down by terrorist activity. When they struck, they wanted to create an atmosphere of fear. And one of the great goals of this Nation's war is to restore public confidence in the airline industry.... Get on board. Do your business around the country.... Take your families and enjoy life, the way we want it to be enjoyed.[12]

After 9/11, it was immediately realized that one of the terrorists' goals was to disrupt American life. The terrorists may have desired to destroy the United States entirely, but a more realistic goal was to topple the way of life that Americans cherished. This would not only dishearten Americans and cause them to feel defeated; it would also presumably undermine American influence on the world stage. From this point of view, the terrorist attacks struck to the heart of the American Dream. And this may explain the reasoning behind George Bush urging Americans to continue with life, in some ways almost as though there had been no attack. Of course, it proved to be difficult, especially in the years when war spread to Iraq, to simultaneously maintain public enthusiasm for military operations, and for the sacrifices entailed in that, while also encouraging the public to continue their lives as though everything remained as it had been before. These contradictory impulses, which could be debated endlessly, would eventually become more apparent than they were at first.

MILITARY RESPONSE TO 9/11

In his initial response to the events of September 11, George W. Bush declared that the attacks constituted acts of war. This characterization perhaps heightened the already emotional national response to the tragedy. Though few questioned it at the time, the president could have framed the assault as horrific crimes against humanity, rather than war. In some ways, this might have made sense given that the enemy in the 9/11 attacks was not a nation, but an amorphous group. If Bush had characterized the attacks as crimes on a massive scale, moreover, it might have implied a different kind of response. This, however, can only be a matter of speculation.

In fact, most people seemed to agree that the attacks did mean war. In the following days, months, and years, the nation pursued a vigorous military response, rather than an investigative-oriented international police operation, which in theory would have been another possible way to respond.

Soon after September 11, the American military verified that bin Laden and top al-Qaeda leadership were working from a base in Afghanistan. In that mountainous and forbidding country, al-Qaeda had been welcomed as guests by the Taliban regime, the extremely conservative Islamic group that then ruled Afghanistan. The U.S. military planned to strike back at bin Laden and his associates. The also set their sights on the Taliban, which appeared to be harboring al-Qaeda.

Operation Enduring Freedom, as the Afghanistan war was called, began on October 7, 2001, just weeks after the assault on the United States. In short order, the Taliban regime was driven from power, at first from the capital city of Kabul and then shortly thereafter from most of the country.

Yet although the mission was successful in these respects, many of the leading figures in al-Qaeda and the Taliban eluded American-led forces. The men identified as the primary targets disappeared into the rugged countryside, or neighboring Pakistan, or elsewhere. In particular, Osama bin

Laden, now the incarnation of evil in American eyes, was nowhere to be found.

A pro-American government under the leadership of Hamid Karzai was installed in Kabul, but its control of the nation was limited and highly dependent on American military and economic backing. Despite continued American and allied military operations in Afghanistan, the situation there remained unstable and largely unresolved for many years.

HOLLYWOOD AFTER 9/11

The Republican Party and Hollywood had a rocky relationship during the Clinton years. Many conservatives had presumed that the film and entertainment industry was contributing to the problems facing the United States. They thought that the works produced had encouraged a breakdown in morality and even an antipathy felt by many Americans for their own country. And they believed that Hollywood tended to side with liberal causes and political views, inserting itself as an active participant in partisan rancor.

Soon after the September 11 attacks, however, the Bush White House recognized that Hollywood might be a useful ally in the emerging War on Terrorism. So despite concerns of the past, the administration began to explore ways that Hollywood might be useful. In this effort, the White House sent Karl Rove to California for a meeting with industry leaders. Rove was a senior advisor to and trusted confidant of President Bush. His participation signaled that the White House viewed Hollywood's cooperation and participation in bolstering the war effort to be important.

Rove met with about 50 Hollywood leaders in Beverly Hills on November 11, 2001.[13] Among the ideas discussed were the possibility of Hollywood producing "public service announcements." Also considered were general proposals for Hollywood-created shows that would travel to entertain American troops, and ways to provide active-duty personnel in the field with access to new movies. Still another aim of the meeting was to find ways to ensure that Hollywood films portrayed the United States in a positive light, so as to bolster support for the war on terror among other members of the international community.[14]

Jack Valenti attended the meeting in his role as president of the MPAA. Valenti was no stranger to wartime politics. He had served as a special assistant to Lyndon Johnson during the early years of the Vietnam War, at a time when American military involvement in that conflict was escalating. (He left his government position in 1966 to assume the presidency of the MPAA.)

After the meeting Valenti reported, "Content was off the table." He meant the discussions were not aimed at giving Washington control over what sorts of messages and stories would appear in film and television productions.[15] Hollywood would remain independent, according to Valenti; it would choose its own direction.

Rove also insisted that this was the case. He said he had come to the meeting only to offer "a few suggestions" and that it "was not our purpose to come here and say this effort should in any way, shape or form be directed by or coordinated by the government."[16]

Still, while saying that the government did not seek to control the messages Hollywood disseminated, some of Rove's suggestions appear to have been consistent with the specific way in which the Bush administration was seeking to frame public understanding of the unfolding conflict. According to an account published in the *New York Times*, one topic discussed was the question of how Hollywood might spread the idea that the new "global conflict" was "a fight against evil rather than a disagreement between nations."[17]

Valenti said that there was "a seamless sense of unity" at the meeting.[18] Rove also seemed to have been pleased with what the meeting had accomplished. Afterward, he reported, "It's clear that the leaders of the industry have ideas about how they want to contribute to the war effort, and we certainly want to encourage that."[19]

At the time, the spirit of unity in the United States was perhaps stronger than it had been at any time since World War II. Because Americans viewed their nation under attack by the dark forces of evil, as embodied in the lurking al-Qaeda threat, the partisan divide lessened not only in Washington, but also across the nation and even extending to Hollywood.

The Influence of Events

Despite the widespread influence of 9/11 on American culture overall, writers have differed in their assessments about how much the event actually changed the way Hollywood did things. As with many traumatic events, it may be that the most significant effects—whatever those may prove to be— did not become clear in the immediate months and years after the event.

Some observers believe that, regardless of how ominously 9/11 loomed in American consciousness, Hollywood did not alter course as the result of the attacks. As Stephen Prince has observed, "The underlying narrative and generic forms of American film did not change in significant ways after September 11. Hollywood kept its genres and story formulas and readily adapted them to the new content of a post-9/11 world."[20] This, of course, is consistent with the ways in which Hollywood had adapted to many crises since the emergence of the modern, nuclear world in the 1940s.

Hollywood had long projected, literally and figuratively, the United States' cultural fears and anxieties emanating from real-world events. This had been the case dating back to the underlying fear of world destruction that became a genuine possibility after the Soviet Union acquired atomic weapons. Traditional Hollywood story forms and genres offer audiences familiar narrative frameworks in which to process dramatic events. As Prince writes, in using these recognizable cinematic narratives, "heroes and narrative denouements provide resolution and closure, and end point to anxieties that seem otherwise inescapable."[21]

More than this, films can be venues in which to express generalized emotional responses to traumatic events in ways that are indirect and offer psychological distance from the specific cause of the fear. This had also been a long-standing Hollywood tradition, with prominent past examples including such well-known films as *Invasion of the Body Snatchers* (1956). Films can thus reflect public perceptions and emotion indirectly through metaphor, allusion, allegory, and other strategies that permit airing of a topic without raising specific details that audiences might shun due to still-raw psychological pain.

Black Hawk Down

Production of director Ridley Scott's *Black Hawk Down* (2001) was already well under way prior to the events of September 11, 2001. The movie deals with the tragic fate of soldiers in the Battle of Mogadishu, discussed earlier, during the American intervention in Somalia in 1993. The particular incident that serves as a focal point for the story, as referenced in the title of the film, were the events after a Black Hawk helicopter was shot down in a dangerous part of the city. The incident claimed the lives of 18 American soldiers and hundreds of Somalis. And to the horror of Americans, the corpse of one U.S. soldier was dragged through the streets as the attackers celebrated their success in downing the American aircraft. That scene was repeated to a global television audience on numerous newscasts.

Despite the tragic events, the film portrays the American troops in a flattering light. U.S. soldiers appear as heroes facing overwhelming circumstances beyond their control. The Somalis, by contrast, are portrayed as "a pack of dark-skinned beasts,"[22] according to a review in the *New York Times*. The movie generated good box office business and many positive reviews. For example, *USA Today* critic Mike Clark reported that the film portrayed "the sheer professionalism of America's elite Delta Force—even in . . . unforeseen disaster."[23] Others were less impressed with the film and with its underlying message. In a February 2002 article in *New Statesman*, for example, Andrew Stephens asserted, "The tragedy of *Black Hawk Down* is that it feeds so many dangerous current American myths."[24]

The Bush administration, which was then working to build support for a potentially long war against terrorism, appears to have welcomed the essentially pro-American, pro-military message that was widely seen in the film. Vice President Dick Cheney, a staunch advocate of an aggressive military response to the 9/11 attacks, reportedly hosted a private screening of the film.[25] Clearly, in the context in which it was released, it was difficult not to read into the film potential parallels or lessons for the new War on Terrorism. One such "lesson" of the film, which may or may not have been an accurate one, appears to be that in the Somali incident, brave U.S. troops were hampered by bureaucracy and poor judgment on the part of American leaders. (This message is somewhat similar to a blatant theme in a very different kind of movie, *Rambo II*, which was released more than 15 years earlier.)

Yet the film can also be seen as more nuanced than this. As Douglas M. Kellner observed, "*Black Hawk Down* can be read as a cautionary tale about the dangers of interventionism in countries that have hostile forces, copious arms supplies, and urban battlegrounds where the U.S. loses its technological advantage."[26]

Shifting Plans

Even before 9/11, Hollywood often had turned to narratives featuring terrorist villains. Such terrorist incidents had been in the news sporadically for decades. Bombings, hijackings, and other crimes, especially in the Middle East and Europe, provided real-world points of reference for such stories, which Hollywood could adapt in fictional movies. In the 1990s alone, high-profile films such as *Under Siege* (1992), *Passenger 57* (1992), *Patriot Games* (1992), *True Lies* (1994), *Sudden Death* (1995), *Air Force One* (1997), and *The Siege* (1998) relied up terrorism story lines. The popularity of these and similar films meant that audiences were well accustomed to encountering fictional terrorism as part of mainstream entertainment.

The context of future films with this theme was altered by the 9/11 attacks, however. As an article in the *New York Times* observed, in the immediate aftermath of the attacks "Hollywood has been handed the gift of actual national villains in the form of Islamic terrorists," but rather than exploit this, as might have been expected, Hollywood "has opted for restraint to avoid accusations of bias and the danger of offending audience sensibilities in an increasingly multiracial America."[27] Indeed, several films in various stages of production were delayed due to the industry's uncertainty about the wisdom of releasing them too soon after the 9/11 attacks. Possibly the most publicized of such films was *Collateral Damage*, which was directed by Andrew Davis and starred Arnold Schwarzenegger. Its release was pushed back to February 2002.

In future years, however, terrorist themes again became mainstream staples in film, as well as television. But in the months immediately after the September 11 attacks, the industry was cautious, as it tried to gauge potential audience reactions.

SETTING SIGHTS ON IRAQ

In his State of the Union Address in January 2002, President Bush laid out a far-ranging vision of which nations constituted the gravest threats to American security. In that speech, he declared that Iran, Iraq, and North Korea were part of an "axis of evil." These were hostile states with programs aimed at developing weapons of mass destruction and arming terrorists who might attack the United States.

Thus not long after the invasion of Afghanistan, officials in Washington were ready to take aim at a new target—even though the Afghanistan situation was not yet complete. To many observers the new focus of attention, Iraq, was actually a return to unfinished business from a decade earlier.

Well before the 9/11 attacks, many conservative intellectual and political leaders in the United States remained very concerned about Iraq and especially about the fact that its leader, Saddam Hussein, remained in power so many years after the conclusion of the Persian Gulf War. Some people second-guessed the original strategy that had resulted in the United States declaring a cease-fire without first deposing Hussein. Even before the 2001 attacks, they were ready to see Hussein and his regime driven from power. The conservative PNAC, for example, called for the overthrow of Hussein as early as 1997. (The term they used for this, which was often repeated by the administration of George W. Bush a few years later, was "regime change.") Following up on this idea, in 1998 Donald Rumsfeld and Paul Wolfowitz, who would serve in the Bush administration, went so far as to send an open memorandum to then-President Bill Clinton, in which they called for the United States to bring about Hussein's removal from power.

It was perhaps not completely surprising, then, that soon after 9/11, with influential members of PNAC serving within and advising the Bush administration, the subject of regime change in Iraq was raised. But there remained the matter of whether Hussein's regime in Iraq had actually been involved in the 9/11 attacks. Surely Hussein was a despised leader in the eyes of most Americans. But undertaking a military operation against him as part of a campaign that was framed as a response to 9/11 was not immediately an obvious decision, unless some relationship between Hussein and the terrorists could be established.

From the PNAC perspective, however, an absolute linking of Saddam Hussein to 9/11 was not necessary. In late September 2001, PNAC had communicated to the president their rationale, stating, "even if evidence does not link Iraq directly to the attack, any strategy aiming at the eradication of terrorism and its sponsors must include a determined effort to remove Saddam Hussein from power in Iraq. Failure to undertake such an effort will constitute an early and perhaps decisive surrender in the war on international terrorism."[28]

In the months that followed the 9/11 attacks, then, there was a strong push to bring about the downfall of Saddam Hussein. Although a relationship between Hussein and support for terrorists was often asserted, a clear connection between his regime and the perpetrators of the 9/11 attacks was difficult to establish. The interest in bringing the War on Terrorism to Iraq remained strong within some quarters of the Bush administration, however.

In that milieu, a new claim was made against Hussein's regime: that Iraq was producing and stockpiling "weapons of mass destruction," which were alleged to represent a clear danger to international security. Colin Powell, the former chairman of the Joint Chiefs in the Persian Gulf War and now serving as the secretary of state, spoke to an assembly of the United Nations in which he claimed the United States had "proof" of Iraq's weapons of mass destruction. Not long after, the United Nations passed a resolution that authorized action against Iraq.

The United States led an invasion of Iraq began in March 2003. As with operations during the Persian Gulf War more than a decade earlier, the Iraqi military's resistance was weak. By the end of the month, Secretary of Defense Donald Rumsfeld claimed that the United States had knowledge of Iraq's weapons of mass destruction, which seemed to validate the decision to launch the invasion. Not long after, Baghdad fell to oncoming American-led troops. The image of what at the time seemed to be a group of jubilant Iraqis toppling a huge statue of Saddam Hussein was broadcast around the world. The Iraqi dictator had fled, and his regime fell apart. By May 1, 2003, George W. Bush announced, "Mission accomplished." It appeared to be the end of another short war.

But things were not as they seemed. The regime had been deposed, but the situation remained tense and violent. Despite an aggressive search, the United States was unable to find the weapons of mass destruction that it claimed to know about and that had served as the public justification for the invasion. Over coming months, these initial claims came under increasing scrutiny, and slowly doubts mounted. Later, it was discovered that there were no weapons of mass destruction and that the intelligence reports leading to that claim were deeply flawed. (Powell later said that he regretted his role in bringing faulty information before the United Nations calling it a "blot"[29] on his record of service to the country.)

By 2004, the situation had deteriorated. The CIA even warned that Iraq could descend into civil war, as battling factions of Sunni and Shi'ite Iraqis violently fought with each other. It was the beginning of a conflict that would drag on until the following decade.

Meanwhile, in April 2004 shocking photographs, which appeared to show American soldiers degrading and abusing Iraqi prisoners at the Abu Ghraib detention facility in Baghdad, were published in the press. The reputation of the United States among many Iraqis and others in the Middle East was already under challenge. The abuses at Abu Ghraib further diminished the reputation of the United States.

THE NEW AGE OF FEAR

The United States thus waged war on multiple fronts in the years following the attacks of September 11, 2001. Meanwhile, on the home front, American culture began to slowly process the new realities of post-9/11 life. Much of everyday existence soon returned to a state of near-normalcy, albeit one in which heightened security concerns were very apparent. But new fears—and new versions of old fears—were sometimes not far from the surface.

After 9/11, Americans seemed to fear for their safety more than ever before. Many measures were put into place in an effort to assure public confidence, but still people remained on edge. For some people, no amount of precaution appeared to be too much. Others were not quite as concerned. But still, anxiety caused by the perception that the world had become dangerous remained strong.

Some Hollywood productions touched on these fears, either directly or indirectly. Steven Spielberg's *Minority Report* (2002) is a science fiction film set in 2054. In this world, the government has developed powerful technologies to maintain law and order. In high-tech laboratories, computers are linked to humans kept in a precognitive state. This powerful combination allows the computers to detect brainwaves of people who are preparing to commit crimes. Armed with this advance knowledge, the police force is able to intercept and arrest the would-be criminals before the wrongdoing occurs.

Although the film is based on a Philip K. Dick story that substantially pre-dates 9/11, the release of the film in the context of the then-new War on Terrorism presented interesting parallels with real-world events. In this new era, the doctrine of preemptive strikes was much debated. The idea that violent attacks should be prevented, almost by any means necessary, was a central goal of the Bush administration's policy. President Bush articulated the idea as early as June 2002 (just days before *Minority Report*'s release) as part of a speech in which he said, "Our security will require all Americans to be forward-looking and resolute, to be ready for preemptive action when necessary to defend our liberty and to defend our lives."[30] In a review published in the *Chicago Sun-Times* film critic Roger Ebert noted the thematic similarity of the movie's preemptive strategy against common murderers and the actual government policy, then new, of using preemptive strikes to forestall attacks on the United States.[31]

How Far Is Too Far?

After 9/11, Americans also grappled with questions about how far the government could or should go to preserve public safety. The potential contradiction of a free society using tools and techniques usually associated with totalitarian states was widely noted. Should "harsh interrogation techniques," which some people equated with torture, ever be condoned? Such questions were much disputed. Advocates of each position were certain that they were in the right.

A film that addressed the possible responses to a dangerous world was *V for Vendetta* (2006). Based on a comic book series, director James McTeigue's film portrays a dystopian society in which a masked hero, V, fights against a fascist government. Facing apparently insurmountable odds, V resorts to violent acts that have all the appearance of terrorism. The film thus implicitly questions whether terrorism is a label that is defined simply on the basis of which violent acts are perpetrated, or if there is ever a justifying context for such violence. As one writer observed, in *V for Vendetta* "protagonists and antagonists employ similar justifications for their actions and use potentially illegitimate violence, including acts of terrorism."[32] Released in the context of public debate about "harsh interrogation techniques," which U.S. forces had engaged in for the purposes of preventing terrorist acts, this aspect of the story touched on then-current contentious themes.

Fearing the Other

The September 11 attacks represented the first major assault on the United States' home soil since the attack on Pearl Harbor nearly 60 years earlier. The 9/11 terrorists were foreigners, but they staged the attack from within. These facts fueled xenophobia, which was a feeling already festering in some parts of the U.S. population. The trauma of 9/11 increased suspicion and anxiety about security at the nation's borders and also propelled immigration into the spotlight as a political issue.

While the initial connection to 9/11 may have been specifically related to the Islamist terrorists who had entered the United States, the issue spilled over to the question of immigration—and especially illegal immigration—more generally. One writer assessed this development by saying that "the country had circled its bandwagons" and that "the Bush administration's War on Terror has slowly spread to a subsequent War on Immigrants."[33]

The controversy over immigration was not a new phenomenon, of course. Racism, ethnic and religious prejudices, and economic competition were among the causes of long-standing rancor on the matter of immigration in the United States.[34] Fear of dangers from the outside after 9/11 seemed in some ways a return to the anxieties of the early 1950s, when Americans were concerned that Communists had infiltrated the nation and were poised to destroy the their way of life from within.

Racism had always been a troubling issue in the United States. In the post-9/11 world, it was an issue with new variations. In a related vein was the movie *Crash* (2005), which was directed by Paul Haggis. It looked at racial and ethnic tensions in a way that many viewers found uncomfortable. On the surface, the movie reveals a jumbled narrative that is based on chance and circumstantial situations, which seem to bring ethnically and racially diverse people randomly into contact with each other. There are Caucasian and African American characters, as well as Latinos, Iranians, and others. In one important scene, two African American men (played by Ludacris and Larenz Tate) randomly carjack a white couple (played by Brendan Fraser and Sandra Bullock), who the carjackers presume are racists.

Other apparently haphazard plot developments then reveal how much prejudice and discrimination infects and affects characters from seemingly every background. As critic Roger Ebert has noted, the people depicted in the film are "all defined in one way or another by racism. All are victims of it, and all are guilty of it."[35] In fact, the seemingly random encounters among characters, which reviewer Ken Tucker called "moral collisions,"[36] explore the depth of fear and loathing that people have for each other, which is perhaps the central idea around which the narrative is built. The film therefore reflects much of the era, in which post-9/11 fears had heightened awareness and anxiety of racial and ethnic difference. The film, while not directly related to 9/11, thus evokes the anxieties that Americans seemed to feel about those who were not like themselves—feelings they were often reluctant to acknowledge.

Natural Disasters

It is difficult to assess whether or to what extent the trauma of 9/11 influenced public perceptions about other types of catastrophes in the 2000s. If the September 11 attacks represented a clear break with past life and traditions, at least across some important dimensions, it is conceivable that this sufficiently altered the context in which events seemingly unrelated to the War on Terrorism were interpreted. In any case, environmental concerns returned to the public debate in full force in the 2000s. As with issues of many other kinds, debate about changing weather patterns was infused with bitter ideological rhetoric.

One Hollywood film that broached the subject of environmental disaster was *The Day after Tomorrow* (2004), directed by Roland Emmerich. A major part of the narrative deals with rescue efforts directed at New York City, which has become encased in ice as the result of catastrophic climate change. Described as the "first major disaster movie in the post-9/11 era," the film attracted a substantial audience.[37]

In 2005, Hurricane Katrina inflicted enormous destruction on the southern coast of the United States and especially on the city of New Orleans. It was evidence of nature's unpredictable power and fury and of the government's lack of preparedness. Indeed, Katrina exposed shocking behavior and pervasive instances of government failure, thus connecting natural disaster and social disaster themes.

Throughout the decade, warnings of coming disaster that would be the end result of climate change were the subject of bitter controversy. The following year, for example, much attention was aimed at a documentary that detailed Al Gore's campaign to raise awareness of global warming—a politically controversial label for the climate change that seemed to be sweeping the earth. Directed by Davis Guggenheim, *An Inconvenient Truth* (2006), sparked bitter debate about the validity of the science on which the claims in the film were based.

AFTER AN APOCALYPSE

Looking back, the attacks of September 11, 2001, can be seen as evoking the sense of dread that had been an undercurrent in American culture for more than a half century. As Mary Manjikian has explained, September 11, was an "apocalyptic moment"—a moment that represented a "singular event, which results in the destruction of the old and the transition to the new."[38] She further suggests that the attacks caused a deep rupture in the American narrative, "a dividing line between a pre-and post-9/11 world" and "a break with order in which the old order will never be fully restored."

But however much 9/11 may have created a dividing line in the American narrative, the attacks are apocalyptic for more than this result alone. Indeed, not only do the attacks represent a dividing line; they constituted a unique and momentous moral event. This was presumed immediately. The assault was interpreted not as mere hostilities between parties that despised each other, but rather as an assault by the embodiment of evil.

For some Christians, the 9/11 attacks were even more than this. September 11 seemed apocalyptic not simply metaphorically but literally. For them, 9/11 appeared to be part of the sequence of events, foretold in the Bible, leading to the End of Days. The attacks, in this view, are thus part of a larger story involving the Second Coming of Christ and God's judgment of humanity.[39] Some conservative Christian leaders further stated that the attacks had been brought on by the United States' bad behavior and failure to observe Christian principles.[40]

Some months afterward, the 9/11 attacks were described as "the defining moment for 21st century US cinema."[41] And surely American life was changed by that traumatic event. But from a vantage point more than a decade later, it appears not only that life had gone on, but also that for many Americans, it had returned to something remarkably familiar. While the details changed, many of the hopes and fears that had been expressed in earlier eras have persisted, albeit with modern, post-9/11 twists.

As apocalyptic as 9/11 may have seemed, especially at first, it does not appear to have wholly disrupted the American narrative. Although Americans stood united in the days immediately following the September 11 attacks, by the middle of the decade the ideological divide that had been building in Washington for many years had returned. Bitter partisanship was widely on display throughout American politics. The 2004 presidential campaign season even dredged up controversies from the long-ago Vietnam War. Democratic challenger John Kerry, who had served in Vietnam, was accused of anti-American activism in the latter days of that conflict. On the other side, George W. Bush's military service was also questioned and criticized. What this seemed to show was that not long after 9/11, long-standing animosity between the staunchest advocates of each major political party had not been significantly altered by the terrorist attacks of 9/11.

Meanwhile, the wars continued. American involvement in the Iraq War continued until December 2011. The war in Afghanistan, more than 10 years old, had by then taken center stage for the American military. Both conflicts burdened the men and women of the armed forces who had volunteered their services. They continued to sacrifice, while most Americans resumed life as if the United States were not at war. Hollywood rarely directly acknowledged these wars. When the occasional film about one of the wars did make an appearance, such as director Sam Mendes's *Jarhead* (2005), audience interest was generally tepid. Movies that touched on post-9/11 themes in a serious way, such as *Syriana* (2005), received critical respect but had lesser impact than more traditional entertainments.

Later, director Kathryn Bigelow's *The Hurt Locker*, which was released in the United States in 2009, told a story involving a bomb disposal unit in the Iraq War. The film was perhaps the biggest exception to the otherwise lackluster attention given to that war as it was ongoing. The film was generally praised by critics and was the recipient of several Academy Awards, including Best Picture and Best Director. Still, like *Lions for Lambs* (2007), *Stop-Loss* (2008), and other attempts to dramatize the war on film, it was only modestly successful in drawing audiences to the theater.

During this time, documentaries, such as Michael Moore's 2004 film *Fahrenheit 9/11*, sometimes challenged the official version of events. But these frequently played to audiences who were already aligned with the ideological inclinations of their directors. Instead, throughout the decade moviegoers flocked to films such as *Spider-Man* (2002), *Shrek 2* (2004), *Star Wars: Episode III, Revenge of the Sith* (2005), *Pirates of the Caribbean* (2003), and *Transformers* (2007). As had been true at times in the past, the lure of escapist entertainment proved powerful in the post-9/11 world.

ECONOMIC CRISIS

From outward appearances, the economy had mostly withstood the impact of the 2001 terrorist attacks and of the resulting wars in Afghanistan and Iraq. By 2007, however, there were signs that American consumers were becoming uneasy. In the following year, volatility in the global oil market raised concerns that the economy might be weakening. Such worries were heightened by the early arrival of the hurricane season that year, which threatened the production of natural gas in the Gulf of Mexico. This again showed that nature's uncertainties, when combined with human actions, had the potential to create serious challenges to the economic well-being of the nation.

None of this seems to have adequately prepared either American leaders or citizens for the economic upheaval that soon followed, however. In September 2008, a report from the Mortgage Bankers Association noted that nearly 10 percent of Americans with mortgages were in foreclosure or behind in making payments. Unemployment, meanwhile, had risen to over 6 percent, making it more difficult for many mortgage borrowers to make timely payments on their mortgage loans.[42]

Just two days after the Mortgage Bankers Association report, the government assumed control of the Federal National Mortgage Association (popularly known as Fannie Mae) and the Federal Home Loan Mortgage Association (known as Freddie Mac), the huge government-backed entities that play major roles in American home finance and mortgage lending. With the situation appearing to the very serious, these steps were part of government efforts to prevent a major economic meltdown. But years of borrowing behavior—in which many people took on more debt than was sustainable if the housing market were to falter—and questionable lending practices—especially with regard to so-called subprime mortgages—had created a situation ripe for a major crisis. Then, the apparently sudden collapse of Lehman Brothers, which had been one of the nation's largest investment banks, and the increasing precariousness of other leading American financial institutions soon showed that the crisis had materialized.

Fearing not just a recession but also an outright economic depression, policies were quickly put into place in an attempt to prevent economic disaster. Although a depression was avoided, the economy was severely damaged nonetheless. The housing market was left in disarray. Unemployment jumped. The stock market fell precipitously. The Dow Jones Industrial Average, for example, had been at over 13,000 in late 2007. By the middle of November 2008, it had dropped to under 8,000.

The economic crisis of 2008 shattered American confidence and prompted many people to ask hard questions. Credit, which for decades had allowed many people to attain home ownership and gain access to the good life of the American Dream, abruptly became much more difficult for average citizens and businesses to acquire. Public confidence in the American economy evaporated, especially as it soon became clear that there would be no quick solution to the economic turmoil. The housing market was slow to recover. Unemployment, meanwhile, continued to rise and by late 2009 was over 10 percent.[43]

The dismal turn in the economy resulted in much social and political unease. The 2008 presidential campaign season was nearing its end as major financial institutions teetered on the edge of ruin and as the Federal Reserve struggled to make quick policy adjustments to avert an even worse situation. The crisis persisted after the election and into the presidency of Barack Obama. The combination of shattered economic circumstances and the resurgence of ideological polarization in Washington created a new era of divisive politics.

As the economy struggled to recover, an amorphous group of economic and social conservatives coalesced around the Tea Party movement. Its influence rose, and many candidates espousing its fiscally and politically conservative message were swept into Congress as the result of the 2010 elections.

But there was a counterreaction. Some months later, a grassroots movement calling itself Occupy Wall Street took to the streets of many cities across the United States. Strongly opposing Tea Party ideology, the Wall Street protesters demonstrated against entrenched corporate interests. And they railed against the rising income gap between the United States' highest and lowest wage earners, which had been widening for several decades.

Although they mostly continued to issue escapist films that replicated traditional outlooks, American filmmakers occasionally presented works that were related to this new economic and political context. Director Tom Tykwer's *The International* (2009), for example, involves a rogue multinational financial firm. The company demonstrates it will take drastic, even murderous steps, to ensure its profitability and market position. The corporation in question is the epitome of an immoral, uncaring behemoth. As film critic A. O. Scott observed, "That multinational weapons manufacturers can be portrayed as more decent, civic-minded and principled than global financiers surely says something about the state of the world."[44]

In 2010, Oliver Stone returned to the financial world he had explored in his film *Wall Street*, which was released in 1987 at the height of the Reagan years and in which the main character, Gordon Gekko (played by Michael Douglas), had once pronounced, "Greed, for lack of a better word, is good." The narrative of Stone's new film, *Wall Street: Money Never Sleeps*, has many parallels to the real-world economic collapse of 2008, including behind-the-scenes profiteering in which insiders benefit at the expense of everyone else. Whether the film added to or changed audience perceptions about the American economy remains an open question. (In his review, critic Roger Ebert said he would have preferred an "angrier" film that was more "outraged," but he commented that perhaps "American audiences aren't ready for that."[45])

Other fictional films with connection to the real-world economic disaster painted similar pictures of corporate greed and a system run amok. Director

Jason Reitman's *Up in the Air* (2009) explored the effects of corporate downsizing. *The Company Men* (2011), directed by John Wells, follows the story of a huge corporation that discards parts of its business that are not profitable. The film reveals the desperation and devastation that result in the lives of characters tossed aside in the name of downsizing and efficiency. Another example is *Too Big to Fail*, a high-profile 2011 HBO cable television production that dramatized the economic crisis.

Perhaps more directly, some documentary films examined the origins and effects of the crisis. Among the most prominent of these were *Capitalism: A Love Story*, the 2009 film from director Michael Moore, and *Inside Job* (2010), a documentary from director Charles Ferguson that won an Academy Award, which explores the connection between the Washington political establishment and major financial institutions.

FEARS IMAGINED, FEARS REALIZED

The first decade of the twenty-first century was marked by severe challenges to the United States and its way of life. The 9/11 attacks, the amorphous War on Terrorism, the more traditional wars in Afghanistan and Iraq, and the economic crisis of 2008 were serious assaults on national confidence that strained the ability of many Americans to hold on to the ideals of the American Dream as they had known them for decades. The toxic political climate of divisiveness in Washington that had evolved over several decades, meanwhile, sometimes reached far beyond the capital. Often it seemed as though Americans increasingly tuned out people whose beliefs differed from their own.

As surprising as the series of traumatic events in the early 2000s may have been, however, the long-standing cultural fear of catastrophic, even apocalyptic events had kept the possibility of American ruin in the public eye for more than a half century. Political culture and Hollywood productions had long repeated the idea of apocalyptic events unleashed on the United States. And with 9/11 attacks and subsequent traumas, these long-standing fears seemed to be realized.

It seems reasonable to conjecture that the anxieties and the implicit sense of doom that had long been a subtext in the American narrative may have increased the intensity of Americans' responses. Undoubtedly, the tragic events of September 11, 2001, would have prompted an intense reaction under any conceivable circumstance. But the thing that had long been feared, having apparently come true, seems to have set off a heightened wave of emotion.

As this review of American film and society in the period extending from the mid-1940s to the 2000s suggests, the evolving anxieties of the culture have been remarkably enduring. Perceptions of the United States' greatness remain strongly linked to fears of its demise and moral failure. But like other forms of cultural production, motion pictures have always had the capacity to conceal and to reveal facets of life that surround viewers. In thinking about the ideals of the American Dream or about the ruin of the nation, then, film has offered audiences ways to reflect upon their world or to escape from it.

Notes

CHAPTER 1

1. John Winthrop, quoted in Garry Willis, *Under God: Religion and American Politics* (New York: Simon and Schuster, 1990), 207–8.

2. Tom Englehardt, "The American Century: That Was Then." *Los Angeles Times*, December 2, 2011.

3. See Leonard Quart and Albert Auster, *American Film and Society since 1945*, 4th ed. (Santa Barbara, CA: Praeger, 2011).

4. James T. Adams, *The Epic of America* (Boston: Little, Brown, 1941).

5. Jim Cullen, *The American Dream: A Short History of an Idea That Shaped a Nation* (New York: Oxford University Press, 2003), 189.

6. Joseph Campbell, *The Power of Myth* (New York: Doubleday, 1988), 5.

7. Ibid.

8. Clifford Geertz, *The Interpretation of Cultures* (New York: Basic Books, 1973), 140.

9. Hughes, Richard T., *Myths America Lives By* (Urbana: University of Illinois Press, 2003).

10. Ibid.

11. Stanley Baran, "Dignity: The Stories We Tell (about) Ourselves," *Bread and Circus*, 2009, http://breadandcircusnetwork.wordpress.com/2009/11/05/the-dignity-series-the-stories-we-tell-about-ourselves/.

12. Dorothy Thompson, "Science Will Make or Break the World," *Miami News*, June 29, 1946.

13. "Fears Atom Apocalypse," *The Windsor Daily Star*, May 2, 1957.

14. "Washington Calling: World Just Step Away from Apocalypse of Nuclear War," *The Florence Times*, September 28, 1963.

15. "Editor's Outlook: 'Peace Now' Cries Ignore History," *Albany Herald*, January 14, 1985.

16. Cal Thomas, "Clinton Policies Bring Israel's Apocalypse Near," *The Nevada Daily Mail*, March 28, 2000.

17. "Confessed Terrorist Confirms America's Fears," *Concord Monitor*, March 17, 2007.

18. "Fighting AIDS in Africa," *New York Times*, February 25, 2001.

19. Andy Geller, "Apocalypse Gets Worse as Epidemic May Double Death Count," *New York Post*, December 29, 2004.

20. Lauren Rudd, "Is This the Investor Apocalypse? Relax If You Can; It Isn't Nigh," *Sarasota Herald-Tribune*, September 26, 2008.

21. "The Horsemen Approach," *The Economist*, December 3, 2011, http://www.economist.com/node/21541016 (from the print edition).

22. George Orwell, *The Collected Essays, Journalism, and Letters, George Orwell: An Age Like This, 1920–1940*, ed. Sonia Orwell and Ian Angus (Jaffrey, NH: Godine, 2000), 523.

23. Tara J. Yosso and David G. García, " 'Who Are These Kids, Rejects from Hell? Analyzing Hollywood Distortions of Latina/o High School Students," in *Handbook of Latinos and Education: Theory, Research and Practice*, ed. Enrique G. Murillo (New York: Routledge, 2010), 452.

24. Thomas Doherty, *Projections of War: Hollywood, American Culture, and World War II*, rev. ed. (New York: Columbia University Press, 1999), 266.

25. See John Whiteclay Chambers and David Culbert, *World War II, Film, and History* (New York: Oxford University Press, 1996).

26. John Emmett Winn, *The American Dream and Contemporary Hollywood Cinema* (New York: Continuum, 2007).

27. Brigitte Nerlich, David D. Clarke, and Robert Dingwall, "The Influence of Popular Cultural Imagery on Public Attitudes towards Cloning," *Sociological Research Online* 4, no. 3 (1999), http://www.socre sonline.org.uk/socresonline/4/3/nerlich.html.

28. Gordon B. Arnold, *Conspiracy Theory in Film, Television, and Politics* (Westport, CT: Praeger, 2008).

CHAPTER 2

1. See, for example, Colin Shindler, *Hollywood in Crisis: Cinema and American Society, 1929–1939* (London: Routledge, 1996).

2. Joseph R. Gusfield, *Symbolic Crusade: Status Politics and the American Temperance Movement*, 2nd ed. (Urbana: University of Illinois Press, 1986), 119.

3. Samuel Eliot Morison, *The Oxford History of the American People* (New York: Oxford University Press, 1965), 900.

4. Motion Picture Producers and Distributors of America, "The Don'ts and Be Carefuls" (1927), reproduced in "The History of American Film: Primary Sources,"

Digital History, http://www.digitalhistory.uh.edu/historyonline/film_censorship .cfm.

5. Hedda Hopper is quoted in: Public Broadcasting System, *The American Experience:* "The Battle over *Citizen Kane*," http://www.pbs.org/ wgbh/amex/ kane2/.

6. Morris B. Holbrook and Elizabeth Caldwell Hirschman, *The Semiotics of Consumption: Interpreting Symbolic Consumer Behavior in Popular Culture and Works of Art* (Berlin: Mouton de Gruyter, 1993), 108.

7. This quotation, from an editorial entitled "The Picture and Patriotism," originally published in the April 21, 1917, edition of *Motion Picture News*, is reprinted in David H. Culbert, Richard E. Wood, and Lawrence H. Suid, *Film and Propaganda in America: A Documentary History* (Westport, CT: Greenwood, 1990), xxiii.

8. One interesting example of war-related American film production was Winsor McCay's short animated film, *The Sinking of the Lusitania*, from 1918, which was simultaneously a short documentary about the sinking of this passenger ship in 1915 and a call to arms against Germany.

9. Aljean Harmetz, *The Making of Casablanca: Bogart, Bergman, and World War II* (New York: Hyperion, 2002), 6.

10. This is shown, for example, in Clayton R. Koppes and Gregory D. Black, *Hollywood Goes to War: How Politics, Profits and Propaganda Shaped World War II Movies* (New York: Free Press, 1987); and in Thomas Patrick Doherty, *Projections of War: Hollywood, American Culture, and World War II* (New York: Columbia University Press, 1993), among other works.

11. This estimate of crowd size is repeated in Bill Bell, "The World Stops Here, Huge Times Square Crowd, Millions Watch from Afar," *Daily News*, January 1, 2000.

12. Tom Brokaw, *The Greatest Generation* (New York: Random House, 2004), xxvii–xxviii.

13. Murray Edelman, *Constructing the Political Spectacle* (Chicago: University of Chicago Press, 1988), 76.

CHAPTER 3

1. Howard Zinn, *A People's History of the United States* (New York: Harper Perennial, 2010), 432.

2. Dennis T. Miller and Marion Nowak, *The Fifties: The Way We Really Were* (Garden City, NY: Doubleday, 1977), 26.

3. George Kennan, "Telegram: The Charge in the Soviet Union (Kennan) to the Secretary of State," Moscow, [Russia], February 22, 1946.

4. Ibid.

5. Harry S. Truman, "Address before a Joint Session of Congress," March 12, 1947, online by Gerhard Peters and John T. Woolley, *The American Presidency Project*, http://www.presidency.ucsb.edu/ws/?pid=12846.

6. Ibid.

7. George C. Marshall, "The Marshall Plan Speech," June 5, 1947, George C. Marshall Foundation, http://www.marshallfoundation.org/library/doc_marshall_plan_speech.html.

8. J. Parnell Thomas, quoted in Nora Sayre, "Assaulting Hollywood," *World Policy Journal* 12, no. 4 (Winter 1995/1996): 51.

9. Testifying before HUAC did little to detract from Bogart's box office appeal. Two of his most popular and successful films were released not long after—*The Maltese Falcon*, in 1941, and *Casablanca*, in 1942.

10. Collins is quoted in Robert Mayhew, *Ayn Rand and Song of Russia: Communism and Anti-Communism in 1940s Hollywood* (Lanham, MD: Scarecrow Press, 2005), 16.

11. Ayn Rand, "Testimony before the House Un-American Activities Committee, 1947," reprinted in Mayhew, *Ayn Rand and the Song of Russia*, 181.

12. Ibid.

13. Ibid., 189.

14. Karl F. Cohen, *Forbidden Animation: Censored Cartoons and Blacklisted Animators in America* (Jefferson, NC: McFarland, 2004), 167.

15. Quoted in Larry Ceplair and Steven Englund, *The Inquisition in Hollywood: Politics in the Film Community, 1930–60* (Berkeley: University of California Press, 1983), 455.

16. Albert A. Einstein, letter to President Franklin D. Roosevelt, August 2, 1939.

17. Richard Rhodes, *The Making of the Atomic Bomb* (New York: Simon and Schuster, 1986), 690.

18. Nikolaus Riehl and Frederick Seitz, *Stalin's Captive: Nikolaus Riehl and the Soviet Race for the Bomb* (Washington, DC: American Chemical Society, 1996), 75.

19. "The Red Danube," *The Rotarian*, February 1950, 39.

20. "The New Pictures: In the Good Old Summertime" [includes review of *The Red Menace*], *Time*, July 18, 1949.

21. C. G. Jung, *Flying Saucers: A Modern Myth of Things Seen in the Sky* (New York: MJF Books, 1978), 13.

22. Ibid.

CHAPTER 4

1. Lizabeth Cohen, *A Consumers' Republic: The Politics of Mass Consumption in Postwar America* (New York: Knopf, 2003).

2. See Jason E. Taylor, "Financial Lessons from 1946," *Forbes*, June 9, 2010.

3. Aaron Brenner, Benjamin Day, and Immanuel Ness, eds., *The Encyclopedia of Strikes in American History* (Armonk, NY: M.E. Sharpe, 2009), 175.

4. Irving Richter, *Labor Struggles, 1945–1950: A Participant's View* (Cambridge: Cambridge University Press, 1994), 47.

5. Cohen, *A Consumers' Republic*, 70.

6. Ibid., 72.

7. Barbara M. Kelly, *Expanding the American Dream: Building and Rebuilding Levittown* (Albany: State University of New York, 1993), 24.

8. Ibid., 31.

9. For a discussion on the practice of redlining, see, for example, Denise B. Rose, "Racial Roadblocks: Pursuing Successful Long-Term Racial Diversity in Oak Park, Illinois, a Metropolitan Chicago Community." PhD Diss., Loyola University, 2007, 22.

10. Public Broadcasting System, "Tupperware!: People & Events: The Rise of American Consumerism," *The American Experience*, http://www.pbs.org/wgbh/amex/tupperware/peopleevents/e_consumer.html.

11. This is quoted in "The Economy: Baby Boom," *Time*, February 9, 1948.

12. Ibid.

13. National Industrial Conference Board, *The National Conference Board Business Record* (January 1948), 10–11.

14. Much of the background work necessary to design the new interstate highway system had been initiated in *Toll Roads and Free Roads*, a report to Congress issued in 1939 and in the Federal-Aid Highway Act of 1944. See U.S. Department of Transportation, Federal Highway Administration, "Celebrating the Eisenhower Interstate Highway System," http://www.fhwa.dot.gov/interstate/faq.htm#question17.

15. Horace Newcomb, *Encyclopedia of Television*, 2nd ed. (New York: Fitzroy Dearborn, 2004), 1607.

16. Most Westerns continued in this way until the 1960s, when the Western genre was reinvented by directors such as Sam Peckinpah and Sergio Leone.

17. Bosley Crowther, " 'She Wore a Yellow Ribbon,' at Capitol, Stars John Wayne as Cavalry Captain," *New York Times*, November 18, 1949.

18. Bosley Crowther, "The Screen: 'The Postman Always Rings Twice,' with Lana Turner in a Star Role, Makes Its Appearance at the Capitol," *New York Times*, May 3, 1946.

19. Ibid.

20. "Cinema: The New Pictures," *Time*, July 4, 1949.

21. Ibid.

22. "The New Pictures," *Time*, October 10, 1949.

23. Ibid.

24. Ibid.

25. Bosley Crowther, " 'Pinky,' Zanuck's Film Study of Anti-Negro Bias in Deep South, Shown at Rivoli 'Strange Bargain' and 'Peddler and the Lady' Other Movies Having Local Premieres." *New York Times*, September 30, 1949.

26. Ibid.

CHAPTER 5

1. Walter LaFaber, America, *Russia, and the Cold War, 1945–1996*, 8th ed. (New York: McGraw-Hill, 1997), 93.

2. Ibid.

3. Joseph McCarthy, Speech to Women's Republican Club, Wheeling, West Virginia, February 9, 1950.

4. Ibid.

5. Robert Griffith, *The Politics of Fear: Joseph R. McCarthy and the Senate* (Amherst: University of Massachusetts Press, 1970), 264.

6. One resulting initiative was the National Defense Education Act, which was signed into law in the fall of 1958. More directly responding to the crisis in confidence that Sputnik elicited was the creation of the National Aeronautics and Space Administration in the same year.

7. Wesley Alan Britton, *Onscreen and Undercover: The Ultimate Book of Movie Espionage* (Westport, CT: Greenwood, 2006), 85.

8. Bosley Crowther, "The Screen: Two Films Have Local Premieres; 'The Thing,' an Eerie Scientific Number by Howard Hawks, Opens at the Criterion 'Communist for F.B.I.' New Picture at Strand Theatre, Features Frank Lovejoy at the Criterion," *New York Times*, May 3, 1951.

9. Mark Sachleben and Kevan M. Yenerall, *Seeing the Bigger Picture: Understanding Politics through Film and Television* (New York: Lang, 2004), 60–61.

10. Ibid., 61.

11. Bosley Crowther, "'The Atomic City,' Low-Budget, High-Voltage Paramount Film, Opens at the Mayfair," *New York Times*, May 2, 1952.

12. "'Invasion U.S.A.': Strong Exploitation Entry Assured of Good Grosses," *Variety*, December 4, 1952.

13. Ibid.

14. Cynthia Hendershot, *Paranoia, the Bomb, and 1950s Science Fiction Films* (Bowling Green, OH: Bowling Green State University Press, 1999), 127.

15. Sidney Perkowitz, *Hollywood Science Movies, Science, and the End of the World* (New York: Columbia University Press, 2010), 96–97.

16. Gregory B. Richards, *Science Fiction Movies* (New York: Gallery Books, 1984), 37.

17. John W. Whitehead, "Invasion of the Body Snatchers: A Tale for Our Times," Gadfly Online, http://gadflyonline.com/11-26-01/film-snatchers.html.

18. Quoted in Ibid.

19. "A Hair-Raiser in a Concert Hall: Hitchcock Movie Sets Its Suspense to Music," *Life*, April 23, 1956, 95

20. Terry Christensen and Peter Haas, *Projecting Politics: Political Messages in American Film* (Armonk, NY: M.E. Sharpe, 2005), 128.

21. Ibid.

22. For an overview of this subject, see John M. Goering and Ronald E. Wienk, *Mortgage Lending, Racial Discrimination, and Federal Policy* (Washington, DC: Urban Institute Press, 1996).

23. In an influential book entitled *The Lonely Crowd* (New Haven, CT: Yale University Press, 1950), sociologists David Riesman, Nathan Glazer, and Reuel

Denney considered the implications of such changes in postwar American society. Riesman, the lead author, became a prominent public figure and subsequently appeared on the cover of *Time* magazine. The following year another book, *White Collar: The American Middle Class* (New York: Oxford University Press, 1951) by sociologist C. Wright Mills, focused additional attention on the realities of middle-class life, arguing that this group had largely become subservient to a "power elite" at the top end of the American economic structure.

24. J. Ronald Oakley, *God's Country: America in the Fifties* (New York: Dembner Books, 1986), 307.

25. Tom Clark, "A Few Pertinent Facts and Figures," *The Rotarian*, April 1946, 21.

26. Flanagan was a famous public figure. His project had been the subject of a popular movie, *Boys Town*, a 1938 movie directed by Norman Taurog that starred Spencer Tracy and Mickey Rooney.

27. Edward J. Flanagan, "Who's to Blame? It's Home and Society!," *The Rotarian*, April 1946, 22.

28. Comic books were also a major target of the investigation.

29. William H. Mooring in "Current Trends and Effects in Motion Pictures and Television and Their Potential Bearing upon Juvenile Delinquency," in *Motion Pictures and Juvenile Delinquency; Report of the Committee on the Judiciary Containing an Interim Report of the Subcommittee to Investigate Juvenile Delinquency, Pursuant to S. Res. 173, 84th Congress, 2nd Session* (Washington, DC: U.S. Government Printing Office, 1956).

30. *Juvenile Delinquency (Motion Pictures); Hearings before the Subcommittee to Investigate Juvenile Delinquency, Pursuant to S. Res. 62*, June 15, 16, 17, and 18, 1955 (Washington, DC: U.S. Government Printing Office).

31. Ibid.

32. Bosley Crowther, "Two Films in Bow Here; 'The Wild One,' Starring Marlon Brando as a Motorcyclist, Is on View at Palace; 'Paratrooper,' with Alan Ladd as Lone Wolf, Opens at Criterion—Young Directs," *New York Times*, December 31, 1953.

33. Darragh O'Donoghue, "The Wild One," *Senses of Cinema* 45 (2007), http://www.sensesofcinema.com/2007/cteq/wild-one/.

34. Bosley Crowther, " 'The Wild One,' Starring Marlon Brando as a Motorcyclist, Is on View at Palace; 'Paratrooper,' with Alan Ladd as a Lone Wolf, Opens at Criterion," *New York Times*, December 31, 1953.

35. Douglas L. Rathgeb, *The Making of "Rebel Without a Cause"* (Jefferson, NC: McFarland, 2004), 92.

36. Bosley Crowther, "The Screen; 'Blackboard Jungle'; Delinquency Shown in Powerful Film," *New York Times*, March 21, 1955.

37. "Bad Boys in the Schoolroom: In 'Blackboard Jungle' Hollywood Gives Exciting If Overdrawn Picture of a Growing Problem," *Life*, March 28, 1955, 49–50.

38. Ibid., 49.

39. Ibid., 50.

40. Mooring, "Current Trends and Effects."

41. Ibid.

42. *Motion Pictures and Juvenile Delinquency.*

43. J. David Slocum, " 'Rebel Without a Cause," *Senses of Cinema* 59 (2011), http://www.sensesofcinema.com/2011/cteq/rebel-without-a-cause/.

44. This review, originally published April 14, 1954, is reprinted in Don Willis, ed., *Variety's Complete Science Fiction Reviews* (New York: Garland, 1985), 103.

45. See David Kalat, *A Critical History and Filmography of Toho's Godzilla Series* (Jefferson, NC: McFarland, 1997), 24–29.

46. Ibid., 32.

47. H. I. Phillips, "A Word for the Long Lost," *St. Joseph News-Press*, May 1, 1956.

48. Bosley Crowther, "Screen: Horror Import; 'Godzilla' a Japanese Film, Is at State," *New York Times*, April 28, 1956.

49. Hendershot, *Paranoia, the Bomb*, 75.

50. At the time, the actor used the name Al Hedison.

51. These figures are cited in Michelle Pautz, "The Decline in Average Weekly Cinema Attendance: 1930–2000," *Issues on Political Economy* 11 (2002): 54–66.

52. Ibid.

CHAPTER 6

1. A resulting trial in the Soviet Union resulted in Powers's conviction. Although sentenced to three years in prison, a year later Powers was exchanged for a Russian spy who had been convicted for espionage in the United States several years earlier.

2. Dwight D. Eisenhower, "Farewell Radio and Television Address to the American People," January 17, 1961, online by Gerhard Peters and John T. Woolley, *The American Presidency Project*, http://www.presidency.ucsb.edu/ws/?pid=12086.

3. Terry Christensen and Peter J. Haas, *Projecting Politics: Political Messages in American Film* (Armonk, NY: M.E. Sharpe, 2005), 136.

4. Ibid., 137.

5. Ray Pratt, *Projecting Paranoia: Conspiratorial Visions in American Film* (Lawrence: University of Kansas Press, 2001), 99.

6. Ibid., 100.

7. This point is discussed in Gordon B. Arnold, *Conspiracy Theory in Film, Television, and Politics* (Westport, CT: Praeger, 2008), 70–71.

8. Michael J. Strada and Harold R. Troper, *Friend or Foe?: Russians in American Film and Foreign Policy, 1933–1991* (Lanham, MD: Scarecrow Press, 1997), 107.

9. Richard Oulahan, "Doomsday Is Better as a Farce," *Life*, October 30, 1964, 12.

10. Ibid.

11. Newton N. Minow, "Television and the Public Interest," speech before the National Association of Broadcasters, May 9, 1961. Reprinted in John Durham

Peters and Peter Simonson, *Mass Communication and American Social Thought: Key Texts, 1919–1968* (Lanham, MD: Rowman & Littlefield, 2004), 467.

12. Harold Morrison, "Bishops Alarmed at Moral Decline," *The Leader-Post*, November 20, 1961.

13. Hedda Hopper, "Hedda Says Money Bags Demand Film Depravity," *Chicago Daily Tribune*, April 19, 1962.

14. "Romney 'Shocked' by Moral Decline of American Life," *The Sun*, June 26, 1964.

15. William Stringer, "Goldwater Repeats Morality Theme," *The Christian Science Monitor*, October 22, 1964.

16. Joseph Sterne, "Rapid Action Urged to Avoid Deepening Racial Split," *The Sun*, March 1, 1968.

17. George Gallup, "Most Americans See Decay in U.S. Morals," *The Hartford Courant*, August 14, 1968.

18. Jack Anderson, "Fear Long-Range Effect of Birth Control Pills," *Warsaw Times-Union* [Indiana], January 6, 1965.

19. Bosley Crowther, "Screen: 'A Fistful of Dollars' Opens: Western Film Cliches All Used in Movie, Cowboy Star from TV Featured as Killer," *New York Times*, February 2, 1967.

20. Ibid.

21. Akira Kurosawa and Bert Cardullo, eds., *Akira Kurosawa: Interviews* (Jackson: University of Mississippi Press, 2008), 24.

22. Peter Krämer, *The New Hollywood: From Bonnie and Clyde to Star Wars* (London: Wallflower, 2005), 48.

23. Ibid.

24. Andrew J. Rausch, *Turning Points in Film History* (New York: Citadel Press, 2004), 172.

25. Ibid.

26. Bosley Crowther, "Film Festival: Heels, Old and New," *New York Times*, September 9, 1965.

27. Lester D. Friedman, *Arthur Penn's "Bonnie and Clyde"* (Cambridge: Cambridge University Press, 2000), 188.

28. These reviews are quoted in Jeffrey H. Goldstein, *Why We Watch: The Attractions of Violent Entertainment* (New York: Oxford University Press, 1998), 116.

29. Bosley Crowther, "Bonnie and Clyde," *New York Times*, April 14, 1967.

30. "Hollywood: The Shock of Freedom in Films," *Time*, December 8, 1967, 66.

31. This is quoted in Laurent Bouzereau, *Ultra-Violent Movies: From Sam Peckinpah to Quentin Tarantino* (Secaucus, NJ: Carol, 1998), 13.

32. *Times Film Corp. v. City of Chicago*, 365 US 43 (1961).

33. *Freedman v. Maryland* (1965).

34. Ibid.

35. Kenneth S. Devol, *Mass Media and the Supreme Court: The Legacy of the Warren Years* (Mamaroneck, NY: Hastings House, 1990), 267.

36. See Joe Russo, Larry Landsman, and Edward Gross, *Planet of the Apes Revisited: The Behind-the-Scenes Story of the Classic Science Fiction Saga* (New York: St. Martin's Press, 2001), 17–20.

37. Ibid., 33.

38. Richard Schickel, "Second Thoughts on Ape-Men," *Life*, May 10, 1968, 20.

39. Eric Greene, *Planet of the Apes as American Myth: Race, Politics, and Popular Culture* (Middletown, CT: Wesleyan University Press, 1998), 80.

40. Ibid., 6.

41. Ibid., 8.

42. Paul Monaco, *History of the American Cinema. 1960–1969*, Vol. 8, *The Sixties* (Berkeley: University of California Press, 2003), 166.

43. Vincent Canby, "Midnight Cowboy," *New York Times*, May 26, 1969.

44. Elaine M. Bapis, *Camera and Action: American Film as Agent of Social Change, 1965–1975* (Jefferson, NC: McFarland, 2008), 111.

45. Stephen Farber, "End of the Road?," *Film Quarterly* 23, no. 2 (Winter 1969–70): 6.

46. Ibid.

47. David Weddle, *If They Move—Kill 'em!: The Life and Times of Sam Peckinpah* (New York: Grove Press, 1994), 6.

48. Ibid., 8.

49. Sam Peckinpah, quoted in Bernard F. Dukore, *Sam Peckinpah's Feature Films* (Urbana: University of Illinois Press, 1999), 73–74.

50. Vincent Canby, "The Wild Bunch," *New York Times*, June 26, 1969.

51. Ibid.

52. See Dimitri Keramitas, "Easy Rider," in *Movies in American History: An Encyclopedia*, ed. Philip C. Dimare (Santa Barbara: ABC-CLIO, 2011), 151.

53. Bernard Drew, " 'Easy Rider' Seen as Requiem for America," *The Evening News*, August 2, 1969.

54. Vincent Canby, " 'Easy Rider': A Statement Film." *New York Times*, July 15, 1969.

55. James Perone, *Woodstock: An Encyclopedia* (Westport, CT: Greenwood, 2005), 41.

56. Barry Farrell, "Gloria! Donald! Countermiracle at the Great Stoned Rock Show," *Life, Special Edition: Woodstock Music Festival*, August 1969, n.p.

57. "Four Die in One-Day Festival," *Palm Beach Daily News*, December 8, 1969.

58. Jack Anderson, "Moral Decay of a Nation," *Ocala Star-Banner*, November 16, 1969.

59. U.S. Department of Justice, "Statement by Attorney General Nicholas deB. Katzenbach Before the Subcommittee on Executive Reorganization of the Senate Committee on Government Operations," August 17, 1966, http://www.justice.gov/ag/aghistory/katzenbach/1966/08-17-1966.pdf.

CHAPTER 7

1. The Gilbert Youth Research Corporation study is discussed in "American Youth Are Skeptical of 'American Dream,' " *Evening Independent*, April 12, 1971.

2. Joseph Alsop, "Threats We Watch: The Smoldering Crime Issue," *The Day*, December 23, 1969.

3. These data are from the Uniform Crime Reporting Statistics project of the U.S. Department of Justice, http://www.ucrdatatool.gov.

4. The Dirty Harry series continued off and on in the 1980s with *Sudden Impact* (1983) and *The Dead Pool* (1988).

5. Dialogue from the film *Dirty Harry*, Don Siegel, director, Warner Bros., 1971.

6. Vincent Canby, "Screen: 'Death Wish' Hunts Muggers: The Cast Story of Gunman Takes Dim View of City," *New York Times*, July 25, 1974.

7. Not long after, the 1973 cease-fire fell apart and the fighting restarted. The war continued, but without the Americans. The renewed struggle continued until the South Vietnamese government fell in 1975, reuniting Vietnam as a single country under Communist rule.

8. Carl Bernstein and Bob Woodward, "Bug Suspect Got Campaign Funds," *Washington Post*, August 1, 1972.

9. Carl Bernstein and Bob Woodward, "FBI Finds Nixon Aides Sabotaged Democrats," *Washington Post*, October 10, 1972.

10. Ibid.

11. Carl Bernstein and Bob Woodward, "Dean Alleges Nixon Knew of Cover-Up Plan," *Washington Post*, June 3, 1973.

12. Tom Wolfe, "The 'Me" Decade and the Third Great Awakening," *New York*, August 23, 1976, 23, 26–40.

13. "Panel Determines Drug Problem Here to Stay," *Bulletin*, March 22, 1973.

14. These data are calculated from Bureau of Labor Statistics data that are reproduced in William Issel, *Social Change in the United States, 1949–1983* (New York: Schocken Books, 1987), 20.

15. Peter N. Carroll, *It Seemed Like Nothing Happened: America in the 1970s* (New Brunswick, NJ: Rutgers University Press, 1990), 131–33.

16. John Cunniff, "American Dream Fades," *Milwaukee Journal*, May 29, 1974.

17. Robert Dietsch, "Record Interest Rates on Way Up Again," *Pittsburgh Press*, June 26, 1974.

18. "Ford Attacks Inflation—Cautiously," *Milwaukee Journal*, October 9, 1974.

19. Gerald R. Ford, "Remarks in Boston at the Old North Church Bicentennial Lantern Service," April 18, 1975, online by Gerhard Peters and John T. Woolley, The American Presidency Project, http://www.presidency.ucsb.edu/ws/?pid=4846.

20. Ibid.

21. Noreena Hertz, *The Silent Takeover: Global Capitalism and the Death of Democracy* (New York: Free Press, 2001), 209.

22. A. H. Weiler, "Screen: 'Soylent Green,' " *New York Times*, April 20, 1973.

23. Rachel Carson, *Silent Spring* (Boston: Houghton Mifflin, 1962), 18.

24. Robin L. Murray and Joseph K. Heumann, *Ecology and Popular Film: Cinema on the Edge* (Albany: State University of New York Press, 2009), 95.

25. Lester D. Friedman, *American Cinema of the 1970s: Themes and Variations* (New Brunswick, NJ: Rutgers University Press, 2007), 148.

26. Chris L. Durham, " 'We Must Be Doing Something Right to Last Two Hundred Years': Nashville, or the American Bicentennial as Viewed by Robert Altman," *Wide Screen* 2, no. 1 (2010), http://widescreenjournal.org/index.php/journal/article/viewArticle/40/88.

27. Michael Klein, "Nashville and the American Dream," *Jump Cut* 9 (1975): 6–7.

28. Stephen P. Miller, *The Seventies Now: Culture as Surveillance* (Durham, NC: Duke University Press, 1999), 99.

29. Gordon Arnold, *The Afterlife of America's War in Vietnam* (Jefferson, NC: McFarland, 2006), 48.

30. David Denby, "Nightmare into Epic," *New York*, December 18, 1978, 98.

31. Miller, *The Seventies Now*, 101.

32. Aljean Harmetz, " 'Deer Hunter': Oscar-Winning Movie Starts a War," *Star-News*, April 29, 1979.

33. This is cited in Arnold, *The Afterlife of America's War in Vietnam*, 51.

34. Frank P. Tomasulo, "The Politics of Ambivalence: 'Apocalypse Now' as Prowar and Antiwar Film," in *From Hanoi to Hollywood: The Vietnam War in American Film*, ed. Linda Dittmar and Gene Michaud (New Brunswick, NJ: Rutgers University Press, 1990), 149.

35. Ibid., 150.

36. Janet Maslin, "Screen: 'Body Snatchers' Return in All Their Creepy Glory," *New York Times*, December 22, 1978.

37. Jimmy Carter quoted in "Carter Seeks New Faith in American Dream," *Pittsburgh Post-Gazette*, January 21, 1977.

38. Hedrick Smith, "Carter Challenges American Dream," *St. Petersburg Times*, April 19, 1977.

39. Ibid.

40. Jack Anderson and Les Whitten, "Senators Ask Pentagon to Join Drug War," *Gadsden Times*, April 15, 1977.

41. The study's findings were discussed in "The American Dream: Many Have Lost Faith, Study Reveals," *The Evening Independent*, March 1, 1978.

42. Jimmy Carter, "Farewell Address to the Nation," January 14, 1981, online by Peters and Woolley, The American Presidency Project, http://www.presidency.ucsb.edu/ws/index.php?pid=44516&st=&st1=#axzz 1rwvqghap.

CHAPTER 8

1. Reagan used this description of the USSR as early as 1975. See Kiron K. Skinner, Annelise Graebner Anderson, and Martin Anderson, *Reagan's Path to*

Victory: The Shaping of Ronald Reagan's Vision: Selected Writings (New York: Free Press, 2004), 513.

2. Ronald Reagan, Remarks at the Annual Convention of the National Association of Evangelicals in Orlando, Florida," March 8, 1983, online by Gerhard Peters and John T. Woolley, The American Presidency Project, http://www.presidency.ucsb.edu/ws/index.php?pid=41023&st=evangelicals &st1=nuclear#ixzz1rxV1TQwD.

3. "Fall of the Berlin Wall: Timeline," *Christian Science Monitor*, http://www.csmonitor.com/World/2009/1108/p25s03-wogn.html.

4. Chris Jordan, *Movies and the Reagan Presidency: Success and Ethics* (Westport, CT: Praeger, 2003), 3.

5. This detail is noted in Janet Maslin, "Film: 'Red Dawn,' on World War III," *New York Times*, August 10, 1984.

6. David Denby, "The Nicaraguans Are Coming!," *New York*, August 20, 1984, 90–91.

7. Ibid., 90.

8. Ellen Farley, "The U.S. Has Surrendered: How *Rambo* Is Taking the World by Storm," *Business Week*, August 26, 1985, 109.

9. Ronald Reagan, "Inaugural Address," January 20, 1981, online by Peters and Woolley, The American Presidency Project, http://www.presidency.ucsb.edu/ws/index.php?pid=43130&st=&st1=#axzz1rwvqghap http://www.presidency.ucsb.edu/ws/index.php?pid=43130#axzz1rwvqghap.

10. Vincent Canby, "Film: Stone's 'Wall Street,' " *New York Times*, December 11, 1987.

11. Ibid.

12. "Stone: Wall Street Nervous," *Gainesville Sun*, March 25, 1987.

13. Desson Howe, " 'Wall Street,' " *Washington Post*, December 11, 1987.

14. Vincent Canby, "Film: Stone's 'Wall Street,' " *New York Times*, December 11, 1987.

15. "Exchange Head Rues Fact That Wall Street Got Stoned," *Spokane Chronicle*, December 16, 1987.

16. See *Hearings on Pros and Cons of Drug Legalization, Criminalization, and Harm Reduction Before the Subcommittee on Criminal Justice, Drug Policy, and Human Resources of the Committee on Government Reform*, House of Representatives, 106th Cong. (statement of David Boaz), June 16, 1999, reprinted by the Cato Institute, n.d., http://www.cato.org/pub_display.php?pub_id=12352.

17. Allan Bloom, *The Closing of the American Mind* (New York: Simon and Schuster, 1988).

18. Tim LaHaye is quoted in Sara Diamond, *Spiritual Warfare: The Politics of the Christian Right* (Boston: South End Press, 1989), 85.

19. Sara Diamond, *Not by Politics Alone: The Enduring Influence of the Christian Right* (New York: Guilford Press, 1998), 70.

20. Stephen L. Carter, *God's Name in Vain* (New York: Basic Books, 2000), 41.

21. David Lynch is quoted in Joseph Maddrey, *Nightmares in Red, White and Blue: The Evolution of the American Horror Film* (Jefferson, NC: McFarland, 2004), 155.

22. Greil Marcus, *The Shape of Things to Come: Prophecy and the American Voice* (New York: Picador USA, 2007), 115.

23. David Denby, "Flesh and Fantasy," *New York*, September 29, 1986, 85.

24. Stephen Hunter, *Violent Screen: A Critic's 13 Years on the Front Lines of Movie Mayhem* (Baltimore: Bancroft Press, 1985), 45.

25. "Thousands Protest Movie about Christ," *The Lewiston Daily Sun*, August 12, 1988.

26. Guiliana Bruno, "Ramble City: Postmodernism and 'Blade Runner,'" *October*, 41 (Summer 1987): 62.

27. Ibid., 63.

28. Sean Redmond, "Purge! Class Pathology in Blade Runner" in Will Brooker, ed., *The Blade Runner Experience: The Legacy of a Science Fiction Classic* (New York: Wallflower, 2005), 173.

29. Mike Davis, *Ecology of Fear: Los Angeles and the Imagination of Disaster* (New York: Vintage Books, 1999), 357.

30. Ronald Reagan, "Remarks Accepting the Presidential Nomination at the Republican National Convention in Dallas, Texas," August 23, 1984, online by Peters and Woolley, The American Presidency Project, http://www.presidency.ucsb.edu/ws/index.php?pid=40290&st=&st1=#axzz1rw vqghap.

31. Vincent Canby, "Review/Film; Nicholson and Keaton Do Battle in 'Batman,'" *New York Times*, June 23, 1989.

32. James Berger, *After the End: Representations of Post-apocalypse* (Minneapolis: University of Minnesota Press, 1999), 30.

33. William Grant, "Reflecting the Times," in *Spike Lee's "Do the Right Thing,"* ed. Mark Reid (Cambridge: Cambridge University Press, 1997), 17.

CHAPTER 9

1. This account draws on Mark Bowden, "Black Hawk Down: A Defining Battle," *Philadelphia Inquirer*, November 16, 1997.

2. William J. Clinton, "Remarks on the Federal Government Shutdown," November 14, 1995, online by Gerhard Peters and John T. Woolley, *The American Presidency Project*, http://www.presidency.ucsb.edu/ws/?pid=87525.

3. James Hirsen, *Hollywood Nation: Left Coast Lies, Old Media Spin, and New Media Revolution* (New York: Three Rivers Press, 2006), 3.

4. Ibid.

5. Ibid.

6. Michael Medved, *Hollywood vs. America: Popular Culture and the War on Traditional Values* (New York: HarperCollins, 1992), 77.

7. Ibid., 71.

8. Ibid., 218.

9. Ibid., 219.

10. Ibid., 219.

11. Kevin S. Sandler, *Titanic: Anatomy of a Blockbuster* (New Brunswick, NJ: Rutgers University Press, 1999), 39.

12. Louise Krasniewicz and Michael Blitz, *Arnold Schwarzenegger: A Biography* (Westport, CT: Greenwood, 2006), 74–75.

13. Sarah Casey Benyahia, Freddie Gaffney, and John White, *AS Film Studies: The Essential Introduction* (London: Routledge, 2006), 150.

14. Daniel B. Wood, "L.A.'s Darkest Days," *Christian Science Monitor*, April 29, 2002.

15. Janet Maslin, "Review/Film; In New 'Terminator,' The Forces of Good Seek Peace, Violently," *New York Times*, July 3, 1991.

16. Richard Brown and Kevin S. Decker, *Terminator and Philosophy: I'll Be Back, Therefore I Am* (Hoboken, NJ: Wiley, 2009), 87.

17. Frederick Buell, *From Apocalypse to Way of Life: Four Decades of Environmental Crisis in the U.S.* (New York: Routledge, 2003), 251.

18. Joshua D. Bellin, *Framing Monsters: Fantasy Film and Social Alienation* (Carbondale: Southern Illinois University Press, 2005), 162.

19. Peter Rainer, "Prehensile Tale: In *12 Monkeys*, Terry Gilliam Has Seen the Future, and It's Murder, Baby," *Los Angeles Magazine*, January 1996, 106.

20. Among the settings where apathy had taken hold were college campuses. For more on this see, for example, Paul R. Loeb, *Generation at the Crossroads: Apathy and Action on the American Campus* (New Brunswick, NJ: Rutgers University Press, 1994).

21. Vincent Canby, "Film Review; A Master of the Universe Brought Down to Earth," *New York Times*, December 21, 1990.

22. See, for example, cases discussed in Michael W. Eysenck, *Psychology: An International Perspective* (Hove, UK: Psychology Press, 2004), 574.

23. Kendall R. Phillips, *Controversial Cinema: The Films That Outraged America* (Westport, CT: Praeger, 2008), 155.

24. Daniel Green, "Natural Born Killers and American Decline," in *The Films of Oliver Stone*, ed. Don Kunz (Lanham, MD: Scarecrow Press, 1997), 259, 270.

25. Christopher Sharrett, *Mythologies of Violence in Postmodern Media* (Detroit, MI: Wayne State University Press, 1999), 155.

26. Ibid., 155.

27. Tarantino's comment, from an article by Gary Susman in the *Boston Phoenix* of October 7, 1994, is quoted in Quentin Tarantino and Gerald Peary, *Interviews* (Jackson: University Press of Mississippi, 1998), xii.

28. Stephen Holden, "Film Review; People Who Dance With Vampires May Find Thrills in a New Vein," *New York Times*, August 21, 1988.

29. Ibid.

30. Matt Drudge, "Newsweek Kills Story on White House Intern," *The Drudge Report*, January 17, 1998.

31. Michael Isikoff and Evan Thomas, "Clinton and the Intern," *Newsweek*, February 1, 1998, 31–46.

32. An account of Hillary Clinton's *Today* show interview appears in David Maraniss, "First Lady Launches Counterattack," *Washington Post*, January 28, 1998.

33. The White House, Office of the Press Secretary, "Remarks by the President, Secretary of Defense William Cohen, and Secretary of State Madeleine Albright at Ceremony Honoring the Men and Women Who Lost Their Lives in the Bombings of the Embassies in Kenya and Tanzania," Andrews Air Force Base, Maryland, August 13, 1998, http://secretary.state.gov/www/statements/1998/980813.html.

34. "About PNAC," Project for the New American Century, n.d., http://www.newamericancentury.org/aboutpnac.htm.

35. Elliott Abrams et al., "Statement of Principles," Project for the New American Century, June 3, 1997, http://newamericancentury.org.

36. For more on the specifically Christian aspects of this subject, see Kirsten Moana Thompson, *Apocalyptic Dread: American Film at the Turn of the Millennium* (Albany: State University of New York Press, 2007).

37. Romesh Ratnesar, "Sneak Attack," *Time*, October 15, 2000, archived at http://time.com/time/nation/article/0,8599,57755,00.html.

38. Ibid.

CHAPTER 10

1. *Rebuilding America's Defenses: Strategies, Forces and Resources for a New Century* (Washington, DC: Project for the New American Century, 2000), 1.

2. U.S. Bureau of the Census, "Median and Average Square Feet of Floor Area in New Single-Family Houses Completed by Location," 2010, http://www.census.gov/const/C25Ann/sftotalmedavgsqft.pdf.

3. *Congressional Record*, Vol. 148, Pt. 15, October 10, 2002, to November 8, 2002, 20669.

4. John Miller, "Talking with Terror's Banker: An Exclusive Interview with Osama bin Laden," *ABC News*, May 28, 1998.

5. Ibid.

6. Douglas M. Kellner, *Cinema Wars: Hollywood Film and Politics in the Bush-Cheney Era* (Hoboken, NJ: Wiley, 2011), 96.

7. Martha Crenshaw, "The Psychology of Terrorism: An Agenda for the 21st Century," *Political Psychology* 21, no. 2 (June 2000): 406.

8. Ibid.

9. Alexandra Marks, "Why GOP Is Going Into a Democratic Lair," *Christian Science Monitor*, January 8, 2003.

10. The unifying effects of perceived enemies are usefully discussed in Murray Edelman, *Constructing the Political Spectacle* (Chicago: University of Chicago Press, 1988).

11. These data are repeated in "New CNN Poll: Pain Remains 10 Years after 9/11," CNN, September 9, 2011, http://politicalticker.blogs.cnn.com/2011/09/09/new-cnn-poll-pain-remains-10-years-after-911/.

12. George W. Bush, "Remarks at O'Hare International Airport, Chicago, Illinois, September 27, 2001," in *Public Papers of Presidents of the United States, George W. Bush, 2001*, Book 2, July 1 to December 31, 2001 (Washington, DC: U.S. Government Printing Office, 2003), 1171–72.

13. A detailed account of the meeting appears in Rick Lyman, "A Nation Challenged: The Entertainment Industry; Hollywood Discusses Role in the War Effort," *New York Times*, November 12, 2001.

14. Sara E. Quay and Amy Damico, *September 11 in Popular Culture: A Guide* (Santa Barbara, CA: Greenwood, 2010), 175.

15. "Hollywood Discusses Role in the War on Terrorism," *Milwaukee Journal*, November 12, 2001.

16. Rove is quoted in Lyman, "A Nation Challenged."

17. Ibid.

18. Valenti is quoted in Lyman, "A Nation Challenged."

19. "Hollywood Discusses Role in the War on Terrorism."

20. Stephen Prince, *Firestorm: American Film in the Age of Terrorism* (New York: Columbia University Press, 2009), 308.

21. Ibid., 309.

22. Elvis Mitchell, "Film Review; Mission of Mercy Goes Bad in Africa," *New York Times*, December 28, 2001.

23. Mike Clark, " 'Black Hawk' Turns Nightmare into Great Cinema," *USA Today*, December 28, 2001.

24. Andrew Stephen, "War Comes Home," *New Statesman*, February 11, 2002, 22–23.

25. Ibid.

26. Kellner, *Cinema Wars*, 28.

27. Rick Lyman, "Bad Guys for Bad Times; Hollywood Struggles to Create Villains for a New Climate," *New York Times*, October 3, 2001.

28. William Kristol et al., Letter to George W. Bush, September 20, 2001, http://newamericancentury.org/.

29. "Powell Regrets UN Speech on Iraq WMDs," ABC News Online, September 9, 2005, http://www.abc.net.au/news/2005-09-09/powell-regrets-un-speech-on-iraq-wmds/2099674.

30. "President Bush Delivers Graduation Speech at West Point," June 1, 2002, http://georgewbush-whitehouse.archives.gov/news/releases/2002/06/20020601-3.html.

31. Roger Ebert, "Minority Report," *Chicago Sun-Times*, June 21, 2002.

32. Berenike Jung, *Narrating Violence in Post-9/11 Action Cinema: Terrorist Narratives and Referentiality* (Wiesbaden, Germany: VS Verlag für Sozialwiss enschaften, 2010), 114.

33. Jonathon W. Moses, "The Politics of Immigration: Introduction to a Special Issue on US Immigration," *European Journal of American Studies* (2009), http://ejas.revues.org/7715.

34. For an overview, see Ronald T. Takaki, *A Different Mirror: A History of Multicultural America* (New York: Back Bay Books/Little, Brown, 2008).

35. Roger Ebert, "*Crash*: When Racial Worlds Collide," *Chicago Sun-Times*, May 5, 2005.

36. Ken Tucker, "Accidents Will Happen: Paul Haggis's Thrilling, Provocative *Crash* Spins a Great Cast into Moral Collisions," *New York*, May 21, 2005.

37. Stephen Keane, *Disaster Movies: The Cinema of Catastrophe* (New York: Wallflower, 2006), 95.

38. Mary Manjikian, *Apocalypse and Post-Politics: The Romance of the End* (Lanham, MD: Lexington Books, 2012), 64.

39. Quay and Damico, *September 11 in Popular Culture*, 5.

40. Ibid.

41. Wheeler W. Dixon, *Visions of the Apocalypse: Spectacles of Destruction on American Cinema* (New York: Wallflower, 2003), 59.

42. This account draws upon E. Ray Canterbury, *A Brief History of Economics: Artful Approaches to the Dismal Science* (River Edge, NJ: World Scientific, 2010).

43. National unemployment data for 2009 are cited in National Conference of State Legislatures, "Unemployment Dips to 8.2 Percent in March 2012," *National Unemployment Update*, April 9, 2012.

44. A. O. Scott, "A Bank That Specializes in Payback (and Not the Kind with Interest)," *New York Times*, February 12, 2009.

45. Roger Ebert, "Money Never Sleeps," *Chicago Sun-Times*, September 22, 2010.

Selected Bibliography

Adams, James T. *The Epic of America*. Boston: Little, Brown, 1941.

Arnold, Gordon. *The Afterlife of America's War in Vietnam*. Jefferson, NC: McFarland, 2006.

Arnold, Gordon B. *Conspiracy Theory in Film, Television, and Politics*. Westport, CT: Praeger, 2008.

Bapis, Elaine M. *Camera and Action: American Film as Agent of Social Change, 1965–1975*. Jefferson, NC: McFarland, 2008.

Baran, Stanley. "Dignity: The Stories We Tell (about) Ourselves." *Bread and Circus* (2009). http://breadandcircusnetwork.wordpress.com/2009/11/05/the-dignity-series-the-stories-we-tell-about-ourselves/.

Bellin, Joshua D. *Framing Monsters: Fantasy Film and Social Alienation*. Carbondale: Southern Illinois University Press, 2005.

Benyahia, Sarah Casey, Freddie Gaffney, and John White. *AS Film Studies: The Essential Introduction*. London: Routledge, 2006.

Berger, James. *After the End: Representations of Post-apocalypse*. Minneapolis: University of Minnesota Press, 1999.

Bloom, Allan. *The Closing of the American Mind*. New York: Simon and Schuster, 1988.

Bouzereau, Laurent. *Ultra-Violent Movies: From Sam Peckinpah to Quentin Tarantino*. Secaucus, NJ: Carol, 1998.

Brenner, Aaron, Benjamin Day, and Immanuel Ness, eds. *The Encyclopedia of Strikes in American History*. Armonk, NY: M.E. Sharpe, 2009.

Britton, Wesley Alan. *Onscreen and Undercover: The Ultimate Book of Movie Espionage*. Westport, CT: Greenwood, 2006.

Brokaw, Tom. *The Greatest Generation*. New York: Random House, 2004.

Brown, Richard, and Kevin S. Decker. *Terminator and Philosophy: I'll Be Back, Therefore I Am.* Hoboken, NJ: Wiley, 2009.

Bruno, Guiliana. "Ramble City: Postmodernism and 'Blade Runner.'" *October* 41 (Summer 1987): 61–74.

Buell, Frederick. *From Apocalypse to Way of Life: Four Decades of Environmental Crisis in the U.S.* New York: Routledge, 2003.

Campbell, Joseph. *The Power of Myth.* New York: Doubleday, 1988.

Canterbery, E. Ray. *A Brief History of Economics: Artful Approaches to the Dismal Science.* Singapore: World Scientific, 2011.

Carroll, Peter N. *It Seemed Like Nothing Happened: America in the 1970s.* New Brunswick, NJ: Rutgers University Press, 1990.

Carson, Rachel. *Silent Spring.* Boston: Houghton Mifflin, 1962.

Carter, Stephen L. *God's Name in Vain.* New York: Basic Books, 2000.

Ceplair, Larry, and Steven Englund. *The Inquisition in Hollywood: Politics in the Film Community, 1930–60.* Berkeley: University of California Press, 1983.

Chambers, John Whiteclay, and David Culbert. *World War II, Film, and History.* New York: Oxford University Press, 1996.

Christensen, Terry, and Peter J. Haas. *Projecting Politics: Political Messages in American Film.* Armonk, NY: M.E. Sharpe, 2005.

Cohen, Karl F. *Forbidden Animation: Censored Cartoons and Blacklisted Animators in America.* Jefferson, NC: McFarland, 2004.

Cohen, Lizabeth. *A Consumers' Republic: The Politics of Mass Consumption in Postwar America.* New York: Knopf, 2003.

Crenshaw, Martha. "The Psychology of Terrorism: An Agenda for the 21st Century." *Political Psychology* 21, no. 2 (June 2000): 405–20.

Culbert, David H., Richard E. Wood, and Lawrence H. Suid. *Film and Propaganda in America: A Documentary History.* Westport, CT: Greenwood, 1990.

Cullen, Jim. *The American Dream: A Short History of an Idea That Shaped a Nation.* New York: Oxford University Press, 2003.

Davis, Mike. *Ecology of Fear: Los Angeles and the Imagination of Disaster.* New York: Vintage Books, 1999.

Devol, Kenneth S. *Mass Media and the Supreme Court: The Legacy of the Warren Years.* Mamaroneck, NY: Hastings House, 1990.

Diamond, Sara. *Not by Politics Alone: The Enduring Influence of the Christian Right.* New York: Guilford Press, 1998.

Diamond, Sara. *Spiritual Warfare: The Politics of the Christian Right.* Boston: South End Press, 1989.

Dimare, Philip C., ed. *Movies in American History: An Encyclopedia.* Santa Barbara, CA: ABC-CLIO, 2011.

Dixon, Wheeler W. *Visions of the Apocalypse: Spectacles of Destruction on American Cinema.* New York: Wallflower, 2003.

Doherty, Thomas. *Projections of War: Hollywood, American Culture, and World War II.* Rev. ed. New York: Columbia University Press, 1999.

Dukore, Bernard F. *Sam Peckinpah's Feature Films*. Urbana: University of Illinois Press, 1999.

Durham, Chris L. " 'We Must Be Doing Something Right to Last Two Hundred Years': Nashville, or the American Bicentennial as Viewed by Robert Altman." *Wide Screen* 2, no. 1 (2010). http://widescreenjournal.org/index.php/journal/article/viewArticle/40.

Edelman, Murray. *Constructing the Political Spectacle*. Chicago: University of Chicago Press, 1988.

Eysenck, Michael W. *Psychology: An International Perspective*. Hove, UK: Psychology Press, 2004.

Farber, Stephen. "End of the Road?" *Film Quarterly* 23, no. 2 (Winter 1969–70): 3–16.

Friedman, Lester D. *American Cinema of the 1970s: Themes and Variations*. New Brunswick, NJ: Rutgers University Press, 2007.

Friedman, Lester D. *Arthur Penn's "Bonnie and Clyde."* Cambridge: Cambridge University Press, 2000.

Geertz, Clifford. *The Interpretation of Cultures*. New York: Basic Books, 1973.

Goering, John M., and Ronald E. Wienk. *Mortgage Lending, Racial Discrimination, and Federal Policy*. Washington, DC: Urban Institute Press, 1996.

Goldstein, Jeffrey H. *Why We Watch: The Attractions of Violent Entertainment*. New York: Oxford University Press, 1998.

Grant, William. "Reflecting the Times." In *Spike Lee's "Do the Right Thing."* Edited by Mark Reid, 16–30. Cambridge: Cambridge University Press, 1997.

Green, Daniel. "Natural Born Killers and American Decline." In *The Films of Oliver Stone*. Edited by Don Kunz, 259–71. Lanham, MD: Scarecrow Press, 1997.

Greene, Eric. *Planet of the Apes as American Myth: Race, Politics, and Popular Culture*. Middletown, CT: Wesleyan University Press, 1998.

Griffith, Robert. *The Politics of Fear: Joseph R. McCarthy and the Senate*. Amherst: University of Massachusetts Press, 1970.

Gusfield, Joseph R. *Symbolic Crusade: Status Politics and the American Temperance Movement*. 2nd ed. Urbana: University of Illinois Press, 1986.

Harmetz, Aljean. *The Making of Casablanca: Bogart, Bergman, and World War II*. New York: Hyperion, 2002.

Hearings on Pros and Cons of Drug Legalization, Criminalization, and Harm Reduction Before the Subcommittee on Criminal Justice, Drug Policy, and Human Resources of the Committee on Government Reform, House of Representatives, 106th Cong. (statement of David Boaz). June 16, 1999. Reprinted by the Cato Institute. n.d. http://www.cato.org/pub_display.php?pub_id=12352.

Hendershot, Cynthia. *Paranoia, the Bomb, and 1950s Science Fiction Films*. Bowling Green, OH: Bowling Green State University Press, 1999.

Hertz, Noreena. *The Silent Takeover: Global Capitalism and the Death of Democracy*. New York: Free Press, 2001.

Hirsen, James. *Hollywood Nation: Left Coast Lies, Old Media Spin, and New Media Revolution*. New York: Three Rivers Press, 2006.

Holbrook, Morris B., and Elizabeth Caldwell Hirschman. *The Semiotics of Consumption: Interpreting Symbolic Consumer Behavior in Popular Culture and Works of Art*. Berlin: Mouton de Gruyter, 1993.

Hughes, Richard T. *Myths America Lives By*. Urbana University of Illinois Press, 2003.

Hunter, Stephen. *Violent Screen: A Critic's 13 Years on the Front Lines of Movie Mayhem*. Baltimore: Bancroft Press, 1985.

Issel, William. *Social Change in the United States, 1949–1983*. New York: Schocken Books, 1987.

Jordan, Chris. *Movies and the Reagan Presidency: Success and Ethics*. Westport, CT: Praeger, 2003.

Jung, Berenike. *Narrating Violence in Post-9/11 Action Cinema: Terrorist Narratives and Referentiality*. Wiesbaden, Germany: VS Verlag für Sozialwissenschaften, 2010.

Jung, C. G. *Flying Saucers: A Modern Myth of Things Seen in the Sky*. New York: MJF Books, 1978.

Kalat, David. *A Critical History and Filmography of Toho's Godzilla Series*. Jefferson, NC: McFarland, 1997.

Keane, Stephen. *Disaster Movies: The Cinema of Catastrophe*. New York: Wallflower, 2006.

Kellner, Douglas M. *Cinema Wars: Hollywood Film and Politics in the Bush-Cheney Era*. Hoboken, NJ: Wiley, 2011.

Kelly, Barbara M. *Expanding the American Dream: Building and Rebuilding Levittown* Albany: State University of New York Press, 1993.

Klein, Michael. "Nashville and the American Dream." *Jump Cut* 9 (1975): 6–7.

Koppes, Clayton R., and Gregory D. Black. *Hollywood Goes to War: How Politics, Profits and Propaganda Shaped World War II Movies*. New York: Free Press, 1987.

Krämer, Peter. *The New Hollywood: From Bonnie and Clyde to Star Wars*. London: Wallflower, 2005.

Krasniewicz, Louise, and Michael Blitz. *Arnold Schwarzenegger: A Biography*. Westport, CT: Greenwood, 2006.

Kurosawa, Akira, and Bert Cardullo, eds. *Akira Kurosawa: Interviews*. Jackson: University of Mississippi Press, 2008.

LaFaber, Walter. *America, Russia, and the Cold War, 1945–1996*. 8th ed. New York: McGraw-Hill, 1997.

Loeb, Paul R. *Generation at the Crossroads: Apathy and Action on the American Campus*. New Brunswick, NJ: Rutgers University Press, 1994.

Maddrey, Joseph. *Nightmares in Red, White and Blue: The Evolution of the American Horror Film*. Jefferson, NC: McFarland, 2004.

Manjikian, Mary. *Apocalypse and Post-politics: The Romance of the End*. Lanham, MD: Lexington Books, 2012.

Marcus, Greil. *The Shape of Things to Come: Prophecy and the American Voice*. New York: Picador USA, 2007.

Mayhew, Robert. *Ayn Rand and Song of Russia: Communism and Anti-Communism in 1940s Hollywood*. Lanham, MD: Scarecrow Press, 2005.

Medved, Michael. *Hollywood vs. America: Popular Culture and the War on Traditional Values*. New York: HarperCollins, 1992.

Miller, Dennis T., and Marion Nowak. *The Fifties: The Way We Really Were*. Garden City, NY: Doubleday, 1977.

Miller, Stephen P. *The Seventies Now: Culture as Surveillance*. Durham, NC: Duke University Press, 1999.

Mills, C. Wright. *White Collar: The American Middle Class*. New York: Oxford University Press, 1951.

Monaco, Paul. *History of the American Cinema: 1960–1969*. Vol. 8, *The Sixties*. Berkeley: University of California Press, 2003.

Morison, Samuel Eliot. *The Oxford History of the American People*. New York: Oxford University Press, 1965.

Moses, Jonathon W. "The Politics of Immigration: Introduction to a Special Issue on US Immigration." *European Journal of American Studies* (2009). http://ejas. revues.org/7715.

Motion Picture Producers and Distributors of America. "The Don'ts and Be Carefuls." 1927. Reproduced in "The History of American Film: Primary Sources." Digital History. n.d. http://www.digitalhistory.uh.edu/historyonline/ film_censorship.cfm.

Motion Pictures and Juvenile Delinquency; Report of the Committee on the Judiciary Containing an Interim Report of the Subcommittee to Investigate Juvenile Delinquency, Pursuant to S. Res. 173, 84th Congress, 2nd Session. Washington, DC: U.S. Government Printing Office, 1956.

Murray, Robin L., and Joseph K. Heumann. *Ecology and Popular Film: Cinema on the Edge*. Albany: State University of New York Press, 2009.

Nerlich, Brigitte, David D. Clarke, and Robert Dingwall. "The Influence of Popular Cultural Imagery on Public Attitudes towards Cloning." *Sociological Research Online* 4, no. 3 (1999). http://www.socresonline.org.uk/socresonline/4/3/ nerlich.html.

Newcomb, Horace. *Encyclopedia of Television*. 2nd ed. New York: Fitzroy Dearborn, 2004.

Oakley, J. Ronald. *God's Country: America in the Fifties*. New York: Dembner Books, 1986.

Orwell, George. *The Collected Essays, Journalism, and Letters, George Orwell: An Age Like This, 1920–1940*. Jaffrey, NH: Godine, 2000.

Pautz, Michelle. "The Decline in Average Weekly Cinema Attendance: 1930–2000." *Issues in Political Economy* 11 (2002): 54–66.

Perkowitz, Sidney. *Hollywood Science Movies, Science, and the End of the World*. New York: Columbia University Press, 2010.

Perone, James. *Woodstock: An Encyclopedia*. Westport, CT: Greenwood, 2005.

Peters, John Durham, and Peter Simonson. *Mass Communication and American Social Thought: Key Texts, 1919–1968.* Lanham, MD: Rowman & Littlefield, 2004.

Phillips, Kendall R. *Controversial Cinema: The Films That Outraged America.* Westport, CT: Praeger, 2008.

Pratt, Ray. *Projecting Paranoia: Conspiratorial Visions in American Film.* Lawrence: University of Kansas Press, 2001.

Prince, Stephen. *Firestorm: American Film in the Age of Terrorism.* New York: Columbia University Press, 2009.

Progress and Feasibility of Toll Roads and Their Relation to the Federal-Aid Program: Letter from the Secretary of Commerce Transmitting a Report of the Progress and Feasibility of Toll Roads, with Particular Attention to the Possible Effects of Such Toll Roads upon the Federal Aid Highway Programs, Including Recommendations with Respect to Federal Participation in Toll Roads. Washington, DC: U.S. Government Printing Office, 1955.

Quart, Leonard, and Albert Auster. *American Film and Society since 1945.* 4th ed. Santa Barbara, CA: Praeger, 2011.

Quay, Sara E., and Amy M. Damico, *September 11 in Popular Culture: A Guide.* Santa Barbara, CA: Greenwood, 2010.

Rathgeb, Douglas L. *The Making of "Rebel Without a Cause."* Jefferson, NC: McFarland, 2004.

Rausch, Andrew J. *Turning Points in Film History.* New York: Citadel Press, 2004.

Rebuilding America's Defenses: Strategies, Forces and Resources for a New Century. Washington, DC: Project for the New American Century, 2000.

Redmond, Sean. "Purge! Class Pathology in Blade Runner." In *The Blade Runner Experience: The Legacy of a Science Fiction Classic.* Edited by Will Brooker, 173–89. New York: Wallflower, 2005.

Rhodes, Richard. *The Making of the Atomic Bomb.* New York: Simon and Schuster, 1986.

Richards, Gregory B. *Science Fiction Movies.* New York: Gallery Books, 1984.

Richter, Irving. *Labor's Struggles, 1945–1950: A Participant's View.* Cambridge: Cambridge University Press, 1994.

Riehl, Nikolaus, and Frederick Seitz. *Stalin's Captive: Nikolaus Riehl and the Soviet Race for the Bomb.* Washington, DC: American Chemical Society, 1996.

Riesman, David, Nathan Glazer, and Reuel Denney. *The Lonely Crowd.* New Haven, CT: Yale University Press, 1950.

Rose, Denise B. "Racial Roadblocks: Pursuing Successful Long-Term Racial Diversity in Oak Park, Illinois, a Metropolitan Chicago Community." PhD diss., Loyola University, 2007.

Russo, Joe, Larry Landsman, and Edward Gross. *Planet of the Apes Revisited: The Behind-the-Scenes Story of the Classic Science Fiction Saga.* New York: St. Martin's Press, 2001.

Sachleben, Mark, and Kevan M. Yenerall. *Seeing the Bigger Picture: Understanding Politics through Film and Television.* New York: Lang, 2004.

Sandler, Kevin S. *Titanic: Anatomy of a Blockbuster*. New Brunswick, NJ: Rutgers University Press, 1999.

Sayre, Nora. "Assaulting Hollywood." *World Policy Journal* 12, no. 4 (Winter 1995–96): 51–60.

Sharrett, Christopher. *Mythologies of Violence in Postmodern Media*. Detroit, MI: Wayne State University Press, 1999.

Shindler, Colin. *Hollywood in Crisis: Cinema and American Society, 1929–1939*. London: Routledge, 1996.

Skinner, Kiron K., Annelise Graebner Anderson, and Martin Anderson. *Reagan's Path to Victory: The Shaping of Ronald Reagan's Vision: Selected Writings*. New York: Free Press, 2004.

Slocum, J. David. " 'Rebel Without a Cause." *Senses of Cinema* 59 (2011). http://www.sensesofcinema.com/2011/cteq/rebel-without-a-cause/.

Strada, Michael J., and Harold R. Troper. *Friend or Foe?: Russians in American Film and Foreign Policy, 1933–1991*. Lanham, MD: Scarecrow Press, 1997.

Takaki, Ronald T. *A Different Mirror: A History of Multicultural America*. New York: Back Bay Books/Little, Brown, 2008.

Tarantino, Quentin, and Gerald Peary. *Interviews*. Jackson: University Press of Mississippi, 1998.

Thompson, Kirsten Moana. *Apocalyptic Dread: American Film at the Turn of the Millennium*. Albany: State University of New York Press, 2007.

Tomasulo, Frank P. "The Politics of Ambivalence: 'Apocalypse Now' as Prowar and Antiwar Film." In *From Hanoi to Hollywood: The Vietnam War in American Film*. Edited by Linda Dittmar and Gene Michaud, 145–58. New Brunswick, NJ: Rutgers University Press, 1990.

Weddle, David. *If They Move—Kill 'em!: The Life and Times of Sam Peckinpah*. New York: Grove Press, 1994.

Willis, Don, ed. *Variety's Complete Science Fiction Reviews*. New York: Garland, 1985.

Willis, Garry. *Under God: Religion and American Politics*. New York: Simon and Schuster, 1990.

Winn, John Emmett. *The American Dream and Contemporary Hollywood Cinema*. New York: Continuum, 2007.

Wolfe, Tom. "The 'Me' Decade and the Third Great Awakening." *New York*, August 23, 1976, 23, 26–40.

Zinn, Howard. *A People's History of the United States*. New York: Harper Perennial, 2010.

Index

About the Author

GORDON B. ARNOLD, PhD, is a professor of liberal arts at Montserrat College of Art in Beverly, Massachusetts, where he teaches film history, media politics, and sociology. He is the author of *Conspiracy Theory in Film, Television, and Politics* (2008), *The Afterlife of America's War in Vietnam* (2006), and *The Politics of Faculty Unionization* (2000). He has also contributed to *Library Journal*, *The Providence Journal*, *The History News Network*, *The BBC Vietnamese Service*, and other publications.